What have We done !!!

A Facebook Timeline

By

Jeff C. Cooper

WW!!! Hello,

Thanks to my Facebook friends, some 4,500 people. I've gotten 54,000 likes on FB.   I've been on FB since 2007.

Published by Create Space, an Amazon company.
Copyright Jeff Cooper 2018

I live in Jacksonville, Florida and was a real estate appraiser for 49 years.   I'm married with a big family.

There is no table of contents because this is a timeline book. Each day's postings on Facebook are condensed herein from 4-6-16 to the end of 2017. Face it was my first timeline book in 2016.

I published 3 books before this one. Buy a Boarded-up House with Contents, Real Estate Dad's Way and Face it. Almost Alcoholic and Dream Lessons are presently in manuscript form.

Thanks to Rachel Maddow, Dan Rather and the Trump Authors. Art of the Deal was his first book and in many ways, the most revealing. Thanks to Jepp Walter, technical advisor. Editor was Kim Osterbrock.

This book is dedicated to Stephanie Lorraine Remisiewicz.

Contact me at jcconrad@bellsouth.net or 904-724-6000

The book uses vernacular as found on Facebook, like T for Trump and ppl for people.   Curse words are bleeped out.

Some liberties are taken with wording and punctuation.
The narrative is conversational like between real people.

My sources include TV, newspapers, magazines and other people. Some of the posts are speculative or suggestive of a future reality. I was not a democrat until Trump. Many posts are suggested by other friends on FB. I have molded them with my own views. Some posts are comedic.
There are no mistakes in this book, only alternate facts.

I have a bachelor's degree in real estate, University of Florida, 1965.

We always watched Fox News. I thought Bill O'Reilly was right most of the time. I didn't like his bullying personality but knew he was smart and well researched.

Then Trump happened and Fox became a screaming advocate. I had always clicked over Rachel Maddow but soon after Trump, realized she was smart and her show had a pleasant format. And she is funny and does not take herself too seriously. Now it is a must watch.

My next timeline book working title is, Blow Hard or Loud Mouth.   I'm on YouTube too. Look under Jeff Cooper, real estate, or Jeff Cooper Face it.

What Have We Done !!! – WW!!!

A Facebook Timeline.   Facebook is great for free speech.   I try to be a culture hog.

4-6-16   My wife Martha is a Trump fan.

Every night I go on the pee patrol looking for surprises and using a roll of paper towels every hour. (We have 7 dogs)

The government targeting the coal industry seems wrong to me.

Pot cures Alzheimer's? I can't remember.

4-7-16   With all the delegate shuffling and electoral college confusion, why bother to vote seems logical.

I now know Trump better than I ever expected or wanted.

Getting old means giving all your money to doctors.

Eartha Kitt's 1953 version of Santa Baby is the best.

4-8-16 Words can only express a fraction of real feelings but that is what great authors try to do.

If not Hillary for president, who? After-all, she rode the subway and spoke to a black person.

Kasich is ahead of Cruz in New York.

Trump refuses to come on O'Reilly's show? O'Reilly dishes sort of a hate light, while Megyn Kelly rains full blown hate, much more honest. Megyn is my hero. Trump's abortion quagmire may actually begin his fall. If so, we owe a lot to Chris Matthews who gave him the question.

4-9-16   Trump has entered Twitter rehab.

Kim and Owen arrive. Kim is Martha's daughter and Owen is a large Scottie mix. Kim is my book editor.

Dad held mortgages but if a buyer got in trouble, he'd lower the payment. This strung out the payoff process and gave dad more interest in the long run while saving the owner's house. Banks, pay attention, you can have a heart and still make money.

You gotta love Bill Clinton, her not so much.

Another Friday, parties, weaving all over the road, getting thrown out of Whisky Ago Ago.

4-10-16   Chris Wallace gets information while Bill O'Reilly beats the interviewee down.

The war on terror is the hardest to fathom in recent centuries.

There are a lot of sick parents who are way too close to their children.

Too many gifts teach a child nothing has value.

Trump reminds me of J. R. Ewing of Dallas fame. Entertaining but not presidential. (Larry Hagman played the wealthy rake.)

4-11-16   Most of the Trump agenda is impossible.

Bernie Sanders will zero the military?

BMW is dropping the standard transmission because they don't give a shift.

Bill has Monica, Hillary has emails and Benghazi, Trump battling insanity, Cruz off the charts. We must pick from the human race.

More Americans die from brooms than terrorists. – Obama

4-12-16   Better to watch a commercial than a Trump speech.

Two of the Trump children didn't bother to register to vote in NY.

The new Republican Party name is ___________.

Trump delegates stolen? Damn Damn Damn

Karen back from Colorado, thanks for my bushel.

My Tesla was recalled before I even got it.

Oscar Pistorius is almost a bionic man.

4-13-16   E-books not as popular as before.

Trump gets caught buying delegates.

Octopus escapes aquarium?

4-14-16   Illegals flooding in before the wall is built.

Trump hit his music teacher because he was no good – Art of the Deal, 1987

The delegate mess turns off young would be voters.

Did going off the gold standard allow our debt to get so high?

Bernie Sanders can't break up the big banks. Sherman Anti-Trust and Dodd Frank already exist for that.

A new legal driver (18 year old) is on the road, duck and cover.

The stagnant middle class has to learn to save money, not wait in the drive through line at Hamburgler for 30 minutes.

4-15-16   Twin Towers in so many movies, I get mad every time I see them.   A newspaper reporter came out to do an article on me and saw the Twin Towers on enlarged postcard and asked, "What are those."

We could have a moon colony by now were it not for our huge national debt.

Disney's Jessie crashes her car driving drunk. What's next? High Barbee?

Trump could generate a military coup of the country. It's hard for Trump to know who the real enemies are because all people are his enemy. He's run a cheap TV campaign but now he needs boots on the ground and he's slipping.

From reading Art of the Deal, his father was just as much a bully as Donald. The oldest son, Robert, did not want to be in daddy's business and eventually drank himself to death. Then daddy Fred cut Robert's kids out of his will. Mean people.

4-16-16   A Corvette sold for $7 million on Mecum Auto Auctions.

So much wind, small trees are in the pool.

The car Mercury equaled Lincoln in looks for 08 only the Lincoln was uglier.

A second Avatar movie?

No Trump impersonator has gotten the hair down right.

Tales from the nursing home: Dad's roommate whacked him with his cane. A cop asked me if I wanted to press charges.

4-17-16   Most voting is an emotional choice.

Trump hiding shady deals by not revealing his tax returns? Imagine Trump vs Jimmy Carter.

Did Bernie Sanders commit a sin by visiting the pope? You could wonder if he was asking for divine help to win election. They were only together 5 minutes so they had to chug their beer.

NASA is adding a room to make their rockets larger and more inviting.

When I get ice from the refrigerator drop thing, I think you could measure the amount of water displacement if you knew the cube size and rate of fall. Maybe this is why I'm not invited to parties.

Enough with the Facebook amens already. Quit asking me to say amen every time you pick a flower.

4-18-16   Me on the $20 bill, you shouldn't have.

Only 1 of our 7 dogs is registered to vote.

4-19-16   Speaking of bad elections, 2000, Gore vs Bush. We've had 16 years to fix this but can't.

Obama does not hate America. Trump on the other hand hates a lot of things.

Just because the voting process is not perfect, you still need to vote.

Ben Carson is hanging around. He likes the spotlight. Maybe he'll get a show like Herman Cain.

An original idea is a precious thing.

Trump has helped to expose crazy election rules that cry out for fixing.

4-20-16   City planners in the '60's built high rise housing but forgot the Seven-11s.

Living above your store is now prohibited by most zoning codes.

The nominee should be voted on within 60 days or he is automatically approved. (Needed new law)

The Supreme Court is now a mini congress.

Trump will sweep the election. (prediction)

Hillary will build a double wall with water and alligators in between.

Is it 7-11 or 9-11, the Trump man does not know.

4-21-16   Florida has approved nude beaches, next door to you.

If Trump is elected, he won't remember what he promised. He will get sucked into whatever rogue nation wants to challenge him.

Remember Gail Storm? And her sister Windy Rayne?

Trump is going to have a tough time with the Florida wall. Florida is fast becoming Puerto Rico central.

4-22-16   Prince was a well dressed rock star, confusing right there. He used his androgyny to rile both sides of the aisle.

There are few hits among many songs. Was Prince better than Michael Jackson?

Bill Clinton's bimbos are once again lining up as well as some new ones to "help" Hillary with the election.

Bill O'Reilly's latest book is: Killing Trump

If you want to add value to a subdivision, when naming it, add e to the end of Point making it Pointe and add the word Reserve to the end of the whole thing.   Spell Harbor: Harbour.   Adding Plantation to the end not so much anymore.

Trump is just auditioning for a role as president.

4-23-16   Prince found in elevator, Elvis in his bathroom, damn.

Trump has a good chance to beat Hillary. Be afraid. If Trump wins, the market could drop 5,000 points.

No more 2' cakes, just cupcakes.

The Sears store at Regency Mall was open 10 years too long.

Prince put himself through such a punishing dance routine, it almost looked like he was trying to kill himself. Art of the Dead.

Hillary has all the qualifications, Trump none. Trump's great strength is he can make people believe lies. His words hang in the air and take on a life of their own. His mean names for people live on in the press coverage. This guy has no class, no clue and lacks the courage to admit it putting us all in grave danger.

4-24-16   Jurassic World too scary to watch all of.

Prince's house functional, not the usual castle.

Trump with no experience would have to learn the job on our backs.

Worse would be if Trump wins the numbers for nomination but it's stolen from him.

4-25-16   One third of voters prefer a racist white maniac over a decent black president.

If you don't want to see Jurassic Park 4, just remember: Don't mess with mother nature.

If Trump turns out to be a good president, then his entire campaign has been a lie.   We will know quickly if he has to go.

Cruz looks constipated – Martha Cooper

Don't know how to use e-gift cards.

Bill O'Reilly hates personal attacks, hate speech and "bomb throwers" yet gives Trump a pass on all of it.

You're on the couch and realize the Kardashians are on TV and the remote is in the other room.   Do you shoot the TV?

At her request, I cut Martha's hair. She said it's too short but isn't that the point of hair cutting?   I say: It looks divine dahling.

4-26-16   Trump on Kasich's table manners: Eats like a pig. But doesn't Trump shovel it in pretty good to get so fat? Maybe Trump has a cookie conveyor belt. Maybe Trump should be nicknamed: Lardo Donald.

4-27-16   The Obama presidency unleashed more hatred than the 1960's civil rights riots.

Two journalists brought down Richard Nixon. How many journalists hate Trump?

You lend someone your pen and it's gone forever.

Pensions and corporate provided health care are on the chopping block.

This is the first presidential cycle I've seen as a retired person so my TV time is greater and the delegate mess is staggering.

My recent book Face It had so many Trumpisms that I had to cut back its size for publishing.   Thanks to Dave Remisiewicz, boy wonder.

Hillary has the FBI investigation and Trump has his University.

To my knowledge, I have never seen a transgender person in a public bathroom but one is tempted to feel their crotches like Crocodile Dundee in that movie.

Trump rubs our noses in the sewer of life.

In 1650 it took 350 men to sail a merchant ship and now it only takes 35, and the ship is 8 times as big. Technology does un-employ people. (Would you have it any other way?) Programmed into the 350 men was the fact that 100 of them would die.

4-28-16   Trump buys all the Botox. Trump is so nasty he can ruin Hillary in a debate. T says bomb the hell out of ISIS killing 90% innocent people. T ok with bankrupting country. After all, it was good for him. We have become victims of Trump's loud and toxic agenda.

Mexican drug lords killed the Ohio 8 – USA Today.

Kicking out the incumbents is not working.

I bought word processing in 1983 and tip toed around the screen afraid the words would fall down.

Fetus can now live after only a few months in the womb, making the abortion struggle even worse.

Prince's lack of a will may cost the estate $100 million. You need a will even if all you have is a phone and clothes.

4-30-16   We are so desperate for an effective leader that we ignore Trump's ugly, immature, bullying personality. T names iCarly as his VP? Carly Fiorina good VP for Cruz, we need more T bashers.

Goodbye spring, hello bugs.

Silver is good too. What's all this fuss over gold? Why not silver?

Rush Limbaugh homeless? He sat on it.

The 1959 Cadillac runs the gamut between classic and crotch itch.

The pope is dragging the church kicking and screaming back into relevance.

Don't order off a picture menu.

The McCain remark alone disqualifies Trump from holding high office.

After T loses, he will watch videos of his campaign like Howard Hughes watching his old movies.

After T loses the election, he won't serve in any other office because he's a selfish prick.

5-1-16   If a young child asks me if there a heaven and hell? I'd have to answer: Maybe.

Ted Cruz: Carly, will you be my VP? Carly; No, Ted, you're an a__hole. T: Yeah, but you'd go down in history and get to bash Trump. C: OK then.

We are waiting on the edge of our seats for the republican convention riots.

Most billionaires I have read about scrimp and save their money, but Trump spends lavishly and tells the banks to go to hell.

5-2-16   Iphone descendants may never physically talk to anyone.   Many don't know how to converse now. Predicted by H. G. Wells in Time Machine where Eloi became simple minded.

Obama funnier than most. Was it his black half or white half that wasn't allowed to be president?

Trump and us both dumb if he wins.

Vietnam vets or their descendants need reparations since the war turned out to be wrong headed?

European maps gave America many of its early city plans. None of these plans anticipated the automobile in such numbers.

5-3-16   All of May's bills are already here, it's a miracle.

A gap year is for travel and reflection between high school and college. For me it would have meant being drafted for Vietnam.

With some talk of redesigning the American flag, I suggest we wait until a new state is added. What are the chances?

Women can and do look better than men in clothes so they should take the time to dress well.

Car styles are: 1. That's just a car. 2. Damn.

Let vets go to any hospital.   Let them sort out the billing later.

War has no consequences to many Trump voters.

Why won't Trump release his tax returns? Has he lied to IRS or to us? Is he worth only a fraction of his stated fortune?   It is too risky to elect this guy.

5-4-16   Cruz quits. Trump will bury Hillary in a mountain of mud. I don't want to risk a T presidency. He takes his playbook from the National Enquirer and O'Reilly looks the other way.   He will be our Khrushchev.

Hillary wants to close coal mines, plays poorly in West Virginia.

Word has just leaked out; Trump will tax tampons.

5-5-16   Trump blew away 16 competitors with hate, vitriol, outrageous statements and stupid comments. The voters are divided between thinkers and malcontents. Trump makes himself rich, not you. Hillary's eating her spinach.

More dems will vote for Trump than repubs for Hillary.

It seems like the American period of greatness was from 1865 to 1955 but that was the era of world wars and robber barons.

5-6-16   Monica Lewinski looks like Bruce Jenner.

The Guggenheim Museum looks good but most curved architecture looks awful.

Paul Ryan vs Trump could mean a party split but I respect Ryan.

ISIS elected Trump. The tide is with Trump while Hillary is just a default candidate.   He is fiendishly shallow. If Trump fails as president, he won't last in office very long.

Those repubs skipping the convention will regret it.

Bernie vs Trump would be more interesting.

Finished off my supply of chocolates by melting them into a bowl of soup.

5-7-16   Reagan has gone from nut to hero. Time filters out the negative.

Perhaps the old republican party needed breaking.

Putting coal out of business seems a poor idea.

Changing Barkley's name to Trump cause he steals other dog's food and is wholly ravenous.

The lab has made a man whose mouth and anus is the same. They call him politician.

The voracious press will find Trump's women.

Trump is a natural politician with good, bad and ugly.

5-8-16   Happy Mother's Day.

Robin Williams egged lil Bush in London. Wish he was here to do Trump. He will testify at his University fraud trial. He knows how to find the suckers. (Trump settled the University case.)

The saddest thing about 1951 Day the Earth Stood Still is that Patricia Neal is left with that awful insurance salesman.

Cantina Laredo gave us a free lunch due to a long wait. Class act.

Does Trump have courage or is he just a puffed up know it all.

We keep useless stuff because it Was expensive originally. On the other hand, how many mothers threw out Superman One comic book?

Do ya think Bill Clinton could get so mad at Trump that shots are fired?

I like some of the two tone car paint of old.

Trump is the ultimate loud mouth. Being a success in business means nothing as to government. Witness Herbert Hoover.

5-9-16 Gassification of one's house is important but I feel solar will save us in the end. Ending foreign oil dependence is high on the list.

You pay your security company money so they/it can harass you. ATT is threatening to raise our rates unless we bundle.

Sarah Palin for VP. Naw, Trump isn't that nuts. Trump's pain is that he can't replicate himself for all the offices. Many repubs will vote dem to avoid T.

The press is hated with justification but we need them or all the treasury would be stolen and we'd be third world.

5-10-16   Bernie Sanders bashes billionaires and Trump won't release his taxes so we take his word for being a billionaire, hah!

Trump is our national medicine we have to take like an enema. He will clean up these bathroom rules. (transgender)

Two million people are in jails. Drugs are often the reason.

One's first car is often a predictor of how his life will go.

We give Trump a pass on his monumental ignorance because of Hillary hate. The woman card is cancelled out by the anti-woman card.

5-11-16   The internet is a wonderful thing but it has encouraged some businesses to lower customer service to the basement.

I'm Prince's grandfather. (He left no will and heirs are coming out of the woodwork.)

Women used to be a minority because they were unimportant.

Obama keeps quiet on coal's destruction, but not Hillary who bellows it from the rooftops.

Friday the 13th looms. Toss salt over your shoulder?

Trump weighs 250 lbs. I want his cartoons in a book. Ben Carson out of T campaign, too honest. Trump has no position you can count on. He could open the door to financial and economic collapse.

5-12-16   Burrito restaurant menu says plural but you only get one.

Remember Mondale had trouble getting a VP. Finally Eagleton accepted but he had had electric shock treatments.

Postcards have value because you stayed there, were married there, born there, educated there, died there, honeymooned there. Stamps may be on the back and signatures of famous people. In Florida, many of the buildings are torn down or replaced. (Fast growth state.)

Trump's tax return is like any other real estate investor's. Buildings are depreciated below market value per IRS rules. But we would like to know if he's mobbed up. And does he have off shore money?

Now that Trump is unopposed, he can really let go. My 3 Trump dreams are: I sold him my car for a can of beans. I was invited up to his penthouse for a drink but had to climb a rope ladder outside the building. He asked me to sell a warehouse. He asked What's it worth. I said $400,000. He said ask $300,000, I want it gone quickly.

5-13-16 Friday. Friends are telling me to lay off Trump. OK, How's this: Obama to park cars after he leaves office.

Trump easily changes his positions. Maybe he's only half mad. If repubs float a new guy in his place, there will be riots.

The '89 crash has a face: Mike Milken, king of junk bonds and Reagan. The '08 crash has no face for the mortgage derivatives except the clueless Bush.

Buy when there is blood in the streets – Baron Rothschild

Make Florida Great Again with bug spray, ditches and air conditioning.

5-14-16 Earth spins in space 4 ways yet our stuff stays stable.

Trump wants blind loyalty from followers. He was his own publicist using an alias? Even if Trump loses, his bad example will remain for decades.

Friday 13th OK for me but my neighbor had a package stolen off his porch.

The bible is not all relevant. Part of it has to give way to modern laws. Old timers who won't let go are going to be difficult for us and themselves.   Old timers think God doesn't change or he'd be wrong, but he does change with us, as we are partners with God.

All the air conditioners and cars running has to be bad for the environment.   It's like smoking. Since when is smoke good for your lungs?

5-15-16   Trump won't accept responsibility for anything. The OJ personality. Lies for a living and for the fun of it. No center.

Does God approve of Lotto?

5-16-16   Bill Maher now a friend since he ridicules Trump. People are voting for Trump because of WTF. Is T a bigot? Don's taxes are public paid documents while Hillary's speeches are private.

Women helped both Trump and Tiger Woods until Tiger got caught and bummed out. Trump is still feeding the flame and benefitting from it while his women must know their place.

Is Reince Priebus an automobile?

Nixon seemed sane but went bad in his 2nd term. Why elect a man who is bad right from the beginning?

Bernie Sanders has done a lot of big things as a campaigner yet the media gives him little credit or press.

5-17-16   Trump out flip flops Hillary 50 to one.

The Supreme Court has been decapitated by Republican neglect. Cases are being sent back to lower courts unresolved because repubs won't approve the 9th justice.

The New York Times alleges 50 women have been abused by Trump. One woman recanted and her statement is repeated 1,000 times. The other 49 are silent. You can't broadcast silence.

TSA lines are so long, flyers are taking the bus. (Transportation Security Administration)

5-18-16 Trump's thug persona is popular but not presidential. He beat the poop out of Megyn Kelly. By ripping her a new one during the first debate, he set in motion the later interview which drew many viewers. Trump can be funny but it's like your hemorrhoid doctor making jokes about your ass.   May he lose with the same percentage as Goldwater lost. He's taken down the civility factor of the entire nation.

5-19-16   Everything is rigged sounds like an admission of failure to me.

Trump's wife has said he is not Hitler. Well, that's comforting.

I would like a tour of Prince's house.

El Faro sunk from multiple human errors.   Sort of a Titanic. Don't mess with Mother Nature. (Cargo ship based in Jacksonville, FL)

5-20-16   Islam not so good for the Middle East.

Keep some of your paper money and coins as it will soon be extinct and collectible.

If you want me to like your page, tell me what city you are located in.

In Lincoln's day, wives were needed to work the farm as were the children.

If Sanders runs as a third party, Trump wins.

Abortion is now illegal in Oklahoma.

Breakfast at Panera Bread with bagels to take home.

5-21-16   People with babies, don't post pictures of them shitting.

Romney, get in the race.

Voters will never allow a deficit cut.   Politics is too toxic for that.

Barkley has had 3 seizures in one day, Epilepsy occurs in dogs.

Trump asked Hillary for her Supreme Court list. I guess it never occurred to dumb ass that she might support Obama's pick.

Hero's Landing Condo on Jacksonville's Beach Blvd was sued by the homeowners assn for $9.6 million for shoddy construction, per the Times Union. Normally, individuals cannot sue in open court but must submit to binding confidential arbitration per terms of purchase agreement.

The 1959 Cadillac seems to make fools of us but I still want one.

Egypt air may have just caught fire but Trump with his all knowing wisdom early on pronounced it terrorism. How dangerous is this man? Since he is the presumptive nominee, he's entered the world stage and embarrassed us all.

5-22-16   Dollar General Coffee cans only filled ¾ of the way up.

Hey Trump fans, character counts. You want shake up? Nero did that, remember?

The Mediterranean Sea where Egypt Air went down is 10,000 feet deep.   I would have guessed more like 3,000'.

Martha has veggie burger at Ted's. Not the same.

Many Facebookers lace their comments with religion and their faith permeates all their posts.

Once you have a good car design, why change it? Why isn't the '56 Ford still available now?

How can War of the Worlds be a stage play? Easy, just have a movie screen above the actors for the Martian tripods to roam around on.

5-23-16   Trump will be like Caesar, stabbed in the Senate. Trump can end abortion with his supreme court picks.

Martha can't find a good fake meat hamburger.

CBS Sunday Morning show on design had a 60 floor skyscraper in New York City on a 75' lot with some wood in its construction. These buildings grow sideways so they are 120 feet at the top.

Bernie Sanders campaign the victim of a rigged system.

The skinny skyscrapers and 6,000 passenger cruise ships are just asking for trouble.   Greed is not good, it can be deadly.

5-24-16   Athene advertises on TV without disclosing their function. I know from personal experience they own life insurance policies.

Hillary will provide steady leadership. Trump will give us OMG and hold your breath. Don't bet more than you can afford to lose. Three Godfather movies and 7 years of Sopranos pave the way for Trump. He has one million positions. His core value is Wear a good hat. You can't make $ from several casinos? Paleezzzzeee.

5-25-16   This is scary: Trump the role model. Millions of younger men emulate Trump's ethics and thought patterns. Jake Tapper of CNN called him a liar. Both Bill Clinton and Trump live in glass houses. (People who live in them shouldn't throw stones.) Repubs paint Hillary with the bloody Banghazi paint brush. This is the ugliest campaign I've ever seen. T sets such a low road that no one can follow and if they do, they dissolve from the stink. This is the perfect storm of slanderous politics.

One bad supreme court justice and we descend into Trump's hell. Dred Scott. Is a negro a man? Today we have gay marriage and the decline of the church. Our present pope has worked hard to keep the church relevant. Does gay marriage spit on God?

5-26-16   Bela Lugosi was Dracula until the end of his life.

Trump will share the US Treasury with himself.

BurgerFi has a better vegiburger than Ted's.

Abe Lincoln paid $100 for a suit.

Bill Cosby to stand trial for unwanted sexual activity. His career is dinged and reputation sullied. Poor way to end one's life.

The Trump University was a financial rape of gullible students. Now they are having buyer's remorse and know they were conned.

5-27-16   Trump is more crooked than Hillary. I like Trump's energy policy but will he do it? $10 million to debate Bernie? How much will he charge us to govern? Obama wrong to bash Trump while in Japan? Trump brings us all down to his level of wallowing in garbage.

Hillary: I am not a crook. (Emails)

Saw a great breast surgery on TV.

5-28-16   Trump has a visceral manner like Babe Ruth farting at the formal dinner. When Hillary trots out Bill as a helper, that give T freedom to pound his past. T kills traditional repubs and Bernie is screwing with dem base.

We had to throw out the flour because of weevils. Tiny bugs barely visible.

Jepp Walter arrives and sends my book Face It for publishing, no problems. He/we stood on the shoulders of 2 failed prior attempts. Henry Ford was ignorant but could summon experts on any subject at any time.

Dogs have no money because they have no pockets. – Jerry Seinfeld

Indians were called heathen savages by the early settlers making them easier to kill.

5-29-16   Could the Trump mouth eat the Trump tail? Trump hyperboled his way to success in the real estate business, then show business and now politics. A logical progression. Trump momentum is huge, Hillary, be afraid.

Obama has cut the deficit but the debt cannot be cut until we run a surplus.

ISIS exists because the Arab kings keep all the money.

5-30-16   Reid Hoffman, founder of Linkedin, says phones take too much time so email is the only way.

Fareed says politely, Trump's campaign slogan Make America Great Again is a lie. We are already greater than the rest of the world in almost all sectors.

The deficit has declined under the Obama administration with republican help but we have to run a surplus before the exploding debt is contained.

I can envision a Mexican border fence with sensors indicating a breach and patrol it with drones and jeeps. The grand Trump wall is too impractical and expensive. It would cause a marble shortage.

5-31-16   Mike says use a national ID card instead of a wall.

Our overgrown yard is ideal for snakes. I see them on occasion.

Self esteem is defined as a dangerous type of vanity while self love is a realistic assessment of our attributes and abilities. – Scott Peck

Part of our dinner last night was grown in Lindsay's garden, thanks.

The apartment manager or maintenance man can have a master key so take care in hiring this person. They can steal, ogle woman or even kill – Forensic Files, TV show.

6-1-16   Trump was afraid of his father and his criticism so now he badgers the press and won't take their questions. Media and politicians who fawn over him have lost their souls. Trump's workers lie too but no one does it with the ease and naturalness of T himself, who has made it his life's goal to lie, exaggerate, deceive and punish.

Financiers delay payment. Like the Geico ad, That's what they do. Some never pay at all.   Trump is one of the world's greatest manipulative actors. O'Reilly is subtly suggesting that he be dictator. Hillary does not understand the Trump steamroller. She should be pounding him about the missing tax returns.

The Formosan termite is 10 times as destructive as a regular termite. Look for mud tubes up trees and buildings.

I have been upset with Christianity for some time. So, the bible is just one reference book on religion. There are others. I have at least 3 books on Lincoln or the Civil War. There is a bible.   Man enslaves inferior men, over 600,000 die to change this, Karma? Greed is not good in this case. The Civil War part of history screams at us what happens when we lose our way. When greed trumps civility.

6-2-16   Backing out of our driveway, I crunched the car parked on the opposite side of the street. Minor damage and the owner came out of his house unconcerned. Still......The insurance companies sure want to know if you drive for Uber.

O'Reilly sides with Trump in that the media is bad. Even tho Bill O'Reilly is a big part of the media.

Little attention has been paid to the fence around the gorilla pit the little boy fell into but it seems inadequate to me. Wanting to give an impression of nature not capture, they skimped on the safety.

Both Hillary and Trump have questionable things in their past.

Two of my favorite movies are KPax and Regarding Henry. They have little similarity but both men have brain alterations. Both are thoughtful and not violent although KPax has a violent flashback.

Half of what you say will be misunderstood.

6-3-16   During the American Civil War, the North lost more men but the South ran out of men.

Fox News is beating a broken drum that the economy is bad. Stats have been improving now for over 7 years.

Trump is sloppy in his speech and his policies. He creates demand by saying Ted is very bad and satisfies it by saying I can get rid of Ted.

Stephanie (my daughter) and her husband Dave will run the iron man in North Carolina this weekend.

Our really big space ventures seem fueled by politics.

Give all people guns and all countries nukes? Trump and the NRA.

6-4-16   Trump supporters are headed toward the bow. Remember the movie Poseidon Adventure when the cruise ship overturned and the only part above water was the stern.   A Trump president could overturn the ship of state, the USA.

Lying Ted is now just Ted, he got promoted.

Today is donut week.   I'll take glazed and chocolate covered with sprinkles.

I had one good course a year in college. Business law, construction, real estate appraising and swimming.

Hillary needs a microphone with her at all times to avoid or lessen her screeching.

If Trump can't think of anything to say, he praises himself.

6-5-16   We spend all of our life getting ready for our 15 minutes of fame.

The tiny house boom is made difficult due to zoning restrictions.

Steady value increases are good. Rapid value increases mean a bubble is going to pop.

After 39 years of putting up with a pink bathtub, we had the color changed to purple, just kidding, beige.

Trump uses the Muhammad Ali tactic of insulting your opponent.

Did Wall Street wreck Main Street?

I did not like Muhammad Ali when he changed religions and dodged the draft. Nobody liked blacks then. So there was a convergence of anti-war sentiment and prejudice. But over much time he captured the hearts and minds of America's people.

6-6-16   I like 1970's TV shows. That is where I left my hair.

Martha is de-cluttering the house.   Many things have gone away, or into my shed or office.   She adamantly opposed me building the shed but now appreciates it. You can't build anything if one tiny bush is lost even though it will grow back.

One listing or sale does not a value make but may point to a trend.

6-7-16   Tropical storm Colin has left the state of Florida. A lot of mailmen didn't work very much.

Obama looking into a restroom: Tear down this stall.

The tub adventure is all but over. One man paints the tub for $300. Takes several hours during which time the air stinks like fury.

Trump using the campaign to malign a judge is abhorrent.

Trump has shown he will mix his business with his politics, perhaps to make himself even more money. Look at the way he talks: I have a very biased judge. Look at my African American, look at him. Many republicans are against a lot of his tactics. Common decency, whether it comes from God or otherwise, is the bedrock of our success as a nation. Our military scores wins by not leaving troops behind. Where does Trump fit in this equation?

6-8-16   If you have a large house, people will move in it.

Hillary wears $10,000 worth of clothes all times.

Repubs fix it now. The longer Trump is allowed to be the "nominee" the harder it is to get rid of him. Trump knows PC is out. (Political correctness) Merely trying to ride the fence or shake off the Trump stink isn't good enough.

OJ Simpson wants publicity so bad he may confess.

Atlantic Blvd at Bowlan closes when it wants to. Sign said back in 5 minutes. It's a Mobil station/convenience store.

Donald's brother Fred Trump Jr. died from alcohol or hatred of his father. Daddy Trump cut Fred's children out of his will. Very mean people.

6-9-16   I saw Hillary at Wal Mart.

Vegetables have sexes. Green peppers, number of bumps.

Bernie Ahab Sanders has thrown his last harpoon.

Trump will cause millions of republicans to apologize. Trump said he will never let us down unless we are Mexican, women, black, crippled, Muslim or POW. (Prisoner of war)   A Trump win means Kim Jung Un bombs South Korea to drag us into a war. Hillary actually thinks she is going to get to say something in the Trump debates.

A cow on the internet, Dudley, has kept Martha from eating beef for over a year.

A seller's market means: 1. Rising house values. 2. Quicker selling times.   3. Marginal homes will sell. 4. Poorly located or damaged homes will sell.

Obamacare may have helped some people but has it also cost jobs and benefits?

6-10-16   Holding a bible does not make one religious. Trump routinely denies payment of his bills usually on some inadequacy of the supplier. The character of a man is far more important than whether he is democrat or republican.

I would have liked to become a scientist and discover anti-gravity working at the Hadron Collider at Cern. Or write, paint, draw, crafts. In the '50's sci fi movies I wanted to be the hero who could have kissed the girl if he wanted but was busy saving the world.

The perfection of CGI, computer generated images, has given new life to sci fi like Avatar and the War of the Worlds remake. The original War and Day the Earth Stood

Still linger in mind as the best. They had the period feel and innocence lost to us now.

6-11-16   Mitt Romney has the courage to tell the truth about Trump. And it isn't pretty.   The narcissist has no trouble immolating everyone for a trivial cause.

Watch Muhammad Ali's Greatest Fight, 2013, great movie about Ali and the Supreme Court. Old white men's view of race at the time and the eventual freeing of Ali. Christianity kept the black in bondage so it was natural to turn to Islam as the good alternative. He had character not obvious to us in the 1960's.

De-cluttering a house doesn't last as the removed clutter is slowly replaced with new clutter.

6-12-16   As Clinton and Trump ramp up the hate, others may come forth like Sanders or Romney. Trump knows his audience well. T isn't the only one to not pay bills. Add to that Chase and Wells Fargo. ISIS originated in Saudi Arabia per Mike Malaghan.

Create Space stayed on the phone with me for an hour while I finalized publication of Face It. This is the first internet company who actually used the phone well.

Democrats say the economy is good, republicans say it is bad. It's both. Like particle physics, the impossible is normal.

Mecum Auto Auctions suggests that your old car could be golden.

With 7 dogs, we have tons of dog hair in the house and in my food.

6-13-16   I made chocolate chip cookies but ended as bowl of dough looking like hamburger. Tasted gelatinous distant of chocolate.

Trump will build Muslim containment camps like for the Japanese during WWII.

As Obama's approval ratings increase, Fox news ratings decrease.

It's easy to criticize, hard to do.

Faye Resnick wrote a book about Nicole Brown Simpson and how she took OJ back after their divorce. She had ample evidence of his brutality and overlooked it. Some would call her stupid.

6-14-16   A president Trump might jail me for anti-Trump remarks. One more shooting by an Arab and T wins.

The Orlando shooter was sexually conflicted, like so many of these killers. Why did FBI take guy off watch list? People go crazy over time and snap one day. Can't anticipate but can make guns harder to get.

Went in hardware store which was full of guns and old white guys.

In second grade we used an outhouse at school, no transgenders then.

After OK City bombing, stobs were placed in front of buildings to keep trucks from getting too close. Nightclubs very bad for safety. Have extra lighting when needed. Big automatic drop doors. Sprinkler system can dampen mayhem. Require windows with shutters. Extra guards. Limit number of patrons. When Jacksonville GMAC office was shot up, they started putting small reception office in front with main office protected in rear. When McDonalds was shot up, they tore the building down to reduce memories.

Hope or Hate, Clinton or Trump – Billboard in Atlanta.

6-15-16   Ban assault rifles. No purchase guns if you are on a terror watch list or no fly list.

O'Reilly lies more now that Trump is running for pres.

New apartments in Riverside just sold for $187,000 per unit, 1,100 sq. ft. Used to be apartments sold for half of house value but now it is equal to house value here in Jacksonville.

Muslims do not tell cops about radicals within their community.

Happy birthday Mr. Trump, a 70 year old insane dictator. Pat Robertson is going to be his VP.

Our weapons are useless in a war on terror. What good is a B-52 over Orlando?

Alligator grabs small boy at Disney lake. Boy was wading in water when eaten. His father right there. Going to cost Disney pretty $. Also lose them business.   Do patrons feed the gators?

6-16-16   Car air conditioning can now be diagnosed with dye in Freon to determine where it is leaking.

Where is Shepard Smith of Fox News?

6-17-16   Obama appears more worked up about guns than terror.   Hoover said the Great Depression will cure itself. Does him going to Orlando embolden future shooters?

Trump pays no tax, so say some people.   A building appraisal might be 5 times higher than the value carried on the return.

Small apartments have traditionally been hard to sell. During the great price run-up of '05, people would convert a duplex back to a house. But, today, large complexes are selling for record highs.

6-18-16   Martha having second thoughts about Trump. A new disease has been named after Trump. O'Reilly is writing a new book: Killing Trump Please.

Kelli had a bird defecate on her head at Disney near where the boy got alligator eaten.

Fridays I kick back and have 2 grape sodas and power belch.

I threw away the new bottle of medicine and kept the old bottle. Had to go dumpster diving to retrieve new bottle. Need warning labels for us: Over 70, watch this guy. As raw garbage slid over my hands, I was reminded of my days in rental house management.

My book arrived from Create Space, Face It, 50 copies. Already sent one out to a guy who said something good about my Facebook posts.

6-19-16   Big lunch at Chilis with enough left over for dinner. That is the standard.

Gave Mike Malaghan's book Picture Bride a send off on my page. Google scan will pick that up and direct readers to his book and mine.

As Trump drops in the polls, he gets more nasty. All the guys out there with ex wives they hate will not vote for Hillary. Friends wish I'd keep quiet about Trump, but I have a duty to educate about the worst candidate in modern history. Trump has some good ideas and thoughts but his negatives are so high that we can't take the chance.

6-20-16   Trump's answer to terrorism is to give everyone a gun. My answer is total surveillance.

Chelsea Clinton's new baby will vote. (someday)

Hillary was walking by a lake and an alligator grabbed her. (Secret wish of many)

Read old unauthorized book on Trump. Party at Mar Largo. Thugs with Uzis in jackets. And these guests were his friends. Trump will need bodyguards because El Chapo has escaped from prison.

6-21-16   Trump's kids are running his campaign. He keeps changing his lines so that he has no story.

Any gun crime is ok with congress.

People stand in the open door and talk.

We need a morgue report showing all killings of all types by town and time. Might help to put some of these terror killings in perspective.

6-22-16   Half the money Trump raises goes to his own businesses.

In the old west, it was the number of notches on the six gun handle and now it's the terrorist body count.

Trump's new book stops at chapter 11.

Magazine scams. You subscribe due to a low rate only to find there are upcharges and hidden fees/agendas.

Just watched at the movie Outlaw, 1943, Jane Russell has cleavage issues with censors so the producer, Howard Hughes, brings in a scientist to measure her breasts with other competing stars and got them in.

Our pool has been invaded by green slime. Reason number 500 why you don't want a pool.

In the dream, dad was too old to be moved off the second floor of his house so Trump advised me to sell the first floor. I said there are problems. He said You want to raise money or not.

6-23-16   We would not want Trump with no experience even if he were normal.

If North Korea lobs an atom bomb into the Pacific Ocean, they will be invaded.

Angel said my real estate book is better than Art of the Deal.

Trump auctions off Christie on eBay. (Trump campaign short of funds.) Trump finds a job for Bernie so he can get Bern's cash.

A new law says all firearms should have the safety on.

The French have raided mosques and found stashes of weapons.

Omar Mateen,30, was rejected by gays so the Orlando nightclub was a revenge killing with ISIS a handy justification.

Cosby raped the women because of his celebrity entitlement, women are nothing in his world, once he got away with it, it was so easy.

6-24-16   Mike Milken gave us junk bonds which blasted corporate America in a blizzard of takeovers resulting in lowered employee loyalty, lowered benefits, lowered wages.

Martha kept a live snake loose in her house when we started dating and I said, One of us goes.

Trump is a great actor and manipulator and he gets the talking heads in a spin, spitting on each other.

6-25-16   Our stock market falls 600 points on Britain leaving EU, European Union. We are one world. Many Americans want the UN, United Nations out of NYC and America but I hope that doesn't happen.

Trump is our Kim Jung Un. (Dictator of North Korea) If the economy falters, the clueless Trump will benefit. Trump says Britain leaving EU is good but market says otherwise. Trump says Take back our country, but every time nationalization rises, we have a world war.

Finally got my Forbes, 5 weeks after paying. Good magazine tarnished by shady sales methods. They wouldn't sent it until I bought another year.

6-26-16   Tony Robbins, super talker, burned some customers by getting them to walk down a bed of hot coals.

A president Trump who hurts other countries invites war. Other world leaders may follow the Trump cult of blowhard personality. Everyone is a role model.   Bush was just stupid, this guy is malevolent. (Evil)

The world is afflicted by too much tax, regulation, and meddling in people's lives.

Jacksonville restaurant, Cruiser's Grill, gets a thumbs up. Good food, reasonably priced with pleasant staff. View of lake. Girl and her dog walked down to water's edge but no alligators were seen.

6-27-16   Trump's financial plan includes the appraiser doesn't have to see the house. Whadda good idea. He would give us a great ride until the country bankrupts. Remember pres. Reagan deregulating the savings and loans. Where are the savings and loans now?

TV commercial time has crept up to 50% of air time.

The 2 party system is not working.   A lot of the present slowness is due to pure racial hatred of Pres. Obama. I thought we were over that, but no. Fox news has fed this beast for too long now. Those who think we can't do worse than Pres. Obama are in for a sad reality. We need good hearted men with good motives, not gasbag businessmen.

The Euro may be gone but we still have the Chunnel.

6-28-16 The Trump wall is now a fence. The Trump brand is now so damaged that his business will suffer. Most Americans would rather have irritable colon than vote for

Trump. He is still a chameleon and can change spots on a dime, say whatever is expedient in seconds, still a dangerous beast.

Hillary probably should have a man for VP.

Many children are pushed into adult situations.   This includes households with loaded guns, booze, pills, drugs, and so on.

6-29-16   The Hubble space telescope was an anecdote to the exploded space shuttle.

Trump makes his listeners feel powerful. He lavishes $ on himself while stiffing others. He would be the Cheater in Chief.

8,000 pages on Benghazi, 4 dead, 200 pages on Iraq War, 4,500 dead.

In the roaring 1980's, I had a corporate, individual and partnership tax return. By 1989, the Reagan recession had cleaned me out.

State Farm insurance raised all auto rates in Florida.

Why did Saudi Arabia get a pass on 9-11? Reeks of guilt to me.

Beginning in the 1950's, US car quality was sliding. The VW and other imports arose. Cadillac fell from being no. 1. Detroit was vacated. US Steel shrank. Today, technology driven new cars could bring us back.

My TV talk of 2005 was about the decline of the Regency
Mall in Jacksonville. In 1981, they doubled their size to 1.2
million sq. ft. Ceilings were lowered, store fronts in the
old mall brought forward, skylights retrofitted, but then
vacancy rose as new competition came from both north
and south sides. People began sleeping in kiosks. No
more floor shows, soon no more restaurants, no movies,
slack management. Roof leaks, floor tiles crack, main
repair tool is duct tape, customers dwindle, vacancy soars
even among key tenants. Now, it is mostly a land value
situation, but still well located.

6-30-16   We got our phonebook pamphlet.

Prince estate cannot collect $ from music sales until all
heirs are named. Brilliant performer but dumb as hell not
to have a will.

Hillary is pulling a Romney and not feeling the mood of the
people.

O'Reilly is re-naming his show: The Trump Hour. A
president Trump will continue the present gridlock.

7-1-16   Fareed says Bernie Sanders should be Trump's VP.
I wonder if any sane person would be Trump's VP.

A horse stepped on granddaughter Emma's toe. Horse is
fine.

Bella, our runner, escaped and Lisa caught her. Lisa old friend of Lindsay's. Lisa used her dog as bait and grabbed her by the ear until I arrived.

SUV's are getting better looking.

7-2-16   Preliminary fireworks going off near my house. Ablaze, rocket's red glare.

Fox News: Obama is stupid. That is all.

My wife Martha, devoted Trump fan, unable to tell me difference between him and Sarah Palin.

Hillary cedes power to Biden who gets Bernie Sanders as VP, crushes Trump. There is no lovable Hillary. Bill has this, gosh did I do that, way but all she has is screech.

Radiation is all around us but most comes from our Sun. This is the great cause of aging.

I believe that if an asteroid is found coming at us, we should nuke it. Many pieces would be created some missing earth. The total energy we'd have to absorb would be less because pieces are smaller and could be traveling slower. As much as half the total mass could end up missing us entirely.

7-3-16   Overall, Bill is no help to Hillary and her campaign.

A vice president Gingrich is no help to Trump. Trump's name calling cancels Hillary's superior ad budget. Especially when Fox News calls her Crooked Hillary, right along with Trump. Trump is a fairy tale, pipe dream turning into Twilight Zone where we are the ones at the bottom of a huge trash can or inhabiting a doll house city managed by a little child.

We are all a shooting gallery for ISIS. We need to hire huge armies of security guards, both public and private. You can't get rid of the idea of Jihad or holy war.   There are too many nuts or poor people willing to buy any way out of their failed lives.

7-4-16   Happy Independence Day! The strings of fireworks sound like a Gatling gun. One of our 7 dogs became scared and crazy over the noise.

The algae bloom in South Florida is our Flint, Michigan.

Are there any shoe shine men left anywhere? Since I buy shoes at Walmart, probably cheaper to start over.

Reporters are now attending a special combat school to interview Trump. He just chews them up like candy. More than one fact checker has quit in disgust. Trump doesn't deal in facts but rather emotion. He's an actor. He avoids real facts and hides from real Q and A. Like his tax returns, hidden from view. Some papers are running the facts beside his rhetoric.   He's friends with Bill O'Reilly, 2 very bellicose men. Trump is the guy who breaks in front of you in line.

7-5-16   There is a great man theory of history. There are also evil men. Be careful who you vote for.

Cheese fries on onion rings, 3,200 calories.

7-6-16   Trump is asking his VP hopefuls for their tax returns. How quaint.   Forbes has a good article on Trumpian tax deductions. Conservation easements. May be worth zero. Real estate is a tax haven.   Trump knows he throws mud at wall and some will stick. There are times when he will catch the IRS asleep at the switch. Trump will always be under audit and we will never see his tax returns. This constant pushing the deduction boundary is expensive and must be blessed by one or more brave appraisers. If the court rules against the tax payer, the appraiser can be fined too.

I miss Shepard Smith and his menopausal meltdowns. (Fox News anchor and Trump hater)

Watched a lot of Twilight Zones over the 4th.

Two of my friends who own condos have lost part of their view due to new construction nearby.

John Rogers was my boss in 1968. I learned a lot about real estate with him.   I learned by watching that one's home is often the best real estate investment you can make.

The media makes stuff up by using the question mark at the end.

Long live the science shows. Probe now at Jupiter, our largest planet. Graphics wonderful. I like science and love the imagery.

7-7-16   Bill O'Reilly, Fox News Anchor, was teetering on the edge of sanity anyway and when Trump became the nominee, Bill fell into a pool of hero worship. VPs include Newt Gingrich who is just like Trump with affairs and bankruptcies. Trump partly right when he said Saddam Hussein should have left him in place. By deposing him, we have left a trail of blood leading straight to the door of George Bush Jr. Lil Bush. The dumb one. Baby Bush. Trump might be a good leader for a year or two. Hitler was a good leader for a year or two.

7-8-16   Picture Bride is now available from Mike Malaghan, an old college chum. It is about Japanese who fought on the American side during WWII.

The black crime and murder rate is so high, cops don't give them as much leeway as they do whites. Blacks want their own language with many curse words, a precursor to violence. And, the willingness of blacks to shoot has inflamed the prejudice of some cops. Legal carry hasn't helped either.

Can a single review close a restaurant? Crab Creek Café may have been victim to this. The last time we ate there, I told Martha the place has sold because there were a few less shrimp and a little more cost.

The number of people with TVs is shrinking.

Talk to the receptionist as long as possible as the person you need to see may come by.

Is TV rife with sexism? Gretchen Carlson thinks so. Ask Roger Ailes. Miss Carlson, former Miss America rose to fame on the back of a meat show and she should be girded for some ogling. Shepard Smith back on Fox after a long unexplained absence. Trump could not only sink the republican party but Fox News as well.

7-9-16   When Trump says Good morning, that is his truth for the day. Top business executives are calling him a dumpster fire. Hillary's emails overblown? Cable news has become a snuff film. Shep back now that Gretchen is gone. Maybe he got more money.

You know it's going to be a long day when you wake up and it's 83 degrees. (Welcome to Florida.)

7-10-16   98 degrees again but at end of day, a tiny rain helped.

Bill impeached, Hillary investigated, Chelsea; pick up your room.

Micah Johnson, first perp to be taken out by robot bomb.

The Trump vs Hillary movie is entertaining. We are the audience and the guinea pigs.

It's fraud to run up debt knowing you are going bankrupt and what about the banks loaning after 2 or 3 bankruptcies in the same city and in the same business? Payoff? (Trump casinos)

A bad waitress will want to clear the table while you are still eating and a real bad one will not give up, making you decide what you are finished with.

Unplug the country.   Too many adjectives spoil the book.

7-11-16   FBI cleared Hillary, didn't want a Trump presidency.

The tiny house craze seems odd. Cheap housing is needed. Manufactured housing is the best deal for this. There are thousands of un-used acres in Jacksonville's developed areas. All we need are sewers and zoning.

My printer ink overflow bucket is full. That's a new one on me. Can't see how to do it without taking apart the entire printer. Jepp Walter says there is no print ink overflow bucket. That's computer for get a new printer.

The Dallas perp Micah Johnson, had sex harassments problems in the army. They gave him an honorable discharge. Many shooters have sex problems, can't keep a girl friend or don't have one. The dangerous age for that is 16 to 26.

7-12-16   A new gun or bullet should be developed. One that immobilizes the perp for a while. The arms we have now are an overkill.

Trump will quit if he perceives he is losing. Yes, his ego is that big.

There is a return to gardening, urban farms and feeding ourselves. This reduces unemployment and gives us a feeling of accomplishment.

The TV show Forensic Files can be gruesome but it is also educational and easy to take in 30 minute segments. Reminiscent of the Dragnet radio show. We believe, the stories are true.

Bruno Hauptmann was convicted of killing the Lindbergh baby and executed in 1936. He never admitted guilt and developed a fan base. So the Lindberghs began to get death threats on their second baby. These same loons are now on Facebook. Nothing ever really changes.

7-13-16   Rain lowered the temperature but created mosquitoes and hail.

Ruth Ginsburg, 83, Supreme Court justice, rails against Trump (rightly so) but perhaps she should remember the dignity of her office. I believe if Trump wins, she will resign. Trump says she's out as VP.

The best apology is changed behavior.

7-14-16   If you are rich like Trump, doctors give you diseases to keep you out of military service. First the Tea Party, then Trump. Trump announces his pick for VP to the tune: Dead Skunk in the Middle of the Road. CNN burns Trump University. Long election cycle lets us get to know candidates. Trump's convention line-up is as follows: 1. Dancing elephants lead by Newt Gingrich. 2. Nakid gurls from Trump's past. 3. Keynote speaker: Monica Lewinski.

If a Chinese food delivery business doesn't speak English, do not be surprised if your eggroll is concrete.

7-15-16   Trump's need for loyalty and secrecy make you nervous? Trump is all the Animal House characters rolled into one, ok at 20 but at 70? Trump's goal is to be worshiped. Ginsburg senile or courageous? Tim Tebow asked to speak at convention to bolster Trump's image, but since it would tarnish Tim's image, he said no.

Rumor says Bill O'Reilly out at Fox News. Will be replaced by King Kong. Asked what he will do with his time, Bill said, chase Gretchen Carlson.

7-16-16   Pence is an anti gay conservative.

Immaturity is central to most over spending – Dave Ramsey

Sarah Palin ran out of gas on her way to the republican convention.

Coup attempt in Turkey caused more deaths than the attack in Nice France.

7-17-16 War has come to suburbia and there are no air raid sirens. Radicalized is just a new word for crazy.

Third time I've been to Dick's Wings and finally learned how to order.

Pence brings some baggage of his own. Some ethical things in the past.

REITs are real estate investment trusts. They hold a lot of property and can be lethargic about management. Often, all that is needed is a for sale or rent sign. A little management can produce big returns on the financial statement.

Buy Face it, Stuff I've said on Facebook now $10 before price goes down.

7-18-16   Open carry to backfire on republicans at convention. Trump campaign could fold after convention. Trump + Pence = Tense. Candidates and the voters all lie. Ferguson kicked off the Black Lives Matter. Cleveland mistake on lake because Cuyahoga River got so polluted, it burned.

Lil Bush drinking again?

7-19-16   Trump has created lots of new democrats. Melania speech stolen from Michelle Obama's 2008 speech? Melanie must have graduated from Trump University. Trump appoints low level administrators with extreme loyalty to T. They adore and worship him and will do anything without question. Trump bathes in their glory. Then they deny they did anything wrong.

7-20-16   I think Melania Trump googled first lady speeches and lifted most of it from there. Her college degree is also fake.

College fraternities have as a recruiting tool libraries of hundreds of term papers on different subjects.

Swagger is not enough. You must do actual work. Roaring is not enough. You must do actual work.

7-21-16   Roger Ailes and Trump two of a kind.

My best car was a 1971 Olds Cutlass, leather wheel, tan color, too bad I tore it up like all my other cars.

Trump people saying things like killing Hillary is ok. Is he a candidate or mob boss? A wall has been built around his Hollywood Walk of Fame Star. Dan Rather was kind to Trump when he said he is like Nixon. His kids like him but they have to, he's their boss.

An old Chicago World's Fair postcard showed something like a zipline across the river. We need that here in Jacksonville.

Trump and Pence are spouting different foreign policies.

7-22-16   Gary Johnson, the third party candidate, could throw the election to Trump. Trump is not hard working, he just yells at others to get it done for him. Lying is the lazy way out. Trump has the highest negatives in the history of elections.

A retro garage door may not operate as well as one that came with the house originally.

If Hillary names Vilsack as VP, there will be jokes about body parts taken out.

Cruz slaps back at Trump for insulting his family. No one can insult like Trump. When others try, they fall flat.

7-23-16   Trump daughters are better looking than his wives. All wives matter. Trump's wives are rented.

Pence so far is a good valet. Trump has drawn out the ugly side of America.

If you order hors d'oeuvres, you will leave half you meal behind. A splendid idea cooked up by restaurants catering to people who can't wait and have no sense of thrift.

Tim Kaine of Virginia is Hillary's running mate.

7-24-16   House values seem back up to '05 levels.

Cruz should have pulled out of the speech at the last minute rather than take up time with no Trump endorsement. Or, he could have given a Trump bashing speech. Either way, Trump is very vindictive.

7-25-16   Roger Ailes could get the best hookers or "friends", why bother to harass the workers at Fox?

Michelle Obama gives both the democratic and republican convention addresses.

Trump and Sanders have broken old party rules and customs.

Trump's 2 ex wives will speak at democratic convention??? David Duke seems to be Trump's bitch.

7-26-16   Hatred for both candidates, Trump and Clinton, will be shown if voter turnout is low. Putin knows Trump is lousy for America which is why he's behind him.

7-27-16   The bedrock of American success is the second opinion, medical and other things.

They have socialism in China where growth is mandated along with the one child per couple rule.

Role models move mountains and are important at any age.

Russia releases Trump's tax returns. Only I have them. Leave $5 million on my front porch.

When house values rise, loan sharks come out of the woodwork. They want the house. This boom could be nullified by rapid apartment construction.

Wikileaks' Assange will be dealt with when Hillary becomes president, he will be taken out.

7-28-16   Trump believes all publicity about him is good. Trump asking Russians to find Hillary's emails a joke say repubs. Hidden tax returns fuel rampant speculation such as bribes and lies. Melania has zero college degree.

Trump is like a religion to his followers. Both VPs are better than these presidents. It's hard to understand the I am perfect mindset that Trump has. Trump is hyperbole defined as puffing the goods to the point of unbelievability. That has served him well in business.

Politically incorrect borders on stupid. Hillary can't lose this race?

Bill O'Reilly of Fox News says slaves who built White House were lucky.

Got my first robocall from the NRA (National Rifle Association).

7-29-16   Trump entered the race at exactly the right time as latent racism toward Obama reached a boiling point. Mike Pence is going to get tired of bailing Trump's boat.

Flag burner sets himself on fire. Damn.

7-30-16   If Hillary loses the election, it will be because she said, I want to put a lot of coal companies out of business. People perceive this as being hostile to business, similar to Obama.

PayPal and eBay have reached a settlement regarding the fraud suit against them. We might get a penny or a farthing.

Fox News seemed a little less rabid now that Roger Ailes is no longer there.

7-31-16   Trump will be in Jacksonville Wednesday. His second visit. It wasn't Hillary who killed the beast, it was Twitter that killed the beast. We are seeing raging mental illness played out on a national stage. CNN is showing Nixon tonight, coincidence? NO voters on the Iraq war were called traitors and cowards but now they are heroes. Similarly, republicans publically against Trump vilified by many will be heroes.

If your enemy is on fire, get a fan. – Jeff proverb

16 dead in hot air balloon crash in Texas.

Dominick Dunne, the crime writer had a prodigious memory for names as did Michael Milken the junk bond king who could remember who held the bond issues.

8-1-16   The "middle class" has to get second jobs or quit wasting $.

The Trump Hillary race seems to be for the least worst. Spence spouts his own stuff because to follow Trump would make him sick. T won't show taxes, won't debate Hillary, a cowardly crook. All Hillary has to do is use T's own words against him for her commercial. Dream, T loses 48 states. T wife Melania was hot and knew how to sell it.

Jacksonville, Florida is well positioned for success.

My uncle Conrad took a lot of liberties with the IRS too.

8-2-16   Polar bears are not endangered, just unlucky –
Sarah Palin. Sarah's hobbies are breast feeding and
helicopter hunting. – Robin Williams.

Fox News should bail on Trump before he drags them into
his sewer. They did agree that T should not have dissed
the parents of the Muslim soldier killed in Iraq. T is stupid
or doesn't want the presidency. When he loses, who will
he sue? A third party can put T in the White House.

Man had sex with pig in Walmart bathroom. Loud
squealing was heard by customers who alerted
management who hauled the pleased pig away.

8-3-16   Trump is crushing Bill O'Reilly of Fox News.
Obama should not diss Trump when traveling overseas.
Melania Trump will strip again for the right debate slot.
Dan Rather to rip T as Fareed Zakaria has already done.
The right wing no longer talks about Trump, just bashes
Hillary. T in Jacksonville today. Get your rotten eggs and
tomatoes from my front porch.

No individual can stand having total knowledge, only God
can do it.

At last a movie about mermen, enough with mermaids
already.

Fear of poverty breeds poverty.

8-4-16   With no tax return, there is speculation that
Trump is not a billionaire. Gingrich shakes Trump Tree.

Repubs may end up in a civil war. Is T afraid to be president? Comparisons to Hitler becoming more frequent. T will quit before he will lose. He's torn his party apart. Frankly, repubs needed tearing.

8-5-16   Republicans are like a beaten wife. He will change, Honest! Trump's most fearful quality his need to control the press. The election is rigged sounds like T is getting ready to lose.   T should release a summary of his taxes. His kids will run the business while he's pres.? Everything is not rigged.

Zimmerman attacked in Florida restaurant after bragging that he killed Trayvon.

Finally, Nixon released his taxes and the result was his famous statement: I am not a crook.

Newspapers are good, Facebook is better.

8-6-16   Mike Malaghan, author of Picture Bride, bought Face It and expects many moments of exceptional reading.

Don't trust a fart.

Monica Lewinski is marketable now, where is she?

Fareed Zakaria says Trump is a bullshit artist (BS). These people lie continuously and make up reality as they go along. They live in a world of their own making and can be very dangerous if given a lot of power.   A lot of Trump supporters are sexist. Even babies are now uniting against T. (He yelled at a baby at one of his rallies.)

8-7-16   The Trump candidacy is hurting his business interests. Fareed says you have to know the truth before you can lie so T just babbles his way through the day making up reality as he sees fit. If confronted with a lie or inconsistency, he says, I knew that or some other dodge and makes up another lie.

Republicans who have come out against Trump to me are heroes. A lot of people and businesses who have supported him are going to get hurt.

There are shows about prison but should there be a prison channel.

Bill and Hillary have some marriage.

8-8-16   If the election is rigged, Trump rigged it. Trump is fighting everyone except his opponent. Fareed said bullshit on the air but we got it first on facebook. Fact checking may not work on T so start drinking heavily.   First it was the Teaparty, then Trump who knocked out the GOP (Grand Old Party). Real life is more scary than any monster movie.

8-9-16   Seems like Barack Obama would be responsible for Hillary's emails. (Harry Truman, the buck stops here.)

Dad never wavered in his love of Nixon so I wonder what he would have thought about Trump.

Would a house appraiser notice if the toilet were missing?

I listened to Trump's speech on NPR (National Public Radio). He referred the audience to his website and told them no more death tax. No one in Detroit pays an inheritance tax now but they all cheered. For Trump, it was a pretty good speech, but can he remember it? At age 70, he's not likely to change. He puts his name on the plane so he can find it in the parking lot.

I wanted a hamburger for lunch but settled for bowl of Cheerios bathed in syrup.

The sub poll measures voter leanings among groups like Hispanic, seniors, and by state.

The makers of exercise equipment sell gadgets that improve part of your body, butt, breast, stomach, etc.

8-10-16   Trump's plans may be fuzzy but by now, his persona is plain. Trump threatens Hillary with his second amendment friends? This is what Fareed was talking about, Bull shit artist. Did he say it or not, nobody knows. If he could knock off Hillary, he could seize power by force. This man is an unknown coward and vicious sociopath.

Secret: Bernie Sanders is rich.

Our 7 dogs control us through: Group bark.

8-11-16   We enjoyed the 2 hour climb up Trump Tower. I was just trying to collect a past due bill.

I've been named Dollar General's customer of the year.

Hillary's emails are boring but Trump's sins are visceral. Did Trump pull down Fox News or was it Roger Ailes? Only Putin and Kim Jung Un want Trump as president.

8-12-16   My videographer postponed my shoot as he had to babysit.

In '07, Trump said declare victory and leave the middle east. That's what happened and now he says Obama founded ISIS. Can't have it both ways. Lying SOB.

Krystal is 90% bread yet they call it a hamburger.

Trump glories in audience adoration so much he says anything and now has a cadre of workers trying to clean up after each gaff.

8-13-16   The problem with Trump saying Obama founded ISIS is that many will believe it.   All channels say Trump is crazy except Fox.

Joan Rivers started the Michelle Obama is tranny thing.

A hacker posing as Microsoft, shut down Martha's computer and then wanted $250 to fix it.

8-14-16   The economy is good now compared to end of the Bush term.

Early on in the Trump campaign, he said, I'd be the best jobs president ever. Wow. His great business talent would boost our economy, but then he hid his taxes and the dream faded and popped.   Tariffs bad since Herbert

Hoover and Trump wants them back?   T hates the media but the media helped him crush 16 competitors during the primary. All the air time was on T's burps and bashes. T campaign unique and we are all on his roller coaster. VP nominee Pence has released his taxes!   Trump has nice kids but they dare not cross him. They are nice to His glory and any benefit accruing to the kids is secondary. The kids are backing off the campaign. Know nothing loons are now defending his policies. Trump has lying/magical thinking, he blames others and has intent to do harm. This is the definition of evil.

The middle class has been hurt since the invention of junk bonds which allowed hundreds of corporate take-overs in the 1980's. Many workers were marginalized. Globalization also hurts jobs but increases buying power.

8-15-16   The press makes a person bigger or smaller. It can turn on a dime.

Soon, there will be mass republican defections from the Trump camp. Trump rails and spews drawing in the press so they don't cover Hillary as much and her failings go un-noticed. When he said he could stand in the middle of Fifth Ave and kill someone and his followers wouldn't care, he believed that and his subsequent statements have proved it.

8-16-16   Why we need inheritance tax: Paris Hilton.

Kimberly Guilfoyle is only at Fox because of Roger Ailes.

Ben Carson can walk free of the Trump cabal.

Trump's tax returns are going to show less than real income. If he owns 100 corporations, their earnings will be partly retained and not taxed to him. Trump may create jobs but we know he creates hate. Trump is learning how to give a pretty good speech scripted but unscripted, he's the Titanic.

Hillary said No boots on the ground. That's a mistake. Roosevelt said the same thing before WWII started.

8-17-16   Dan Rather finds himself an advocacy journalist against Trump. I cheered him on by saying politicians and pundits who embrace him are guilty as sin of country corruption.

Obamacare should have been a Medicare tweek.

Roger Ailes now working for Trump. What a duo.

Rush Limbaugh also subtly advocates people killing others. Drive by media is likened to drive by shooting made popular in the '20's by use of Tommy guns. (machine guns)

Teachers know by fifth grade who the criminals are going to be. Behind every criminal is a mother who excuses his actions and says you don't know him or he's a good boy.

8-18-16   Hillary is killing Trump with ads using his own words. Trump's remarks will linger in the air for 100 years

like a super turd. His bile now sanctioned by a new staff.
T has given Rachel Maddow a new reason for living.

Media gets it wrong all the time. Look at their ignoring of
Tesla.

Sanctioned hate is very popular and extends wars.

8-19-16   The president's job is to instill pride in our
country.

A dude in Walgreens browbeat the cashier into giving a
$10 unwarranted refund saying Youall have all the money
and I don't care if I go to jail.

Rezoning is like a divorce, expensive and very emotional.

Facebook has taught me to question everything.

Corrine Brown falling faster than Trump. Crooked
politician for 2 decades in complete denial about her guilt.

I thought Trump might give us some inspiration but the
first debate dispelled that notion when he talked about
Megyn Kelly's blood. The cartoon media loves Mr. Trump.
Nude Trump statues have appeared around New York City.
Bringing Breitbart on board paves the way for Himmler,
Goebbels and Eichmann. If Trump loses, he'll get even.

8-20-16   Donny is brave to run exposing his many faults.
Trump apology weird and unhinged. He put his penis size
in play during a debate for God's sake.

Corrine Brown says she does not have to defend herself.

Teach the middle class how to handle money, from driving to washing laundry. Money courses should begin in 5th grade. Use good role models like Warren Buffet, not crude greed merchants like Trump.

8-21-16   Ben Carson should do well once he gets out from under Trump's thumb.

Pancakes, ice cream and pie in one day.

Trump was not ready for prime time.

If you have pie, why fix dinner?

My neighbor, Robert, carried in our new bookcase. God bless.

Let the market decide the fate and future of coal.

8-23-16   Hillary resigned from Secretary of State in 2013. Why wasn't her charitable foundation crooked then?

The Trump campaign is characterizing Hillary as weak, sick and ineffectual. Is that because she's a woman? To me, a third party is Hillary's biggest threat. Trump tells blacks how bad they are and then asks for their vote. What about all the blacks that aren't bad? Many Trump voters were cheated as now it turns out most of his positions are "in flux" or to be determined.

Prince and Elvis should have Just said No. (Nancy Reagan's slogan) Happened upon the Bucket List movie and enjoyed it. My first grape gum is history, not so good.

8-24-16   Trump is a money grubber. What he wants is a TV show. Trump's doctor says he's good to go. Trump defined by his own words and it ain't pretty.

Andria Tantaros filed sexual harassment suit against Bill O'Reilly?

The famous Goldfinger movie of 1964 had as its plot destruction of America's gold supply at Fort Knox but America went off the gold standard 7 years later under President Nixon.

Fox News pundits like O'Reilly and Hannity have made themselves targets since they are aligned with Trump.

Face it, Stuff I've Said on Facebook is now in the Jacksonville downtown public library.

During the primary debates, Trump bombed the other candidates and the media helped him, but with Hillary, it'll be one on one and he will be expected to know something. Trump changes positions faster than I can spit gum out of the car window.

Hillary's foundation accepts political contributions. Politicians have always accepted contributions.

Went downtown Jacksonville but had to rush back to feed parking meter rather than shop.

8-26-16   What is West Coast Style? One of the morning news anchors has it.

After 8 years of dems, you'd expect the pendulum to swing back to repubs, but with these candidates, not so much.

Dreamed Trump would give an atomic bomb to every white American male over the age of 18 to be used at his discretion. Furthermore, the cross country system of canals abandoned in 1820 will be reinstated and bomb laden barges will carry their cargo around waiting for an attack.

8-27-16 The biggest surprise and tragedy was when Trump blew away 16 other good republican candidates with the media fanning the flames.

Barkley, our Chihuahua/hound on Phenobarbital for Epilepsy.

Last chance to buy face it, Stuff I've Said on Facebook before the price goes down.

Trump has gotten many journalists off their objectivity.

Hillary should place the foundation in trust until she either loses or is no longer president.

History repeats, only the names change.

Trump's doctor it turns out was the hemorrhoid doctor in the Burt Reynolds road movies.

Nothing is worse than pushing an idea whose time has not yet come. - Al Gore

8-28-16   Trump gonna stop the gang violence in Chicago? Uh Huh.

As we load our truck with stuff to take to Good Will, I think, please this Christmas, gift cards, not stuff.

Dems played the nuke and race card against Goldwater in 1964 and it worked.

Millions of voters have evaluated Trump and found his psychic inadequate. He lies to the media and when they confront him, he says the media is crooked. You cannot fix that kind of psychosis. I love you so much I'm hurting you. He would be our first wrecking ball president. He has drawn out people who have never voted before in their lives. His followers think he is a messiah.

8-29-16   Cleaning out the garage has benefits. I did not know we had a chainsaw. I called AAA to get the car out but lo and behold, it started. I built a pantry out of small bookcases.

Trumps signature issue, immigration, is now a wet noodle.

8-30-16   Trump is the Weiner of politics. May he get cut off.

Mike's book, Picture Bride came in today, beautiful.

GOP (Grand Old Party) now wishes they had picked someone else besides Trump.

Use ownership maps for Chicago gang neighborhoods and use National Guard to clean it up. They confiscate guns and anyone arrested serves longer time in a special jail like Gitmo built for this purpose. Jail could be wire screening in a public place heavily guarded. It would invite escape but death if seen. Special laws would have to be written for this as many rights would be suspended but political correctness has gone on too long. If successful, the same plan could be used in other infected cities.

Taking out the trash, I heard a rustle like I had knocked something over, then a loud bang and I knew the rustle was electricity build up just before the lightning strike.

My video at 8 minutes is too large to send by email. WTF.

The chocolate man died, Willie Wonka.

Watch CNN for dirt of Fox.

Eight boxes of dishes and 2 china cabinets to be put in storage.

Some people use the gun as furniture, a decorating accent, a charm, like a lamp or trophy. These people usually are not a problem.

Dollar General didn't have it. CVS didn't have it. Finally, Winn Dixie had one but at high price $2.50 for the toilet paper holder with spring load.

Should you throw away everything to make it easier on your heirs?

8-31-16   Creepy clowns invading woods of Greenville, South Carolina? They may pose a threat to children as in kidnapping.

The middle class was killed by unions and easy credit. The union did not respect the labor market and easy credit is enslaving. People have quit respecting jobs and are merely putting in time until a better one comes along.

Corrine Brown and Angela Corey both voted out of office. Corrine is currently on trial for charity fraud and Corey was in my opinion an over zealous prosecutor charging death when life in prison would do.

9-1-16   Happy birthday to my daughter Stephanie (Taffy) Remisiewicz.

Trump's debate preparation is to get his shoes shined. It took courage (balls) to go to Mexico but speech was all hat, no cattle. Trump traveling to flooded LA and Mexico are good photo ops and Hillary better start spending. Show her foundation feeding the hungry and giving medicine to sick children.

We get dog food delivered now but hard to lift the 80 lb bag.

I bought a can of beans from Trump Grocery. Upon opening it, water poured out leaving only 2 beans. Is this legal? He didn't say how many beans were in the can.

In 8th grade, I loaned a kid my lunch money. He swore on a bible he'd pay me back. Turned out the bible was a dictionary.

9-2-16 What is the formula for time?

Trump wants to be the bellower in chief.

9-3-16   What Hillary said: What difference does it make? Wipe my server? You mean with a cloth? We are going to put a lot of coal miners out of business.   What Trump said: 10,000 lies and smears. Prepare for a 5,000 point drop in the stock market if Trump wins.

Technically, it's Obama's fault Hillary's emails are messed up.

Emotion rules candidate selection so minds are very hard to change. Fans get emotionally involved and invested in their candidate so facts matter little.

9-4-16   Negative advertising lowers voter turnout?

Trump says he picks the best people, people like him, Mark Burns, disgraced preacher. Roger Ailes.

9-5-16   The number of Trump lies boggles even Nixon aides. If Trump wins, I will admit the will of the people has been served unless it's rigged which is something he has talked about. One or two candidates on the republican stage might have even been worse so take comfort in that. If experienced people can't do the job, then let's elect someone with no experience.

You know it's gonna be a bad day when your wife hands you a list of things you can do better.

Martha discovered it's Bentley who at night pulls the toilet paper from the bathroom to the bedroom.

9-6-16 2016, the campaign of lies. If everything is rigged, education is valueless. Trump gets voodoo doll from Haiti and sticks Hillary. Hillary killed Kennedy, just damn. Al Sharpton ok when he disses Trump. Trump's plan is to spend billions on a wall and deportation while cutting taxes.

Pens appear and disappear from my pocket. JibJab is still around. Vantage Press gone as of 2012. North Korea's sole purpose is to threaten others. For many weeks, my Canon printer told me to empty the paint bucket and now it's tipped over and won't work at all.

Early copiers came with a repair man (like today's computers). God help you if you work on the weekend and it failed on Friday. In 1970 a copier cost the same as a car, about $5,000. My first electronic calculator cost $1,000. Before that was the slide rule or abacus.

Drones create some great surfing videos. When your ball point pen leaked all over your hands, did you wipe them on the back of the kid in front of you? Publishers, editors and agents kill a lot of good books. Uncle Kenneth's book on 1920's bronk riding for example. He was told to put more women and sex in it. There isn't any women or sex in it.

Dreams suggest that we remember everything from birth and that the future has already happened, in God's mind.

Ben Carson due to his non hysterical manner, has a chance to hang around in the media long after Trump's Turkeys are gone.

9-7-16   Gretchen Carlson got $20 million from Fox News and Roger Ailes for sexual harassment.   Think of the hookers Roger could have had for that much money. Greta Van Susterin out as well. Trump paid $25 million to get rid of Ivana, his first wife. Are women just commodities to be bought and sold? Rich men's toys?

Dad never admitted Nixon was wrong so he'd be a Trump voter. Trump wants third party candidates in the debate to provide distraction from his own lack of knowledge, like in the primaries. Fox seems to be cracking up due to support of Trump and maybe Roger Ailes. Trump fails to pay 3 tween girls who danced at his rally? Look at the damage George Bush did and then think of what Trump could do to us.

9-8-16   I wish I could live to see our first space alien. ITT Tech folded in 2012. I'm on YouTube, several videos.

No politician is talking about health care, the 900 lb gorilla. – Steve Forbes.

Ted Turner owns 2 million acres of ranch land, a real billionaire, not some glitzy, self serving ass pincher.

Ordinarily, Hillary would lose, but with Trump opposing her, not so much.

9-9-16   Many smart people choose Trump because they hate Hillary, so emotions rule over sense. Trump is a square boat.

Our yard man, Alan Love, has been here hundreds of times but to the dogs, he is always Genghis Khan.

9-10-16   Wells Fargo did an oopsie. Regions lied to me to get me to open a credit card I did not need or want.

Trump is the Houdini of language. If caught in a lie, he replies effortlessly and without hesitation.   Not since Caligula have we had such an evil dictator within reach of power. He has so much debt he can't pay his suppliers. His post election business brand will be limp.

Matt Lauer not doing a real debate. The media wants a close race, better for ratings.

Will self drive cars allow texting and driving?

9-13-16 Hinkley freed, tried to kill President Reagan. No sense to that decision.

Hillary berates ¼ of the electorate with her Basket of Deplorables. That is one stupid move.   You insult the candidate, not his followers.

The world makes a path for the person who knows where he is going.

Three restaurant meals in a row, loud children have been near us.

If a person won't sell his property even tho offered a high price, there may be a dead body buried thereon. – Columbo.

A half dead Hillary is better than 1,000 Trumps. If both Hillary and Trump died, Kaine is 1,000 times better than Pence. Pence eats Trump's shit, smiles, says this isn't shit and I'm lovin it.

Kim and Jepp, two great techs, installed 2 videos in one day for me.

Hillary is sick but gets sympathy and praise for working anyway. Nixon was sick before his debate with Jack Kennedy. Listeners on the radio thought Nixon won but watchers on TV knew better. Roosevelt couldn't walk but he did fine.

Stephanie flew on 9-12-01, there were 4 people on the plane. I tried to work on 9-11 but kept looking toward our naval base at Mayport for the atomic cloud.   At lunch in McDonalds, a woman screamed, Kill all the Islamics. I wasn't sure what an Islamic was. My house inspection was on that day was half assed.

When Galileo was declared a heretic, the nuns burned his papers. Thus much of his life was lost to history.

9-14-16   People calling on the phone should not use your first name.

Martha, a Hillary hater, says she has Parkinson's. Pneumonia is the current diagnosis.

I hope coverage of pre-existing conditions can be salvaged out of the crumbling Obamacare.

Pence deserves an Oscar.

Trump needs a blood test made public.

When Geraldine Ferraro ran for VP, her husband John Zacarro was a real estate man in New York City.   He rented to a few hookers and the media chewed him up. In Jacksonville, I rented to a topless dancer who paid the rent on time with small bills and coins.

Trump is a born mudslinger but not the other candidates and when they fire back at his level, they sink.

Colin Powell said Bill Clinton is still bedding bimbos at their home but I prefer to think of it as just giving the maids a thorough inspection.

We old people do get mail, funeral homes, drug companies and hearing aid hawkers. Being retired means never having to go to the laundry.

Trump shows his medical report on Dr. Oz, a TV doctor, he needs to lose 15 lbs. More like 55 lbs. He took someone else's blood test to the exam? Some doctors become pushers. Trump making most of Hillary being sick. This campaign teaches us and our children the truth matters little.   This campaign should have been written by Carl Hiaasen.

All real estate people get in trouble sooner or later. The bigger they are, the harder they fall. In Harry Helmsley's case, the trouble turned out to be Leona.

My failed printer costly. Ink cartridges must have leaked somehow.

9-16-16   Trump is exciting. People who attend his rallies bond like a cult member. A-bombs are exciting. Trump uses hyperbole; lying while smiling.   (Art of the Deal) Harmless lying he calls it.

Corrine Brown needs $ for her defense. Please send to me and I will see that she gets it.

9-17-16   Trump calls lies hyperbole but they do stink and burn. Just because a person has money and has been on TV does not make him fit for high government office. Some reporters are ragging him and losing their objectivity.

9-18-16   Tesla died in 1943, the year of my birth and I stayed for 2 days in the Hotel New Yorker where he died.

No alien races will be met until we can go faster than light.

Wells Fargo manager may have said, I want more new accounts. The worst 2 of you will be fired. And that's all it took for hundreds of fake accounts to be opened.

We ate at Sweet Tomatoes Buffet, a guarantee of over-indulge.

Trump's love and hate of the media is legendary. They give him millions in free time but point out his faults making him squirm. I wonder if polls aren't being skewed in his favor to keep the race going. Tight makes it more interesting.

9-19-16   Our personal room cleaners arrived (granddaughter) and took away 3 cabinets effectively emptying a sun room off the kitchen. Will it be a new dog bathroom?

YouTube is a second TV for me.

I took photos of the old Women's Club building off Riverside Ave in Jacksonville. The imposing 2 story brick house sat vacant and was eaten by termites. By the time they were discovered, it was too late and demolition was required.   Neglect was expensive in this case.

Trump is licking his chops over recent bombings/terror attacks in NY and NJ. He thinks that is his way into office. He is a masterful language twister. Did he say kill Hillary Clinton? We are not sure, but we should not have to wonder about it.   A Trump win would be the biggest dumb down in our history.

9-20-16   Comcast gave us new TV remotes and boxes. Channel scrolling is now more cumbersome.

9-21-16   Moby Dick is true, sort of. In 1820 the Essex was rammed and sunk by an enraged sperm whale but most escaped in the life boat and eventually made it back to New Bedford. Herman Melville appeared in the movie and Moby Dick was born in 1856. Historical fiction at its best. Whales are thankful that the discovery of oil in Pennsylvania alleviated the need for their oil, used for lighting lamps.

A man has a charity foundation, uses $2 million for personal needs, pays IRS fine of $500,000 and he's still ahead as none of the money was his in the first place.

Trump and Putin both revered by their fans. So much in common.

Wells Fargo and Regions Bank near the top of the list for complaints. - USA Today

9-22-16   Bill would be a help if Hillary wins but not during the campaign. Too many loose bimbos.

Trump is hiding his taxes from his ex wives. YouTube parodies of Trump not funny because he is already a parody of himself. Cartoonists, on the other hand, are doing very well.

Robert Fulghum, author of All I Needed to Know, I Learned in Kindergarten now travels and lectures.

California has hired a manager of cow farts.

Trump resembles a mafia don and soon he may get the big enchilada. TV and movies have glorified the mafia and now it is close.

9-23-16   Trump has to lie to be competitive? Since both Trump and Bill Clinton, have a lot of bimbos, that will probably be the poison gas of this campaign and not used.

After several years of waiting, I've finally scheduled cataract surgery for Nov 2. Yesterday, I had the preliminary exam with 500 or so pictures of my eyes being taken.

9-24-16   They are preparing a cell for Trump beside Bernie Madoff's. Most white color crime goes unpunished. Trump not in Bernie's league yet but he's not president yet either. Trump is a Martian with an army of tripods waiting in hiding. Ragging on Hillary is not going to fix Trump. Any media that calls Trump out is guilty of being crooked, slanted, rigged and un-American.

Bentley has gum disease and Bailey has lost hair on the tail. A vet's delight. Dogs are living longer as more people spend more money on their meds.

Is Obama slighting his white half? A white person worrying about a "bad" cop is like worrying about a plane crash. No point.

South Korea needs to fix the Kim Jung Un problem to the north.

It's Friday night, let the partying begin. Broads. I just hope I wake up with someone I know.

9-25-16   Begin the battle of the bimbos. Welcome to the debates, Jennifer Flowers. Wasn't Monica available? As a surprise treat, Monica will perform fellatio during intermission.

The debate game show: Hillary walks onto the debate stage, gets settled at the podium, looks at Bill a few seats back, After the crowd quiets down, she says to him: Won't you come back and live with me? He, stands up, Walks fast up to her, they hug, This marriage can be saved. America is thrilled, Trump's bimbos look ashamed.

People will be able to subscribe to police camera recordings at any time of their choosing.

Rodney King is the poster boy for police brutality. A Rosa Parks sort of.

Petsmart reeks of overcharge. Their dog brushes cost $10 but the same brush for people at CVS is $5. We bought tail spray for Bailey's bare spot.

9-26-16   Well over half of the Fox News team is able to put lipstick on the Trump pig. A ground swell of history has pushed the undeserving Trump to a high level. The right barker at the right time. Reagan had character, not Trump. The first debate is the most important.

About 1980 we bought a Video Writer, a typewriter with a screen and word processing as the only program. It used ribbons in cassette and square disks. It cost $800 and after a few years, the ribbons became unavailable. And no one would fix the machine. It was after five years useless. I miss it.

9-27-16   Hillary hates Trump's womanizing and Trump does not want to be on the same stage as inferior Hillary. Wags say T had a nip of cocaine before coming on. Hillary in red, Trump in blue. Read T new book Hitler and Stalin were just misunderstood. This election is all about equality. Any felon can be president. Any Godfather can be president. Not many saw it but Paula Jones threw her undies on stage. T continues to lie about why he can't show his taxes. I guess he owes China and Russia one billion dollars. When he first came on, his eyes were closed while Hillary remained bright and perky.

Both candidates were arrested while on stage. Pence beamed up by aliens. Sanders and Kaine left to duke it out over who is pres and who is vp. T lost points when he banned fat women from the debate room. Thousands died during drinking games over how much he lied.

Lawyers have ravaged the medical profession. You can't get a wart taken off without an EKG.

Our own history shows high taxes for the rich often coincide with periods of great prosperity.

So who won the debate? Hillary did but he's still in the game. There is no substitute for knowing things.

One of my friends said, She had a student like Trump who hit another kid and lied about who did it even though 30 other classmates said it was him.

This was my first debate with big screen and high definition. Stunning.

Using the split screen was effective as both candidates were shown while one spoke. T looked pained and Hillary looked cheerful.

9-28-16   Trump decided not to ask Sarah Palin for debate advice next time. T cares for himself, not the country. T is a predator businessman, a greed is good man. If he helps you, it's an accident. She smiled, he dripped. There is too much Trump in Donald Trump.

A minimum tax could be passed so no one pays zero tax.

9-29-16   Michelle Obama is at long last, pulling her weight.

Reagan did a Trumpian tax cut but Big Bush then had to put it all back.

Dems offer free stuff while Repubs bore with tax brackets.

Trump's tax returns probably involve hundreds of partnerships each with its own return exposing the names of other investors, ie, his client list. His clients could be audited and raiders could try to steal some of them. Rockefeller hid too but ironically, he made more money after the government broke up Standard Oil.

Either Christie knew about Bridgegate, or he's dumb as a rock.

Alicia Machado, Miss Universe, was probably hit on by Trump and rebuffed his advances unleashing a life long vitriol against the woman. He never forgets a slight.

Trump pays zero tax? Leona Helmsley said, Taxes are for little people. She went to jail. Trump has no major newspaper endorsements.

Readers said So what? Some of the papers are republican. No one reads them anymore anyway. (Such is the mind of a Deplorable.)

9-30-16   Larry Flynt, Bernie Madoff and Donald Trump. One is in jail. Flynt and Trump both have planes, money and operate at the edge of the law.

Christie is working on Trump's ethics and Palin on his grammar.

TV news is often just a commercial for their website.

Don't buy a house from a builder who is getting a divorce.

Kellyanne Conway, Trumps manager, says he lies because he does not know the truth.

10-2-16   I've got the Trump/Miss Piggy sex tape, leave $50 on my front porch.

We've never had a mentally ill president, but now, it's possible. Trump has given us ample warning, heed. If Trump wins even one state, I'm depressed. USA Today has joined the never Trump movement. Trump would be our first president no one can believe. Trump knows a thing or two about sex conquests. Maybe Fred Trump was so abusive, lil T decided not to grow up, but, whatever the reason, he is developmentally challenged.

Carole Westberg has given us the following Trump descriptions. Witless cocksplat, hell beast, bloviating flesh bag, tiny fingered Cheeto-faced ferret wearing shitgibbon. This when he went to Scotland after the BREXIT vote.

Videos show long lines waiting for a Trump rally. There are a lot of desperate people in America. The Trump candidacy has given new life to MSNBC and a problem to Fox News.

A wrong number called very concerned asking if I am alright. I said I think so and she realized she had a wrong no. but not before I said, And you?

The Allstate Mayhem guy is funny. (TV commercial)

Happy birthday to Lauren, my medical student granddaughter.

Lunch at V Pizza where Martha gets ribs and I get stuck. Just once I wish we could split a pizza.   (Spouses talk to each other on FB)

10-3-16   Trump fans seem full of anger. Marla released the taxes. She was married to him in '95 so it's her return too.

The Trump brand will suffer when the depth of his corruption sinks in. T shoots messengers routinely. His tax deduction is creative. The promise not to build on something has value so he deducts it as a gift. The IRS is hampered for years sorting it out. Victor Posner was jailed for inflating the value of donated land.

I'm surprised unpaid subs haven't killed Trump. A Trump spokesperson must be loud. If he really did lose a billion dollars, he needs a new gig, like the presidency.

Appraisers must bless all donation values and some depreciation schedules.

10-4-16   The heart of tax minimization is lying and Trump is good at that. New York State Attorney General pulled Trump's charity for inadequate paperwork. Trump said he would fix Obamacare, not get rid of it. Not very conservative. Trump is right in that he can be nastier than Hillary.

Saw a 230 lb Mastiff at the vet's. At first, my brain recalculated what a dog could be. It was a genuine "taken aback" experience.

Journalists either want to talk or get information.

Kim Kardashian robbed of $10 million in jewels? Publicity stunt?

We are expecting Youge payoffs from Pay Pal and Pfizer. Why work when you can sue? – Trump University

10-5-16   Mike Pence (Trump's running mate) says the sun goes around the earth and that the earth is flat. Pence will run the country while Trump travels around looking for photo ops. No Fortune 500 CEO has recommended Trump. After Trump loses, he will be known as Donald Tramp. If Trump earned $3.5 million in 1995 and the prime rate is .035, then he's worth one billion $ not the 10 B he says. Cash strapped, he will look for money from any bank or country.

Hillary's basket of deplorable was wrong headed. Trump's fans are simply star struck. He's a teen idol, a flawed James Dean. (Jett Rink) Fans identify with him and they love him. Trouble is love goes out the window when the storm comes.

Picture Trump in charge of social security. Hooo boy. The man puts gold on everything. No wonder he lost a billion dollars.

10-6-16   The supreme court put Bush in power so why is it decapitated now. (Only has 8 members as republicans have refused to consider Obama's nominee.)

Romney was a real businessman who didn't brag.

Don't live near a construction project during a hurricane.

Some say Trump passed Marla around. She may have the whole tax return to release, she signed it.

10-7-16   Sunday's debate has to compete with football and Hurricane Matthew. Officials err on the side of danger to get you out of harm's way. We will now find out who followed building codes. Jacksonville's coastline is indented or recessed from the main coastline, helps a little.

Pence lies for his boss. Trump's lawyers are getting lawyers.

10-9-16   Hurricane Matthew gone. We lost power one night. Branches down all over but no big damage.

Trumps remarks on women demean us all. Bar for president sickeningly low. A misogynist believes men are superior to women and if a man and woman are up for the same job, the man gets the job. There are more demeaning words about women than men.

Trump picked a good time in history to run but is blind to his past and its effect on citizens.

10-10-16   My wife Martha's birthday. Happy birthday Trumpette.

Trump has created the greatest show on earth. Believes it's easy to win an election against a woman. Gathered some of Bill Clinton's exes in one room just before the debate. Trump knows he's losing and must kick a hail mary. Pence was seen trying to escape the campaign bus and might drop out of the race. This president gig should/could make T a lot of money.

Even Nixon knew when to quit. Which is worse, DUI or groping? A million times the conversation has been switched from something T said to how bad Hillary is. Trump would overspend terribly. Country trumps party except for now.

Many wish Trump would get his nose drip fixed. Guess he can't afford it. After all, he did lose a billion dollars. T said his groping not as bad as ISIS. Thanks for clearing that up.

Trump and many other rich people zero their income taxes via aggressive deductions and inflated values of things donated to charities. Fareed Zakaria said on his Sunday show how for a $1,000 lunch, you can get your own line of tax code. The US tax code sucks.

Dozens if not a hundred top republicans are voting for Hillary Clinton.

10-11-16   Trump is the drop your pants candidate. Get media attention, no matter what. Born of media, now hurt by it. He is now our Watergate, the long national nightmare. Hannity: Hillary has killed millions. I hope Trump is senile by 2020 but how will we know?

10-12-16   Could Trump lead a revolution against America in a hostile takeover? T is now at war with dems, repubs and media. Hitler lost because he could not fight on 2 fronts. Mr. Stupid pissed on all his friends, then fell down.

The army teaches recruits to cuss as part of being a man. How did Trump learn it?

10-13-16   Some believe Trump is inciting violence against Hillary. Most of the electorate is seeing T as a psychotic molester of women and teen girls. T and his followers all seem angry. T collects enemies like a beachgoer collects sand. Trump and Bill Cosby both curse the damn crooked media; which made them in the first place.

Isn't this just the bimboest campaign ever?

Loyalty not fealty. Trump demands both but both should not be given. Sexism is the root of Hillary hatred. Trump and Cosby are now the Boobsey Twins. Played doctor all over the world. People naturally adore the rich and famous. Why else do the British have royalty. Martha says mashers were normal in her youth and women should just get over it.

So many people still like Trump one wonders if democracy can survive. Michelle Obama found her stride fighting for women's rights. Dad said don't kick people when they are already down but he didn't know Trump.

Trump: I am not a sexual predator.

Nixon: I am not a crook.

Nixon: If the president does it, it's legal.

Trump: Suspend the laws that offend me so I can be god king.

Trump has skills such as calling his campaign a movement. A campaign is just a sales pitch but a movement is a grass roots ground swell of need. Skipping a debate to raise money for veterans was smart except he kept the money. Bringing Bill Clinton's exes to the debate was smarmy but consistent with his gutterism.

Trump must be insecure in his manhood to project this feminine war. If he gave up women, he'd probably gain a lot more weight.

Victims of sexual harassment are called bimbos. Typical blame the victim, but it's probably true in Paula Jones case.

10-15-16   Trump thinks the media shorts him at rallies. His ego is more important than the country.

10-16-16   It was telling when Trump said that woman is too ugly to molest. He's no strongman, just a bigmouth. He's promoted himself to his level of incompetence.

Trump's been ragging on the media since he began his campaign. So they turn on him, what a surprise. NBC leaked the tape at the right time to do the most damage. They beat T as his own game.

A flood of bimbos is erupting over Trump's lies so big not even Hugh Hefner could handle.

Most Trump supporters are not deplorable, they are misguided and frustrated. (Word used by Hillary Clinton to describe half of Trump supporters.)

Trump has tapped in to the comfort zone of many people. They settle down at his rally like a good ole fashioned ole time religious haranguing. Trump deflects all criticism aimed at him and the crowd eats it up. He's James Dean, Elvis, Hugh Hefner and Larry Flynt.

10-17-16   I have never seen such idiocy played out on a national scale before. Evil people create more evil people. Maybe Trump will emerge with a TV show. After all, he's buds with Roger Ailes. Trump will cost republicans votes for 100 years. If he loses, he said we'd never see him again, our punishment is not to see him. He has made me a democrat and changed some of my TV shows. And now this rigged election scapegoat. Not since the Cuban missile crisis has the world been this dangerous.

10-18-16   Larry Flynt is offended by Trump. Media is all over T because he's a circus act.

10-19-16   Trump decided to run for the top office, not governor, not senator, the top job. He opened blustering and kept getting worse. Grist for books and talk for decades. Trump bringing Obama's brother to debate. He would bring his own brother but he died of alcoholism.

Trump and Putin best buds?   No doubt T would like a system that allows complete control. Claims satellites are helping to rig election against him.   This guy should write comic books.

Post Hurricane Matthew only involves picking up ½ million piles of branches and disposing of it all.

Chuck Berry is 90. In the '50's, he slept in his Cadillac because he could not or would not use the white owned motels. Still, white girls crawled in the car to be with him.

10-20-16   Judging by the last debate, I expected Trump to wrestle Hillary to the floor. They should put a wall between them. A wall of taco trucks surrounded Trump's hotel. Trump would put his kids on the supreme court. Sniffles are a part of body language, learn from it. Hillary not interrupting him because the more he says, the dumber he appears.

Existence is the ultimate lotto.

Most of our mail is geriatric; health insurance, medicines, burial, stair chairs, walk in tubs, miracle meds, stopping diarrhea, hemorrhoids, cremation.

There are no blond jokes about men.

10-21-16   They hate Hillary for being a woman as they hated Obama for being half black. Obama ignored his white half?

Chinese delivery good, easy to store the leftovers.

The Trump show has Limbaugh twisted up trying to fit it to a logical pattern.

Trump has a better job now. I agree. Being president is hard and you have to think and everything.

1.5 hours of debating and the only thing we have to show for it is Trump might not accept the results of the election. He could build his own white house, with gold dome.

10-22-16   As T refuses to concede his loss, thousands of angry white supremists will swarm the nation.

Walmart creates welfare recipients and crime waves as customers think theft is normal.

Come by San Marco Books for discounted prices on Face it, Stuff I've said on Facebook, Real Estate Dad's Way and Buy a Boarded-up House with Contents. Signing this Saturday.

10-25-16   Sold 2 books, one real estate and one face it book. Women don't buy books. Kids like books. Young women liked my no Trump sign and took pictures of it. To some I was automatically famous.

The Jacksonville Jaguars play like mercenary soldiers fight.

If Trump wins he will sue sue sue.

My first jury trial was of a hooker. All her friends showed up and regaled me with promises of favors.

My second jury trial was of a guy who didn't sign in as sexual predator. Guilty. This trial is about cocaine possession and petty theft. Black guy wants to make a point, has no lawyer.

Walt Disney had it bad growing up and delved into a play world of his own making and control.

Get your Columbo T-shirt or go straight to Nerd.

Bought a half gallon of chocolate milk, my first. Has 2,000 calories.

The hand dryers in the court house blow so hard it sounds like a 747.

Have you noticed the 8 to 10 am repair window is never at 8.

10-26-16   Best outcome if Trump wins is he turns it all over to surrogates. In his rallies, he gives himself god like powers.

Trump is a billionaire and the system is rigged, yeah right. The media makes the good better and the bad worse. If you're into grabbing women's body parts, then coverage by the media will grow and glow.

Finished half gallon chocolate milk in 3 days.

There was a law passed in the '60's prohibiting "block busting" or introducing blacks into white neighborhoods.

In the 1960's the Trump organization discriminated against black tenants. But in fairness, so did most other landlords or sellers.

10-27-16   Voted early, first time in my life. Did not want to wait 2 hours.

Hillary's agents distributed bedbugs in all of Trump's hotels.

Marco Rubio, Newt Gingrich and Rudy Giuliani have all fallen into the Trump mud.

Megyn Kelly now looks like a boy according to wife Martha. She did cut her hair. You remember she earned Trump's ire right out of the gate with her debate question on women abuse.

It's not easy when one's wife is a Trump fan.

10-28-16   Guilty. I was one of a 6 person jury. Man entered Fresh Market where he usually panhandles but this time his pant legs were tied and he put $200 worth of frozen meat down them. 2 managers tried to detain him. Just then, an off duty cop rolled up in uniform driving his squad car. Put him on the ground as he was trying to ride off on his bicycle. Found box cutter and cocaine on him. There were no video cameras here. Man had no attorney. Career criminal with 13 convictions. Perp used prosecution witnesses, 2 cops, 2 store employees and a chemist. Tried to use mistrust of police as an excuse.

$100 million courthouse takes breath away. Judges pushed expense. So bright you need sunglasses. Seven story atrium with opaque dome, looks like they ran out of money.

Soon, the supreme court will be down to 7, then 6, then 5..........

10-29-16   A new email dump on Hillary's close friend and wife of Weiner. Holy cow. Trump to Comey: Weiner, how do I love thee, let me count the ways. Trump feels confident enough now to grope a new woman. He never gropes blacks or Hispanics, prefers Scandinavians, they are the best.

Anthony Weiner just gets bigger and bigger and ....Weiner decides election?   Oh, my head.

The wheels of justice grind slowly but grind they do.

Trump had quit giving money to his campaign, why throw good money after bad? So had most of his followers. But now Weiner causes new hope to stand erect.

10-30-16   Should men with thin hair wear it short or long?

Huma Abedin is the new 15 minute fame woman, friend and confident to Hillary and ex wife of Anthony Weiner. If no indictment, FBI should have remained quiet about Hillary's emails.

All the 1950s space invaders were radioactive.

Trump has said he would sue each of his accusers. So we can expect detailed coverage of court testimony where he slid his hand up and up until he reach the P___ and then, oh my.

Two FBI agents died from touching Weiner's computer.

Do not talk politics with a barber with a razor at your neck.

10-31-16   Happy Halloween. We don't participate anymore. We have 7 dogs and Martha goes to bed early. I used to play the Halloween theme music out the window and one year I dressed up. Don't need the candy either.

Still time for Trump to complain about crooked media or maybe his prostrate and that damn Mexican doctor.

Target sent me two $5 off tickets, one for grocery and one for entire store. I cleared with customer service that entire store meant grocery, right? She said Oh yes. Happily filled my cart, but, wait, not so fast. Cashier said you can't use both of those. I said Yes I can, pointing to customer service. Then she seized on another ploy, the card hadn't started yet. The card begins in the future. I never expected that one. Stunned, I left cards behind and all food on the conveyor or in the basket.

Then I remembered when they tried to give me the red discount card. They asked for enough info to check my credit and that's when I asked if this was a credit card. The cashier feigned ignorance or was really ignorant. I paid full price whistling as I left, because I love to pay full price. Don't you?

Another maddening retail tactic is pricing. 5 for $9. How much is that for one?

Wiley banking tactics have seeped into retail. Stores are trying to become clubs. Family.

Points. My bank sent me an email saying I've got 8,000 points, Excited, I pressed the button to activate them. I was told to visit the website or call. After listening to a machine for hours, a person told me the value of 3,000 points is roughly 45 cents.

Republicans are becoming irrelevant especially with Trump at the helm. Hillary has a new Morgan Freeman ad dissing T. With God and the President against you, give it up!

11-1-16   Without blacks, women and Hispanics, Trump can't win. He has relied almost completely on personal appearances. Truly a campaign on the cheap. He is perhaps the best liar ever to hit the campaign trail. Born for the lower scummy side of politics.

I've got cataract surgery tomorrow. Dreams I've had include receiving a bill in the mail for my funeral and a pharmacy prescribing a can of gasoline. Fantasies include men in a burning cage and a 40 ton laser machine coming lose and falling all the way though my face.

11-2-16   Day of the surgery. Got up at 6 but I had not seen the part about where this is located so 3 buildings later, we found it, Not late tho after 7:30. Two hours paperwork and prepping. The put a blood spatter robe on me and I don non skid socks. Take my blood pressure and monitor my heart whole time. I resisted my inner Trump and did not grab a nurse's boob.   The doctor wrote my name or his name on my eye. The laser was a small deal on swing arm. It only took a few minutes of flashing blue lights for it to be done. Two hours of prep and 30 minutes of real work. Martha drove me home but not before I ate her milkshake and mine too. Hard to sleep with massive bandage on my left eye. Copious aids helped get me through it. Tested this am, could see the barn's broad side.

Trump is building a wall around his Walk of Fame star.

Buy Mike Malaghan's Picture Bride book.

Many voters are sick of minorities, first Obama and now Hillary.

Most high up repubs sold their soul for Trump but they will have time for regrets.

Hole in roof discovered by yard man who was up there cleaning it off. Recent Hurricane Matthew caused the loose tree branch to fall. Luckily, Pete came by that

afternoon to pay his mortgage money and since he is a
roofer, he got up there and patched it.

Hillary said half the Trump supporters are deplorable.
That means the rest of them are gullible. Actually, I think
most of them are gullible.

Kelly Anne Conway, Trump manager, said he lies because
he doesn't know the truth. It's worse than that. He lies
because that's who he is and he's good at it. Actually, he
lies more than anyone on earth, certainly more than any
candidate I've ever seen. He lies because he is mentally ill.
Magical thinking is one of the legs of evil.

11-4-16   Nobody is more surprised by Trump's campaign
success than Trump himself. Except maybe Melania. She
has surely gotten much more than she ever bargained for.
Trophy wife and Trump stereotype.

They say Jacksonville is Trump country, a polite way of
saying this is a hick town. Irene said the same thing about
Pittsburgh. The paper, The Times Union has come out in
favor of Trump but only 2 days before the election.

11-5-16   Fox News hides behind the idea they are not
main stream news, but they are. By portraying themselves
as the little guy, it excuses their excesses?

Julian Assange is now handing down stone tablets.

Christie, Trump, Putin, all lined up in a neat row.

Unemployment is 5% but Trump says it's 10%. What is this, humiture or wind chill?   Trump's taxes wouldn't make any sense either.

When Jimmy Carter got elected, that was it, his biggest accomplishment. – Tip O'Neill

Melania Trump says no bullying. Does she even know who she's married to?

11-6-16   Mark Woods, Times Union columnist, defended paper endorsing Trump. Paper also serves south Georgia market.

Business news is also provided by Financial News and Daily Record and the Jacksonville Business Journal.

If our election is like 2000 and it goes to the supreme court with 8 judges, see the problem. Thanks, republicans.

Trump demonstrates the cult of personality. They will name a disease after him. He thinks his faults are virtues. People are praying for him to win. The FBI and IRS have been politicized since Nixon. There are facts and then there are Trump facts. Millions of people believe what he says. Millions of people are now spouting erroneous "facts".

The story of the year is how Trump blew away 15 other good candidates right off the stage with bullying, name calling and loud insults.

11-7-16   Four turnovers and the Jacksonville Jaguars lose the game.

The Jacksonville paper Times Union has made us a laughing stock by endorsing Trump.   W. S. Morris IV, owner of the paper, accepted a full page Trump ad. Hey fool, Trump wants to control the media. Businesses rarely survive third and fourth generation owners.

Trump will keep on bashing Hillary as a private citizen. Martha is tired of me being right about Trump. He is a god in his own mind.

FBI Director Comey seems confused, pressured, disorganized, maybe not right for this job. Both IRS and FBI have been hurt by bias.

Kellyanne Conway has aped the Trump method of being interviewed. Talk all the time so questions you don't know the answer to can't be asked. Kellyanne is the Trump campaign manager. (Good luck getting paid, sweetie.)

Trump: Help me take America back to 1300 where I am the king and you are the serfs.

11-8-16   Election day. Glad I voted early. RIP Janet Reno. She took responsibility for the Waco disaster on the same day it happened. I respect that. She was the first woman attorney general appointed by Clinton.

Our talking TV told me to shut up.

Roger Ailes has gone the way of Jimmy Hoffa?

I know more about Trump than the generals, believe me.

Donald's taxes will cause some new laws to be written.
Trump should have run as a younger man. He came close
in '98. That's when Doonesbury discovered him and his
hair. He had the same ignorance then but would be young
enough to learn from his mistakes yet didn't his mistakes
propel him to the top?   Anyway, he could have run again.

Trump facts are what you want them to be. This childish
approach has won him many converts. All five year olds
know the truth is whatever you want it to be.

Neck and neck in Florida, guess the Jacksonville paper's
endorsement of Trump wasn't that stupid. A Trump loss
won't hurt the GOP. This campaign and Facebook have
taught me that people will believe anything.

Zero political experience, blew away 15 good candidates
with 200 years combined experience. All by huffing and
puffing.

It's not perfect, has been changed to, It's rigged.

Maybe Obama wasn't so smart to help Hillary, maybe it
backfired.

11-9-16   I stayed up until 11 and it was looking bleak. Got
up at 5:30 and Trump had won. Where were the polls?
The movie Candidate comes to mind.

Obama didn't create racism, that was done by his
opposition. I guess Hillary gets a real estate license.

Facebook creates friends, brings back old ones, but also divides and discards some people. One person in particular is very zealous of his time and preferred a different venue for keeping in touch with old friends and being highly educated, looked down on Facebook. He also voted for Trump. A PHD voted for Trump. Gawd.

Lots to say on the Trump victory. Outrageous? Longshot.

11-10-16 Thurs. Went on Facebook tear. Deleted one guy who told me to stuff it up my wrinkly ass. I don't allow personal abuse like that.

Hillary won the popular vote I think, some states too close to call. Demonstrations in major cities. Polling is dead? People don't level with pollsters and often don't know until they get in the booth.

Ben Carson, relatively untainted by the Trump stink, will have an important role to play in new administration.

Still rigged, Donald?

Putin sent Donald Kiev as a good will gesture.

Cartoonists are happy. Nixon on steroids. Trump was the most surprised. Eight years of a black president was enough, the tide went out. A black Muslim pres. Going off script seemed to help Donald so is he going to be unhinged all the time now? He's really going to pay no taxes now. In case you are tempted to ape Trump's actions, say grabbing women, don't. Rules don't apply to him. Who will be the next first lady?

Is Trump still going to run his business? A real danger is another Vietnam as he knows more than the generals.

When Hillary denigrated coal miners, she cursed at all working men.   God blessed half the electorate and turned his back on the other half. The pope knew what he wanted but had little influence.

This Trump mess, what an odd brew. Will the Weiner rise again? We wanted change so we elect a madman? Baby Bush is smiling and saying, Miss me?

11-11-16   Veterans day. Uncle Gene was shot down in the Pacific WWII and so was father in law Hank. Both men rescued by US Forces.

Trump could be more hated than Obama. I feared a Trump loss would spark riots. Novelists can't make this up.

You can't move to Canada unless you have a job there.

Bill Clinton did not help her campaign.

Can Christie get the transition done before he's jailed?

Will Trump lift a candelabra from the White House? Can Michelle and Melanie wear the same clothes?

How many of the street protestors didn't vote?

Bad optics for Obama to use Air Force One to campaign for Hillary. Did Trump steal his plane from the US government by not paying taxes?

The pollsters seem to have gotten swept up in the tide of anti Trump feelings while doing their work.

11-12-16   Trump hounded by supporters (KKK) and detractors alike. T will have high staff turnover. His every move will be watched. T is changing the name of the country to: Trump Colossus.

Scott Adams (Dilbert) said T speaks in simple word pictures.

More women are being groped and more minorities are being punished.

No phones were lost when they had cords.

Democrats burn buildings, republicans throw golf clubs.

We can get Trump interested in science by telling him NASA will put the name Trump on the Mars rocket.

God does not care about our elections or sports outcomes.

11-13-16   Sun. Since Trump is fond of naming people, I have a name for him: King Kong.

Trump would rather live in his tower than the white house. Trump's wife says who he is. Someone said Barron doesn't know English.

Half the people didn't vote and now they are bitching. The second string candidates might have swayed the election.

I asked the Ale House waitress, an older white woman if the election suited her and she proudly stated, Yes, she voted for Trump.

The Reagan tax plan whipped the economy up and then down. Nixon is smiling and asking, Miss me? Pence's new book, Living with the Inquisition, is selling well.

The future of religion seems in doubt. So many biblical admonitions have been killed either by science or culture. We've seen the Muslims and their view imposed on others violently.   Liberals don't respect life as in abortion.

11-14-16   Fox News workers leave to work for Trump.

Let's run someone we all like, say Tom Hanks.

And now, What he really meant._____________________

11-15-16   Tues. Steve Bannon, Trump's sidekick, is toxic. Maybe Trump's answer to the "crooked media". Our first Twitter president. Trump's wall will be how long?_______ He's having a high learning curve.

I wish people would quit saying, Going forward. Bannon has the look of a heavy drinker.

Nixon resigned, Clinton impeached, yet we accept Trump? He will get super rich. Kids running business with security clearance, oh my. Trump is a man who pays no taxes. It would be foolish to think he wouldn't line his pockets given the chance.

It is likely Trump worked harder than Hillary did on the campaigns. Trump does well as the underdog. If there can be wisdom in ignorance, then Trump could shine.

11-16-16   Wed. Country seems more divided now than when Obama took over in 08. Maybe we should have a candidate in their 40s.

Trump should go to Flynt, MI and fix their water.

Ruth Ginsberg will hold her position on the supreme court until she is old as God.

No ship is unsinkable. No nation unwreckable.

11-17-16 Thurs. Megyn Kelly has new book describing Trump and his henchmen trying to influence her. Go girl.

Ben Carson kicked out by Bannon?

If Trump works on his business, we will know about it.

Has anybody else got Trump stomach?

The leader sets the tone. The subordinates usually set a lower tone.

11-18-16 Fri. The ACLU has gotten tremendous boost in recent days. Membership money is flowing in. ACLU is the American Civil Liberties Union. They stand up for individual rights and are expected to lead the fight against Trump's oppression.

The Trump name has been taken off 3 New York buildings. Tenants did not want to be associated with him.

Obama is overseas now apologizing for Trump in advance.

It's time for my annual ear job, wax removal. It's not surprising that ear doctors speak loudly.

11-19-16 Sat. On Venus, it rains lead, among other things.

In old movies, they pay for drinks with pocket change.

Trump settles the University suit for $25 million.

Trump should live at white house, not the tower. Tower not made for security and not fair to others nearby.

Romney would make a good secretary of state. If the past vitriol can be swallowed.

11-20-16 Sun. Trump whined about the rigged election for months only to be benefitted from the "rig". (Electoral College) Twice presidents have lost while winning the popular vote. We must not love the constitution blindly.

11-21-16 Mon. Toilet paper cores have gotten bigger. When I worked at the toilet paper factory, the guns blowing the rolls full of air sounded like a war zone.

How many diseases do TV ads have a cure for?

The Trump victory shows people only look at campaign material the last 2 weeks when T was fairly on point. Trump fails to pay subcontractors part or all of the money. 80% write it off. 20% sue. 5% collect. Billionaire math. It pays to stiff people. Obama was a good president but he came at a high price. Melania Trump now being satirized. She's arrived.

11-22-16 Tues. After beginning writing my obit, I fell in the hall. Slipped on a patch of dog pee. Went down on one knee. Glass in right hand broke off but I wasn't cut or hurt.

Martha has a personal shopper.

11-23-16 Wed. The school bus driver who killed 5 kids in a crash in Chattanooga had prior accidents.

Slowly, Christmas gifts cover the dining room table.

Headline 2-98: Winfree Wins Beef Beef. Oprah was sued for what she said about unhealthy hamburgers.

Flipping best done during times of inflation. Read about it in Real Estate Dad's Way. Dad and I were in the real estate business together.

As we touch 70 years of age, our age becomes part of our name.

Trump cannot be himself if we have a free press. Some think the election is still going on. If there were no electoral college, the election would be dominated by Florida, Texas, California and New York.

11-24-16 Thurs. Happy Thanksgiving. Hillary leads by 2 million votes. Will there be a recount? Was fraud involved?

I thought stocks would dive if Trump won but they did not.

It hurts me to have a movie with Santa in it rated R.

NASA called. They can see neighbor Ray's Christmas display from space.

Ben Carson head of HUD? (House and Urban Development) He's a medical doctor but I hope he can clean up the fraud and corruption.

Millions of turkeys are having a very bad day today.

11-25-16 Fri. Hillary has applied for a job at the car wash. Sign in laundry mat: For sale, 40 pantsuits, cheap.

Eat whipped cream right out of the spout.

As kids, we'd listen in on the party line. Give them advice. Back in the '50's, phone lines were cheaper if shared with other users and if they were using, you could hear them when picking up the receiver.

Got home from Thanksgiving to 3 police cars across the street. Group of people in distress. Probable meth lab being operated in shed behind the house. Man found dead inside house by 12 year old son. Two men lived in the house across the street from us. As dark fell, hazmat truck and TV crew arrived. No TG for him.

11-26-16 Sat. America's dog Jasper is an immigrant.
Jasper is owned by Fox's Dana Perino.

Barron Trump is autistic? Rumor backed up by video going
around.

I don't shop on black Friday. One time I walked the
Regency Mall on that day. So many people I could not get
up any speed. Today that mall is a tomb.

Trump invented fake news. Ima build a wall.

Martha has a picture of her brother Jack in our office/BR.
He was a highly accomplished man and very down to
earth. I met him several times and wish it could have been
more. Even tho he was 85, he left way too soon. He took
a flyer on a new heart procedure and felt great for a week,
then boom. He did not want to live impaired.

11-27-16 Sun. Millions of species on the earth. It all just
happened?

Castro dead at 90, seems like 190.

Four birthdays celebrated at Outback last night. Lindsay,
Leslie, Heather and Justin. Three children all well behaved.
Charlie, Emmalyn and Madison, 1, 3 and 9.

11-28-16 Mon. No Christmas tree no more. We have
plenty of other decorations.

Hillary's, We are going to put a lot of coal miners out of business was a stupid thing to say. Romney's 47% of voters won't vote for me was second.

Tweeting Trump bashing vote recount. We want to know the truth, right? The 2000 election made the Florida voter into Mr. Stupid. It seems things would be more fair without the electoral college and 3rd party candidates. Democracy is a messy beast.

The Florida Times Union printed my letter but they changed my joke about Trump's 6" wall to a 6' wall which doesn't make sense. Crooked media.

One thing stands out this year, the corruption of the truth.

11-29-16 Tues. CNN says Trump lies to manipulate the press. Dan Rather says he believes his own lies and that is frightening. The Green Party elected Trump. Don't take his tweeter away, we need to know what he is up to. As 2016 fades away, I say Goodbye truth, I will miss you. I think Fareed Zakaria also said Trump believes his lies.

How many citizens of Cuba did Castro kill? Probably 10,000. I blame him for the deaths of all those trying to leave. Trying to float to Miami on a beer cooler.

My Walmart shoes have slowly turned into bedroom slippers.

11-30-16 Wed. People are doing bad ass stuff just because they voted for Trump. Voters have thrown a brick through the glass of government. The dance of Trump vs Romney, queerer and queerer.

Tennessee is now the burn capital of America unseating California.

Can or will Obama close Gitmo before Trump takes over. I have an idea Trump will find Gitmo very useful.

Auditors agree, paper ballots are better than e-voting.

I have the cure for thumb sucking. Leave the money on my front porch.

Going through my parents old checks. Gas $4. Laundry $3. Church $2. University of Florida $168, tuition for half year. Relatively expensive.

12-1-16 Thurs. Jill Stein is better known now than before the election. (Green Party candidate) Jill is heading a recount in 3 states where Trump won.

Trump's extreme vetting implies a sort of magic. Looking into the future to see who's going to go bad.

Bernie Sanders might have beaten Trump.

Trump hires all of Fox News people.

Doctors have installed a new heart in a patient. It is the first heart to be made of Legos.

Nancy Pelosi just leads and leads and leads.

12-2-16 Fri. Trump is hosting a $100,000 plate dinner. Call me for tickets.

If Trump can win over Romney, then he is superman? Is Romney Trump's Lex Luthor?

Wife Martha and I now both have personal shoppers.

One thing all Trump appointees have to remember, their job is tenuous as snow in August.

12-3-16 Sat. Cool. The robber barons of 1890 had more money that the government. Trump has not missed this fact. Gen. Mattis (Trump pick for sec. of defense) has been compared to Patton. Patton would have kept WWII going longer fighting the Russians.

We will learn to ignore some of the Trump bad tweets just like a Miley Cyrus video. Trump sure doesn't lack confidence. The economy could get overheated. Now is not the time to simulate it.

A Japanese restaurant instruction book includes the passage: Americans eat like pigs. The clatter of 1,000 spatulas sounds like a machine gun firing range.

Asian cashier speaks poor English making it hard to close the deal AND she's rude too. Asian woman are supposed to be compliant but once they get hardened, stand back.

12-4-16 Sun. Breathe deep, fart long. It's all good for you. – Forgotten source.

Oops, another Indiana company is moving to Mexico.

A month's worth of pills fit in the bottle cap.

The open house host never put down the potato chips and never gave me a card. I gave her my real estate book card and told her what I thought the place was worth. (It's overbuilt and almost a zoning violation) She told me they would have no trouble getting it appraised for what they wanted.

Real estate agents: Even if the open house looker lives next door, you don't know when they might buy or know someone who will buy, and anybody can complain to the real estate board.

Trump has given us new truths: True, almost true, nearly true, maybe true, oops, no way, GD lie, pants on fire, Trump Truth.

You can boil marijuana and obtain THC, a powerful derivative which can blow your head off.

The trouble with going to the Walmart pharmacy is all the interruptions by people looking for toasters, hamburgers, trees, spray and deodorant.

12-5-16 Mon. CNN: Trump lies all the time even when it serves no purpose. Honorable mention goes to Nixon and Johnson who got a big Vietnam war going.

Winston Churchill invented fake news to throw off the Nazis. Now the Nazis are gone but fake news remains.

Forrest Gump Trump is hoping all ends well like the movie.

High death toll in Oakland, California warehouse fire packed with occupants living there. Sanctuary mentality very dangerous.

Sooner or later it'll be Trump vs America. There is a 30% chance he won't finish his term. Trump is like Bill Clinton raised to the power 100.

Hillary was boring, forced, fake, strident and scripted. Bernie had conviction but the simple Trump ran away with it.   His rule is act like children to get what you want.

12-6-16 Tues.   Lose weight drinking my special eggnog. Leave money on front porch.

Is it stupid to send Christmas cards? Some people send notes and pictures and their hand writing says something about them. Some don't have ready computer access. We could be the last generation to send cards, although greeting cards in stores are numerous and amazing.

The eye doctor is happier about my progress than I am.

Martha says she doesn't want any gift cards. There goes my only idea.

12-7-16 Wed. Memorable repossession appraisals: Man cleaned and worked on his motorcycle in the living room. Another man got new floor and threw the old carpet in the swimming pool.

When did cars get so expensive?

What do you think about the movie Uncle Buck?

Trump never quits running for office and campaigning.

I bet mailmen hate the Christmas season.

90% of news is speculation or repeated.

If you can't spell their name, they don't get a Christmas card.

The hurry up style of management makes for many mistakes.

Trump is so corrupt, he'll be gone in a year – MSNBC

December 7th 1941, a date that will live in infamy. Who said it?

Today is the 75th anniversary of the Pearl Harbor attack.

12-8-16 Thurs. Finally got Martha's gift, a fake Hope diamond. No one will know.

For 2 days, I've been spitting into my ancestry tube. What a gift that is.

Trump admits he has a short attention span and easily gets bored. Loves turmoil. Sold all of his stock. Only 3% of his wealth.

Megyn Kelly's book might be worth buying.

Someone please assemble the reindeer for our deck. We don't need outside lights, just a sign pointing next door to Ray's.

12-9-16 Fri. Trump got away with not showing his taxes so he will continue with the business/real estate conflicts. Fake news elected Trump. – Rachel Maddow. Ivana wanted to party but Trump was a homebody – Surviving at the Top   Ivana got 3 prenup raises since he did so well in the '80's.

Trump's hate for the press happened when he divorced his first wife, Ivana. Up to then he lapped up their attention. But soon, he was looking down the barrel of full blown tabloid journalism.

Schools should teach fake news classes. Witness the 1938 broadcast of Martians invading Earth. It was just entertainment but millions believed the story.

Hitler told his people Jews were bad, and many believed the lie so it helped later with the persecution.

12-10-16 Sat. Trump continues with his businesses, he will be a part time president. Bill Clinton with his sexual escapades, helped give us Trump.   Trump is the classic journalist; loud, never mind about the facts and never at a loss for words.

Some gas pumper drove off with the pump in the car. I parked there for gas, went in to pay and was told I had to use a different pump. Back out and re-parked at another pump. My bad, I did not notice the missing pump on the first one and their bad no out of order sign was used. Friday Christmas traffic to boot.

Trump suffers from, Is that all there is, syndrome. Only he thinks it's a good thing.

12-11-16 Sun. Look! Fireball Vodka miniatures at ABC Liquors for only one dollar.

The Russians tried to throw the vote to Trump and Hillary won the popular vote. That is a formula for mayhem.

Thanks God, at long last, Santa got a bathroom on the sleigh.

Applebys and Fridays, a mountain of mediocre.

The paper mill had labor saving devices unused due to union rules. Ultimately the union lost. Jobs have gone overseas or been replaced by automation.

12-12-16 Mon. The Gold Member gentlemen's club has been torn down. The 4,000 sq. ft. building is to be replaced with a 7,000 sq. ft. building. No word on how many extra poles that is.

The Jacksonville Jaguars cannot win by order of a new law.

I put all my crayons in a sauce pan and melted them, trying to invent a new color. The new color was mud.

Gift cards are easy to lose. Please put the recipients' name on the gift.

Long beautiful hair is an asset to anyone's appearance.
How many years does it take off Trump's age?

Leaving Dollar General at the same time as a fighting
couple. Get out of there quick. You never know who is
armed or will shoot.

12-13-16 Tues. Ben spent $30 for chicken bone candy.

Our house is stuffed. We have 10 Santas to begin with.

Boy was I wrong about the market diving. Business loves
low wages and Trump is king of that.

Trump says the CIA was wrong about Iraq weapons so he's
not gonna worry about Russia. Pence is Trump's intel
back-up.

Some people won't answer their phone, they just do texts.
I have never texted.

McArthur, the Florida billionaire owned an insurance
company and would not consider a claim the first time.
They'd have to send it a second time before he'd even
think about paying it. So it is with Trump and his suppliers.

I don't wrap gifts but Martha using a glue gun takes 30
minutes to wrap one package.

Wait till he's president. Trump hates the media now, just
wait until then.   He's gonna make Russia a state?

It's likely Jill Stein cost Hillary the election. It chaps my ass
to hear Trump say he won by a landslide.

12-14-16 Wed. First Hillary loses to an under qualified half black guy and then to an overstuffed aged lying businessman. OMG

Trump is the only person who doesn't want to know if the Russians interfered in our election.

I was stabbed at San Jose Antiques. A candle holder without the candle got me. Drew blood on my finger.

Trump calls his lies hyperbole. The book 1984 had the government changing language and history. Reality was whatever government said it was. The press will be our last line of defense against this.

The constitution put Trump in office (electoral college) and the constitution could take him out (emoluments). No president can accept money from a foreign power. Trump will get richer from his position.

Unplugging the Keurig seemed to break it.

I acquired 5 acres in Colorado. It was part of one of their land boom tracts. I ended up trading it in for down payment on a car at Key Buick.

12-15-16 Thurs. Kelly Anne Conway is starring in a movie where she plays a tree.

The most oft uttered phrase in our family is, Don't tell Jeff.

Trump support shrinks? Some holding nose, others licking boots. He's gonna keep one foot on the rock of business and the other on the rock of governing. He will go with one if the other gets too hard. His 3 kids will make for a shell game, interchangeable with the boss. Likely we will have a part time president. He's easily bored.

Melania Trump will stay in NYC. She has a reason now to be rid of him. The president's term should be 6 years to reduce constant campaigning.

12-16-16 Fri. Two hairs at the end of my nose defy scissors.

Dylann Roof is dead whether the jury gives it to him or not. (shooter who killed 9 blacks in a Charleston church.)

Jaguars should have won 8 games.

Lunch at Ted's with Ted. No matter if you order cup or bowl of soup, you are going to get one ladle.

Capt. of el Faro knew more than the navigators and lost his ship in Hurricane Matthew. Greed kept him going?

We can blame the Syria war on the Iraq war, right?

12-17-16 Sat. We blew it toppling Saddam in Iraq and ISIS battled in Syria on our side against "the murderous dictator Bashar al-assad". Russians fighting for Assad. Against us?

Where is it written that we have to be reminded of our mistakes twice?

Alaska has 1 million people, California has 40 million. They each have 2 senators. The electoral college works like that too.

Next to Don't tell Jeff, it's, Don't give Jeff candy.

Christmas takes over our lives.

Trump is like Johnson, knows more than the generals and escalates the Vietnam war to a monster in US clothing. Also both good at influence peddling and arm twisting but Trump uses Twitter.

General Custer knew more than his scouts and sent 300 men up against 3,000 Sioux.

12-18-16 Sun. Reliving the JonBenet killing serves? The end of Witness, Book retrieves the shotgun from the grain bin. Would it even fire? Would it penetrate a man's body? Old Law and Order, Lenny and Carver were defense attorneys.

Robert Fulghum says use crayons, not bombs.

Even good credit cards can go bad. Any gifting problem can be solved with buckets of cash.

12-19-16 Mon. The big gift wrap is over. Steak dinner, unusual for us.

Greg Gutfeld show, wordy, right wing, inside jokes, frenetic, verbal slapstick.

As a boy, I spit off the Empire State building. Hiked up on the parapet wall and watched it go down until wind dispersed. Went back and steel fence prohibited that. Now I'm told it's all encased in glass.

Maybe Trump will Gump his way through his presidency.

We have so many gift cards, we ate one. (Used it at a restaurant)

Himmler to be ambassador to Israel.

12-20-16 Tues. Trump will eliminate selected news organizations. Rachael Maddow should watch her back.

Trump will fight for his version of the truth knowing it is fluid. California is developing a secessionist mindset.

Zsa Zsa Gabor is the reason for the pre-nup.

Kids need to learn that some truths are absolute and some are not so easy.   Is the tree upright or cut down? Absolute. Is bad good? Could be argued forever.

Many jobs are being invented as old ones die.

Every 15 minutes, 100 toenails from 7 dogs clatter across our wood floor to bite the mailman or some other badman.

Our Keurig is Kaput.

Trump won 83% of US land area.

Hillary will never be hungry again.

One can't say Bill killed her campaign but one can't say he helped her either.   Bill's bimbos set the bar so low, even Trump seemed almost normal. Bill impeached for what Trump does all the time.

Does Trump tweeting all his discomforts endanger national security?

Only 5 days left to buy my book before the price goes down.

12-21-16 Wed. Trump library burns, both books destroyed.

Cookies, Reeses, eggnog, chocolate, heavy cream, love Christmas.

Matthew, Karina and Matty Matt celebrate Christmas with us.

12-22-16 Thurs. Merry Christmas Stephanie, Dave, Ben, Emma.

All I want for Christmas is half a front tooth, Cataract surgery to go well, lose weight.

Cold cuts went over big, at least with me, and no huge leftover problem. Shortest day of the year. Buying over, opening left.

12-23-16 Fri. Trump thinks nuclear proliferation is a good thing. Records will be played at his inaugural. With his hair, Trump could have been a musician.

TV helps create thought but also blocks it.

The Sovereign of the Seas, 16th century wood warship was victorious in many battles but was undone by an overturned candle. Don't let that happen in your house.

12-24-16 Sat. This is Christmas eve. Martha shopped all day yesterday.

Trump thinks nukes are shiny hotels.

Marshall Dillon nuggets: One white woman is worth 5 horses. The Calvary had trouble telling one tribe from another. Dillon slept with his hat on.

Believing strongly in a certain faith is not ignorance but rather indoctrination.

John and Shelia Antonio had their picture made with Michelle and Barack Obama after a media dinner. I knew John as a 6 year old. He's now head of programming at CNN. Shelia is Mike's sister who I knew in college. Shelia is John's mother.

Perfume ads can be and usually are sexy but Carl's Hamburgers had the most sexy ad I've ever seen on TV.

It seems to me that newer cars are getting more chrome, reminiscent of '50's cars.

12-25-16 Sun. Merry Christmas. Warm in Jacksonville, Florida. Jaguars won a game proving there is a Santa Clause.

Rest in Peace, Jake Jacoway and Billy Odom, two friends of mine. Billy was a child and high school friend and Jake was more important to my dad but I did buy 2 houses from him.

May 2017 be good to us and the world.

12-26-16 Mon. Given a choice, kids will always open gifts first and eat later.

As a family we got a drone and smart vacuum. (Rumba)

Do not date a professor who is dating another one of your professors. – Back to School.

12-27-16 Tues. The NRA (National Rifle Association) is now in charge of our nuclear program.

Dinner was turkey, pistachios, cashews and peanuts.

Row well and live, Forty One. – What movie?

Music is very generational. Martha and I both have albums but none in common.

First, remove old stuff, clean where it was, install new stuff.

12-28-16 Wed. Addiction allowed Carrie Fisher to have a career but ended her life early.

Save the swamp.

You're a pro if you shop the liquor store using a grocery cart.

RIP Gary Shandling.

Dad invited everyone who stopped by to eat dinner if it was dinner time. Mother got mad.

Old cigarette ads proclaim the king size cigarette safer because it's longer and filters the smoke. The key is quality.

What is the IRS doing about the Trump Foundation?

Don't dos by Peter Lynch, author of One up on Wall Street: If you don't know anything about it, invest your life savings in it.

We have 15,000 nukes many of which are 30 years old. Maybe Trump is going to inspect them all. Putin is now president of two countries.

12-29-16 Thurs. Do you stomp the kitchen garbage once, twice, more?

Only a one mile road would connect Windy Hill where Martha used to live with Town Center, the busiest shopping center in Jacksonville.

Big Weld – What movie?

Each side in the campaign seemed to admit their candidate was crooked but not as crooked as the other person.

12-30-16 Fri. During Obama's last days, he is giving Trump plenty to do.   Putin bought a unit in Trump Tower?

Our Christmas Victrola is set up and cranking. 50 year old albums clear as a bell. We need to find the 45 speed records.

Five Reeses too much to make a glass of chocolate milk.

Jesus and other greats of religion are guideposts along the way of our evolution trying to change us from violent to peace loving.

I spent $1,500 extra for laser surgery to get rid of cataract left eye and now I need more laser surgery to get rid of the scar tissue.   Not an exact science.

12-31-16 Sat. Freezing in Jacksonville, Florida. First of the winter.

Martha gave me 3 chocolate covered cherries, delicious.

Alvin and the Chipmunks to perform at the Trump Inaugural.

Following in the Melania tradition, Trump will use Obama's inaugural speech.

2016: Trump won. Face it, Stuff I've Said on Facebook published. Ben and Matthew get first cars. Friends and relatives visit. Jack died.

Trump throws mud at people until it sticks. He will be badly muddied by that "fact" that Putin elected him.   One Thousand lies a week.

1-1-17 Sun. Fireworks less than some past years.

Put tiny houses in back yards and let caretaker live there as baby boomers age.

Obamites and Trumpers both have magnified the other's problems and outright made up problems and lies.

Twilight Zone on TV all day and all night.

Trump says we should know when he's lying.

Carrabba's sausage and lintel soup now has sausage so fine it can't be seen.

I hope the dems won't block Trump as the repubs blocked Obama.

1-2-17 Mon. Three times I've melted Reeses for chocolate milk. The mess is less but so is the taste. Big chunks left over.

Impeaching Trump could be the new gridlock.

Maybe we humans are the progenitor for the entire universe.

100 Twilight Zones and counting.

Black eyed peas, collard greens and biscuits.

Happy New Year!!

1-3-17 Tues. What will Obama do after he leaves office?

Ann Coulter is so tough she sexually harassed Roger Ailes.

Record high temperatures today.

In two years Trump will lose his majority in congress and he will be forced by law to release his tax returns so we can see who he is obliged to.   But he will never release all of it.

1-4-17 Wed. A teen mob rushed a St. Augustine Outlet Mall store, stole 46 handbags worth $400 each and there was no surveillance.

You look like you been whooped with an ugly stick. – Bo Diddley

Real estate developers go broke all the time.

Hard cover books have no cover once you lose the dust jacket.

Drain the swamp? That kills all the animals.

Maybe Obamacare will be suspended with no new insured's, leaving the present ones intact. Then they can add new parts to the law, one at a time.

I went to 3 first grades. Why don't people who have trouble getting work move to a more prosperous area?

1-5-17 Thurs. Obamacare was passed without knowing what was in it and now it going to be scraped without reaching its full potential.

Politicizing intelligence is a very bad thing to do, Donald.

We will have to peel Obama's cold dead fingers off the White House door knob.

Do I file Megyn Kelly under M or T for Trump?

Give Dylan Roof life in prison where the homeboys will take care of him. If we execute him, it could rally other martyrs to the cause.

Trump knows more than the generals because that's what he wants you to think but at the same time you have to know he's lying.

Charles Manson regrets that he is too sick to attend the Inaugural.

1-6-17 Fri. Chicago's great red spot is the gang violence unstoppable by a police community where life is cheap and will is weak.

Repubs can leave Trump high and dry like many did before the election.

Trump has many legal distractions and lies during depositions. Megyn Kelly and Greta Van Susteren both moving to more liberal networks.

Stores will have holography to display goods not really there. You will punch in what you want and it will appear but don't know how you would try it on. Machine would take your digital measurements.

Auto insurance rates are climbing due to texting and driving.

We have passwords written on little slips of paper in all rooms and in all drawers throughout the house.

1-7-17 Sat. Martha tinted her hair a ravishing brown color.

Trump said Mexico can pay for the wall later. Ooops.

Trump has a new book out: Flexible Facts R Us

There are many old factories among my postcard collection. Wonder how many of them are still in operation.

Welcome to the world's first fully automated cruise ship. No worries, we know more than the hurricanes.

Trump made a career lying but the world will call him out.

1-8-17 Sun. Freezing in Jacksonville. Summer not so bad. If it's going to be this cold, might as well have snow.

Dems need to get off Trump's faults, they are well known. Instead, promote something new like free college. – Mike Malaghan

Trump begs the question, are honesty and ethics really necessary? Ask yourself that when going in for an operation.

1-9-17 Mon. Jacksonville weather is pretty good. Six days of freezing and long springs and falls.

Watching the '89 set of Columbos. They are using young unknown perps. Why pay name stars when Peter Falk is the attraction?

Trump walking in his long coat reminds me of Darth Vader. He has proven that ratings trump character.

The mentally ill and guns. Whaddya gonna do?

1-10-17 Tues. Detroit assumed Hillary would win and didn't bother to turn out for the vote.

Gas bags pop. Tweet storm a comin. Trump may last 2 years. When he feels power slipping away, he'll make an audacious grab for it.

God takes care of us but remember, he gave us legs for when the Velociraptor appears.

Leftovers tend to gather in one large bowl.

Kellyanne Conway is the wicked witch of the tower.

Businesses used to answer their phones.

I stopped for gas. On the way in to pay, found a dime. No sooner had I picked it up when a beggar ten feet away asked for money so I flipped the dime to him. Did he say thanks, no, he cursed.

Trump administration feels like a civil war brewing.

Had to borrow one dollar and repay it so bank would not charge inactivity fee. (It's in the contract, they said) Banks bounce checks on purpose.   It's the way their computers are rigged.

People are talking about Meryl Streep dissing Trump. Trump apologized once, didn't he?

Many toddlers wear diapers all day as their only outfit.

1-11-17 Wed. Both my daughter and granddaughter are sick.

"Only little people pay taxes." – Leona Helmsley and Donald Trump

We found the 45 speed records.

Err on the side of good.

Obama will work hard for democratic causes and occasionally throw a stick at Trump.

1-12-17 Thurs. Putin told Trump I'll make you president if you will make us a state. Wadda deal. T forgets he won by a minority vote so when he pisses on CNN, he wets himself. Russia blackmailing T over sex? Pleeze.

Diddja ever lay down in the back seat, stick your feet out the window and lose a shoe? That would be before car air conditioning.

Goodbye elegance, hello crude.

Vietnam cost us 50,000 dead, cost them one million, yet we lost the war. Must have been a war by electoral college.

The Trump bubble has to pop.

Weather forecast is only accurate for the next day.

We accept that Trump will get billions richer by being president, but just don't ruin the country.

Trump always wins in the short run. He crushes reporters with gushes of bullshit. His press conference was just like his campaign.

Don't frame pictures. It makes them bigger and more space hogging. It tries in some twisted fashion to make them immortal. And it burdens the giftee with the need to hang the damn thing. It presumes you know the decorating taste of the giftee.

The one who calls others crooked all the time is the real crooked one.

Some journalists will die during the Trump term.

Fox News has the legs. Gals show more than any other network. Thanks Roger.

Isn't eating rice with sticks a fool's journey?

1-13-16 Fri. Had new frozen dinner in a sack.

Voice mail forces customers to email. The eradication of thinking from business sure is efficient but soulless and usually under serves the customer.

Dan Rather is THE Trump basher.

In the end, Hitler refused to surrender costing another million lives and he blamed the German people, not himself.

Jim Acosta of CNN is the new Megyn Kelly?

It's the fool's turn at bat.

If growing up in public housing qualifies Ben Carson to be secretary of HUD, them I'm mayor of Pittsburgh.

Often children have to take over aging parent's life policies. The company will encourage these kids to drop the policy for obvious reasons.

1-15-17 Sun. OJ Simpson took the stand during his liability trial for killing Nicole and Ron. He blathered on just like Trump does with no regard for the truth.

The people of Chicago have legalized silencers so they can get some sleep.

We have never elected a truly bad president, so the people assume we cannot.

A foreign corporation could buy one of Trump's buildings giving him a huge profit and evoking the emoluments clause of the constitution eliminating Trump as president.

The 1958 Fly is a good movie while the newer one is just gross. Why hasn't there been a serious movie about teleportation.

Rachel Maddow of MSNBC just comes flat out calling Trump a liar.

Obama had some verbal missteps in 8 years but Trump does that in 10 minutes.

Fukushima argues for going solar or wind and the Tesla battery may make it happen.

Dead malls tend to fill with churches.

Run from a wet friendly muddy dog.

Before you spend that gift card, find out how much $ is on it.

I had a dream that Key West and Venice were inundated by rising waters.

Russia did not elect the beast, it was voter apathy that elected him.

Remember Frankie Lane? Mule Train, Boot Hill

Some workers when faced with a cut in pay, quit the job and receive nothing. Then they blame the stupid economy.

1. Have a will. 2. Keep it up to date.

Only about 10% of counselors care. Caring can make all the difference.

1-16-17 Mon. North Korea, backed by China, seems to be our worst threat.

Avonlea Antique Mall thinning? Interest in antiques or old stuff has waned.

Columbo catches high class criminals but Forensic Files deals with real life.

The fact that some worry about Trump lining his pockets via the presidency proves he's the wrong man for the job.

I'm loaning Trump my Victrola for his inaugural along with my Adolf Eichmann records.

Dylan Roof tried to start a race war but Trump is the man to get it done.

Trump is putting his name on all the inaugural potties.

Trump's bullshit is being exposed as lawmakers try to enact it.

Methinks when Trump finds out being president is hard, he will let Ivana take over.

1-18-17 Wed. Bob Beckel is back on the Five. Juan Williams must have been too coherent.

As a private citizen, Barack Obama is going to Chicago to fight crime.

Save circus jobs, Mr. Trump.

Has Justin Beaver thrown any feces on houses lately?

Don't all Pit Bulls live in trailer parks?

Manning sentence commuted? What was a private in the army doing with classified information anyway?

Trump only has a 40% approval rating but Rush Limbaugh says that is fake news.

A president Trump will probably commute OJ's sentence so they can work together.

Trump and Putin seem cut out of the same cloth.

If Trump is as bad as Bush, we are done for. Wars, depression, exploding debt.

Twitter will be Trump's press conferences.

1-19-17 Thurs. Hillary is wearing a stunning pink pantsuit to the inaugural with cut outs. She has rented the Champagne room at the hotel. Last words were, Keep em comin.

Once you pass 90 in age, all the doctors see is a corpse.

Trump is ruled by his penis. It's defined him. Will he show it to us to put to bed rumors of its tiny size?

The pharmacy is where we go and the medical insurance company is our source of mail.

Trump's cabinet embodies rule by the rich, well born and corrupt.

Trump has turned Rachel Maddow at MSNBC into a powerhouse.

At my age, all women are girls.

1-20-17 Fri. New President today. Trump wants to see Jesus' birth certificate as well as his re-birth certificate.

Roosevelt packed the supreme court, which is still going on today.

Trump will cut a lot of programs' funding. If he stays in his own hotel, the press complains about free publicity. If he stays in another hotel, the press would say his own has rats.

To end war, program all guns and missiles to, Return to sender.

Trump has a bad case of "Is that all there is?"

Bernie Sanders is stuck in a rut of calcified thinking.

Trump voters will turn on him?

Let's see which side cannot appoint a supreme court justice the most.

The only way to stop a game is to stop it. – Scott Peck

1-21-17 Sat.   Trump doesn't have to sell all his properties if he is honest. (giggle)   He stopped former Pres. Obama's FHA rate cut so is that a raise? If Trump can bring back the coal industry, he can walk on water. Trumps first 2 wives probably wish they were first lady.

Glad I live in Florida and America no matter who is president.

Dems and the press with break Trump or make him better.

Rugged individualists and evangelicals support Trump. The man has almost never seen a bible. In fact, every time he goes in a church, fire breaks out and demons writhe.

El Chapo Guzman will build the wall. It will have tunnels with admission fee. (Shorty is a huge Mexican drug runner.)

Trump voters think they have elected Dirty Harry.

Blacks won't tell who shot them. They hate the police too.

Melania and Barron will never leave the tower in NYC.

Trump is Putin's bitch is payback for 8 years of birthing Obama.

Trump is having a hard time getting out of campaign mode.

1-22-17 Sun. Trump's fight isn't with the media but with facts. Trump facts are changeable but not when we have video.

After only 2 days as president, we have the CIA speech and "press conference." Scary.

Tornadoes can smell a trailer park.

If Trump causes a recession as large as Bush's, we may not have enough money to fix it.

Outfits can't be original. Neither can buildings. There is only so much leeway.

A powerful idiot creates many other like minded idiots.

Kimberly Guilfoyle of Fox News could hardly keep a straight face while lauding Trump's virtues.

1-23-17 Mon. A crossover is a station wagon.

The ocean lot I used to own in Flagler Beach is likely gone.

Trump to drain the Everglades?

I've got hundreds of audio books both fact and fiction. Some I've heard a dozen times but always get something out of it.

Kellyanne Conway gives us the "alternate truth".

Trump lying in business served him well but not so much in world politics and government.

Failing septic tanks can be smelt from the street.

Is Trump Batman? Mystical figure swoops in black helicopter, saves mankind.

1-24-17 Tues. Could the CIA/FBI take out Trump? Trump's "take the oil" motto combined with an Exxon Secretary of State makes one wonder. Rachel Maddow could be at risk also.

Joe Dirt II is soon to be with us. The movie.

1-25-17 Wed. Jepp Walter is our tech advisor and hero.

Are hackers making Facebook crazy?

Trump hair looks white. He forgot the yellow or as he calls it, gold.

Many people know Trump is a zero including my daughter, Karen.

One year old Charlie has discovered the joy of straws.

Nobody talking much about TPP, Trans Pacific Partnership trade deal which Trump killed.

Pollution is greatest in our oceans, then air, then space. I like pipelines. Let solar get so good it renders oil uneconomical.

Trump gags EPA. No regard for laws.

I worry about Trump's minions coming for me in the night.

So the pipeline Obama killed for 8 years is back. No leader is all bad.

Trump says millions voted fraudulently in California. Millions were at his inaugural parade. Etc. Is he going to start his own church where we all worship him?

1-26-17 Thurs. Melania's ok, she's got a good son, money but no back door man?

65 is not too late to plan retirement. 75 is not too late to get fit.

Kellyanne Conway tries to keep up with Trump's lies but can't quite make it look real.   Hard for her to keep a straight face.

20% of the men tortured turned out to be the wrong man.

$20 billion to build the wall, another $5 billion a year to man and maintain it. I can imagine it crumbling and neglected. Communists build walls in Berlin. We are going to have a 2,000 mile dragon. It's just so 11th century.

Did pharaoh worry about pyramid cost? Neither will Trump for the wall. It will be "T" shaped in honor of its creator and to make it harder to scale.

In only one week, President Trump has already created 50,000 new psychologist jobs.

Many people believe whatever Mr. Trump says.

1-27-17 Fri. Trump will legalize pot all over to pay for the wall?

The original Twin Towers were architecturally barren but the fact that there were two of them outshines the present offering of one.

Just build a road and fence along the southern border.

You may have a drinking problem if the bartender knows your name and what you drink.

Trump will benefit states who voted for him.   Mexico will pay for the wall if we give them California, oh, we already have.

Many of my favorite novels I've never read, just heard.

Trump is brazen, bold, has some good ideas, incompetent as to the workings of government, insecure, all about the short run, image and lies. He is a potential tyrant. He needs worship.

1-28-17 Sat. Trump has some good people, Mattis, Pence, Ryan but also some crazies Bannon, Conway. Where is Sarah Palin? Too bad Robin Williams isn't here to see this.

Trump should open a Go Fund Me page for his wall. Hillary can't believe Trump is using a private phone.

I flew airplanes out the car window. Lost a few doing that. We did not have car air conditioning until I was in college.

Up until Bill Clinton our presidents were closeted
Methodist ministers but Bill opened the door for Trump.

If millions of illegal voters went for Hillary, then the
Russians hacked our election in favor of Trump. You can't
have it both ways. History will record Trump as the
illegitimate president.

1-29-17 Sun. Dan Rather has emerged in the nadir of his
career as the preeminent Trump opponent. He excoriates
him basically on the issue of decency. His venue Facebook
is widely read and of course inter-active. He never had
that at CBS.   Long live Dan Rather.

John D. Gartner of Johns Hopkins University has diagnosed
Trump as a malignant narcissist. Incurable. This is a very
dangerous person who will stop at nothing to validate his
own glory. The article appeared on Facebook and US
News. The book 1984 is a hot seller again.

If your property is over assessed, and you get it lowered,
there is still no refund for prior years overcharge.

Trump's executive orders are just signed tweets and they
look like menus. – Bill Maher

Bill Clinton opened the morals door for Trump. He dated
the only Jewish girl who couldn't get a stain out. – Robin
Williams

1-30-17 Mon. Even Dick Cheney hates Steve Bannon.

Trump won't own his own mistakes. – Mark Cuban

I never liked the ACLU until now.

Canada is building a border fence, a hedge.

Trump's anger is fear based, fear that we all will find out he's a dipstick.

Trump does what he promised and everyone goes nuts. He did win, didn't he?

Trump has turned off the light in the Statue of Liberty. – Fareed Zakaria

Books a Million puts stickers on books that won't come off with any known solvent. Also have to ask for bags.

1-31-17 Tues. Some Nazis went insane too. Trump's mother was an immigrant maid. The Muslim ban is likely to cause a terror attack. Bannon has a gin blossom nose? Trump may not see 100 days.

Trump used the media to pursue and dump women. Ask Marla Maples. He required his dates to be HIV tested during the Aids scare. "Most people aren't worthy of respect." Trump from the book Never Enough by Michael D'antonio.

Nixon fired his attorney general. Trump loves him a low information voter.

J. Edgar Hoover, the first director of the FBI, sent his rebelling agents to Idaho.

2-1-17 Wed. Trump outlived or outlasted many of his dissenters.

Fox News is now the state TV. CNN can't play.   The truth is what Trump says it is.

Can't have Muslim ban so we have a Muslim pause. There is big bucks in finessing words like this.

The elderly actress, Kim Novak should sue her plastic surgeon. – Trump

I was bored when Marla was walking down the isle. – Trump

No place are people more vicious than with the opposite sex. – Trump

2000 Bush v Gore, presidency decided by one vote. It was 5-4. 2016 Merrick Garland never considered by Republicans. So the rule is only republicans can nominate a supreme court judge. So the court becomes a repub pocket congress thwarting the will of all the people.

The good news is sometimes supreme court judges don't always do what's expected of them.

2-2-17 Thurs. Fox News lies for Trump until they get caught?

The president's manner seems to be starting holy wars in Texas and Canada. Outrageous statements won Trump the nomination and now he's after an Oscar?

Back in the days of full employment, the workers carried the king down the road.

Bush and Trump are the home wreckers. Not theirs, yours.

My bills arrive with 99.99% accuracy, thanks US mail.

What to do about Chicago: Determine the infected area on a map, cordon it off. Send in the guard with full military. Suspend ordinary laws and impose martial law in the infected area. Use rubber bullets. Put prisoners on public display. Stay the course, You can check in but you can never leave. Have extreme political courage.

Iran shoots missile. Trump calls Putin for instructions.

Narcissism can hardly be called a disease when millions of people photograph their food before eating it.

The constitution presumed reasonable men would run the government. A reasonable man does not withhold a hearing on a supreme court justice for a year. A reasonable man walking down the street calls in a fire if he sees one. The reasonable man theory presumes we all have a moral center and conscience.

Trump's mother spoiled him and he had a tyrannical father, just like Hitler. When the president lies, the whole system is in peril.

2-3-17 Fri. Trump is a dog with full bladder and the world is his bush. – Greg Gutfeld

Trump has created the dept. of paranoia in his head. In one week, he has pissed off Iran, Mexico and Australia. I hope his people do all the work and he messes with TV, Twitter and junk food.

Putin kills his opposition. Hope Trump and Tillerson are ready for that.

Fake news is funny to the educated but believed by the ignorant. Memes circulating about a military coup against Trump. This scare gives him the incentive to shut down the media.

A strong man is just disorganized and simplistic with many victims.

2-4-17 Sat. The biggest thing since Trump won are the protests. See what happens when you don't vote.

Christie was cleared in the Bridgegate scandal but nowhere to be seen in the Trump administration.

Dad learned it's fun to fish but not fun to own a fishcamp. Read about it in Real Estate Dad's Way.

Truth and good works are everything.

One of Trump's henchmen will kill a media personality. Is the Trump wall just another Maginot line? Where is Pence lately? Who's reading the briefings?

Are sanctuary cities a copout against enforcing existing immigration laws?

2-5-17 Sun. Chili's restaurant poorly managed in Jacksonville.

Trump's habit of demeaning judges is going to hurt.

Interstates are a good example of progress hurting some. Some were cut off, bypassed or rendered less important.

I read Art of the Deal when it came out in 1987. While it showed Trump to be aggressive, it took the campaign to reveal he's batshit crazy. Lies destroy the soul and can kill people. No one can lie and insult like Trump. When underlings try it, they are crushed. He'll be forced out when half his supporters turn on him.

Most of the lakes in Keystone Heights, Florida have dried up. Still the land has value and if there are utilities, a buildable site is always worth money.

2-6-17 Mon. We don't notice good actors, only bad ones.

Lawyers on TV are sucking social security dry with disability claims.

Tax preparers anymore are just loan companies.

Trump speak with forked tongue. Legal problems to multiply. Be careful overthrowing him. Don't want to set a bad precedent.

Immigrants come here with little and work hard.

What did he say? Trump speaks obfuscation. A commander must be clear in his orders. Trump will collect lawyers and litigation like a snowball.

2-7-17 Tues. Ship 2 Shore good restaurant on Southside Blvd.

Rachel Maddow compares Trump to Putin and finds little difference. Post Trump required exams to be president will include: Reading, spelling, grammar, telling time and proper diet. The Muslim ban has been changed to: Bannon's World.

Robin Williams on W. Bush: And they named the smart one Jeb.

It's time to place orders for my new book: Farting with Class.

400 diet commercials and auto insurance commercials a day on TV.

The capt. of the El Faro ignored warnings of bad weather.

Get your huge burnin hunk of love Teddy Bear from my front porch, only $500.

Trump tax returns would almost surely show ties to Putin.

Mom's new boyfriend, a convicted felon, left his gun in the apartment while they went shopping leaving 2 kids home alone. The 8 year old shot and killed the 6 year old. Both adults being held in jail.

A couple is being sought by police for having sex in our courthouse. It's so bright you need shades and so many cameras you have to step over them.

Give Brady an inch and he'll take the Super Bowl.

In a war between Trump and the judiciary, he's got the army.

2-8-17 Wed. Trump holds puppy by its tail out the window. No, that's a lie. Obama did it. Vagina Americans are marching. Trump says his wife is not a hooker and never was a hooker.

Obamacare cannot be touched by republicans. Something like Dracula and crosses.   There are facts and then there are Trump facts.

The media is covering up terror attacks? Maybe the media is not covering them enough? Wrong ones? One thing's for sure. Trump has his own Benghazi, known as Yemen.

Elizabeth Warren may be the next president.

2-9-17 Thurs. When the economy slumps, drug use goes up. Should be the opposite.

Trump has this joke presidency but he is building a hard right administration.

Pie gone in two days.

Sanctuary cities, cop free drug gang zones. You can't make this up.

When the phone rings, dogs bark to go outside because no one can hear otherwise.

Religion pays big bucks to many people. Jessie Jackson asked for resources to solve the Chicago gang violence problem. Maybe Trump can build a factory there. His first made in America venture.

Trump needs judge support to get his immigration bill passed so what does he do? Insult judges.

2-10-17 Fri. Will a political pope endanger the church's free tax status?

51% of Trump supporters think he should violate a court order.

Trump faces defeat at the hands of the judiciary. Can he learn? So called judges gave him a wedgie. Boss Trump learns politics 101.

Through-out the land, there is great buyer's remorse, take it back, has the return date expired?

The dogs are going to build a park and the cats will pay for it.

What happens when taxes are cut. Deductions are cut. Other taxes increase. In 2 years, there will be a big increase. The only net effect is the tax code gets larger.

For 20 years I was incorporated. It cost money but today I'm still getting pens with the company name on it.

Martha thought Trump would quit saying stupid stuff when he won, ha ha ha ha.

A stolen Lincoln Navigator tore into a house killing the lady who was watching TV. Not possible with a Ford Escort.

Newly appointed education secretary DeVos has flattened all the globes in all public school classrooms.

The Trump administration is too understaffed to make good policy at this time. After only 3 weeks, most positions are vacant and he let Obama's people go.

2-11-17 Sat. The guy who carped most about rigged elections and polls is himself now the suspect of colluding with the Russians to rig his own election to the presidency.

By his own admission, Trump likes to fight. He would complain about people's breath just to get the upper hand. A true gutter puncher.

With the press and judiciary as enemies, where is this going? It's likely the court heard and considered Trump's order to make the Muslim ban legal.

An Afghan immigrant waited months to enter our country. He was asked, What's the first thing you're going to do? He said, Go to Golden Corral. (All you can eat buffet)

2-12-17 Sun. It's nice that our diseases are given nick-names, like part of the family, Hep-C and A-Fib. If they can't name the malady, they get a cute redhead to play it.

The republican party has been set back 50 years.

We got rid of the carpet because it was soaked with dog pee. Now all 7 of them pee on the re-finished hardwood flooring. Twice I have slipped and partially fallen because of the puddles. I used to worry about Trump's army coming for me but now it's this slippery hazard looming large.

Another thing, Martha got a smaller kitchen garbage can with step flip lid. Used to be I could walk by and lob trash into can but now it's stop, step and drop. And it's too small to stomp.

Reading, Trust Me on This, by Donald Westlake, it occurred to me that the readers of the newspaper, The Daily Galaxy are the same people who voted for Trump.

Formal dances in high school can be agony.

Ted's good place for me, Martha, Matthew, Karina and Matty Matt.

My dog pee slip/falls have been dramatic. In the hall my left leg went away and I made a 3 point landing; right knee and both hands.

In the Living room, again left leg lost, right leg pushes down, spin to left, become airborne, slam landing with both feet flat footed, arms extended, a pirouette.

2-13-17 Mon. Vietnam was full of bad communists who had to be killed and now Muslims have to be vilified.

China, take North Korea, please.

Trump tweets are ok by me as long as national security is left out of it. Who doesn't want to know where the Trump women buy their clothes.

Steve Bannon is the heart and soul of the Trump administration. – Fareed Zakaria

2-14-17 Tues. Happy Valentine's Day.   Dollar General has cards for $1.

The Trump administration careens from one obstacle to the next. – Rachel Maddow

As the California dam falls apart, will Trump withhold help due to their sanctuary status?

Trump is a successful businessman and a flim flam man.

In the old days, aristocratic families "finished" their kids with music, foreign language training and sports. Trump was finished in fart school.

White privilege was countered by affirmative action but poor whites were left out of this equation and so voted Trump into office.

VW had a scandal and goes on with advertising like nothing had happened. Their ads are so good, it almost zeros the pollution.

The case against Michael Flynn, the national security advisor, is that he told Russia don't worry about Obama's sanctions. You help Trump get elected and we will lift them. Now that he resigned, the next step is more house cleaning?

Pence is more scary than Trump to many people. He's got experience in government. While he's subject to extreme religious beliefs, he's still sane while Trump is not really sane to me.

2-15-17 Wed. Dennis Miller is worried about Trump's future and is giving him advice. Repubs now don't want to see his taxes. Obama trying to overthrow Trump? Dan Rather says the Flynn flap is Watergate. Kellyanne Conway one of the faithful.

Playboy nakid again.

Imagine a leader whose sole purpose is to prepare for an attack from the United States.

Journalists Johnson didn't like were allowed an interview while Lyndon was on the toilet.

If partisanship trumps truth, we are all done for.

Joe Kennedy was coarse and got his son elected president. Trump is coarse and got himself elected.

A waiter at Mar Largo whispered to Trump, nuke North Korea so T made him national security advisor. (Michael Flynn's old job)

Lawyers for Bo Bergdahl, the deserter, could get the case dismissed for lack of ability to get a fair trial since Trumper said he was a traitor on the campaign trail. Big mouth unhinged does damage.

2-16-17 Thurs. The FBI/CIA does not trust Trump. Some republicans are beginning to smell a rat in T. The thugier one is, the better chance of being a T aid.

If Trump starts or escalates a war, that would keep him in power.

A good example of media hype was in 1944 when they stated, Robots are coming, referring to the German V-1 or Buzz bombs.

When Jackie first visited the Kennedy family she was rudely awakened. She said she had always wanted to be a ballet dancer. Ethel said, With those feet, better stick with soccer.

Michael Flynn is not the only high Trump official to go. Our intelligence community seems to be a war with T.

Mexico is readying a $200 catapult in answer to Trump's $200 billion wall.   Granny is weeding her garden when 100 lbs of cocaine comes flying over the wall.

Steve Bannon was arrested for beating his wife back in the early '90's.

2-17-17 Fri. Obamacare in peril.

Trump had a very critical father which is why he now hates the media?

Trump is a toxic mix of demagoguery and nonsense. – Rick Perry

The defining statement made by bankers is: We want it all.

Trump talks for the questioner. He is afraid of a real question. Very insecure. Always campaigning. Press conference is now an audition.

Fence or wall. One is $10 billion, the other $30 billion.

The snow storm in Chicago has put on hold 300 killings.

In Oklahoma, it took 45 minutes to put a prisoner to death. Drug mix up I guess.

Jackie Kennedy or Melania Trump best first lady. We don't think Melania has yet shown up for work.

Historically, big killers have been autos, prohibition, diet and worry.

Warren Buffett is Mr. Capitalism.

Jeb Bush was ruined by his stoopid brother and the crowd wanted Showboating.

Health nuts must feel bad to die over nothing.

Ruth Bader Ginsburg can't quit lest Trump replace her. Maybe she didn't think through her promise to quit if Trump won.

So far, Gorsuch seems ok. (Trump's Supreme Court nominee)

Can you have real leaks and fake news?

2-18-17 Sat. Trump is suing the newspaper that said Melania was an escort. Using same lawyer that put Gawker out of existence.

Repubs approved Scott Pruitt head of EPA before his investigation was complete. As an oil representative, he sued EPA many times.

Coming to a movie house near you: Apes of Wrath.

At the trial of Capt. Queeg, lawyers assumed no captain of a U. S. Navy ship could be a coward, therefore he must be crazy. Similarly, no U.S. president can be stupid, therefore he must be crazy.

Rodney King was the first police beating recorded. In 1992, it was on TV constantly. I had to explain it to 8 year old Lindsay. Twenty years later he died of alcoholism. It was video on phones and small cameras that exposed police brutality more than Obama ever could.

Thomas Jefferson had a slave girl friend but no one said anything. Where was the media?

In 3-08 Ann Coulter said Eliot Spitzer, governor of New York, should resign for using prostitutes but when Trump does it, it's ok.

Is Trump the Dr. Kevorkian of politics? Dr. Death.

Paul Ryan's father died of alcoholism at 55. As his kids grow up, he'll have more time for politics, but will the Trump stink follow him?

2-19-17 Sun. Much of our national energy and treasure will be spent correcting the Trump errors.

The 15th century inventor Leonardo da Vinci has come up with exactly what we need, the Trump stomper.

I posted the First Amendment to the Constitution, free speech and a free press. Trump attacking the press is a spear into the heart of our country.   The press calls Trump a liar. (true)

First the "fat" Trump and now the "little" Trump. Comics love him.

I saw a report that said Trump owes $1.8 billion to 150 lenders. He may not have any net worth at all.   High leverage has been the bane of real estate men over the ages.

My friend Leonard Alterman has come out against Trump. He is a very polite reserved Jewish man who no doubt is upset about the Nazi gangs running the streets and posted a full page of anti-Trump facts.

Trump is fond of saying, "This is a movement, folks." Well, there is a "movement" growing against him and I hope he does not survive.

2-20-17 Mon. If the tip of the iceberg principle applies to Trump, imagine what we don't know. T is Jabba the Hut and Melania is Princes Leia. The media tells more lies than Trump is a weak argument. The person saying the press is crooked is more crooked. Sweden called Trump a liar.

North Korea gonna blow. Get ready.

A dullard leader tends to dumb down those around him.

I saw our Cadillac in a 1990 Columbo TV show.

Russia was afraid of Hillary and her staff so the Trump election was good news to them. Trump is too proud to ask questions (admit he doesn't know).

Trump's first month as president has been a freak show. — Fareed Zakaria   He did round up some illegals. I am surprised at the amount of sympathy for illegals.

2-21-17 Tues. Trump taking his time getting going. He has the full force of the government around him as insulation and encouragement, but some will turn on him and he won't finish 4 years.

Some of us rejoice in no winter. Enjoy it before the flood.

I wish Schwarzenegger could run against Trump. Then we could have the terminator vs the prevaricator.

Put $ into an ETF. Exchange Traded Fund. This follows a well known index like the DJA. Dow Jones Average.

Trump is the best liar in the world. He has honed it to a finely tuned art. The Art of the Deal is based on it. He can't tell truth from fiction. He's a black hole of narcissism. If he says it, it's real. Believe me.

Sold an ebook, making 9 cents.

2-22-17 Wed. Trump is good at deportation, causing pain.

Hillary must not run again. How about Sally Yates?

First the Muslims and now the Jews. Is Steve Bannon behind this?

Cracker Barrel pancakes do weigh one down.

Trump and blacks in the same room? Isn't that like Dracula and the cross?

Martha bought some diamond encrusted Capri pants.

Are people leaving a Trump administration faster than he can appoint them?

2-23-17 Thurs. Trump likes to fight, by his own admission, but with our friends? Why are so many people surprised he's an ass? Did they sleep through a year long campaign?

Leaking pipes in your house is part of a class action lawsuit?

As to sex, there are 3 types: 1. Straight. 2. Normal gay people. 3. Everyone else. For centuries we had no problem with who went in what bathroom, why start now?

Pelosi should go. Her plastic face and stupid remarks are a millstone around the democratic party.

Trump needs to show his taxes. To keep it a secret is a blot on his record. We need to know who he's in bed with. (figuratively)

He is shining light on the immigration problem. As the Joker said, You can't make an omelet without breaking some eggs.

2-24-17 Fri. Priebus is cooked.

ACA (Obamacare) will become some modifications to Medicare.

Steve Bannon was released and spoke on live TV, then he ate a cat.

Most of Trump's appointees are doing their jobs so Trump is just noise.

The 1974 movie Towering Inferno was a precursor to 9-11. No one could have dreamed up what really was to happen.

Sanctuary city or den of law breakers?

2-25-17 Sat. W. Bush stupid. Trump cunning. Johnson worst. Trump has no interest in the truth.

Running air conditioning in February.

If Trump can blame his mistakes on the fake media, he is absolved in his own mind of any error. They never happened.

The economy is on a roll, up from the depths of the Bush crash in '08.

Trump defunds PBS (Public Broadcasting System) because they might tell the truth.

Trump is a bad mentally disturbed child.

2-26-17 Sun. Could Trump be even more stupid than we think? Yes.

In 1970, I bought a recorder to answer my phone and I had thousands of messages from dad who passed in 1998 and I never thought to keep any of the recordings.

Me thinks Trump does not know about Nixon and the media.

Inspector Clouseau not funny when played by Steve Martin.

Wedding this afternoon. I have three suit jackets and no matching pants.

When people get invested in a position, they will die for it.

Getting there is all the fun. The Mars mission if it's like the moon mission is not about science but rather political and military power.

2-27-17 Mon. Do eye doctors run blurry commercials?

Why do murderers talk to their victims?

Trump: I am the most inclusive guy in the world, believe me. F__U media.

Trump cancels media dinner 2 months early. Double dumb.

Don't leave guns in unlocked cars and don't leave Trump in Fort Knox unguarded.

2-28-17 Tues. Russia needed Trump well before the election as a means to laundry money. The election was an unbelievable bonus.

Fixing Obamacare not so easy. Trump is admitting, this stuff is hard.

If the U.S. won't steal Iraq's oil, Trump will.

The pill box is twice as big as the pill bottle.

Once Trump became president, watching Rachel Maddow on MSNBC became a necessity.

Trump no doubt thinks he is doing a good job. Malignant narcissism at work. The media peeks light into Dracula's cave.

3-1-17 Wed. Trump not showing his taxes violates transparency.

A speech from a liar is meaningless. He will do whatever is easy. He is a lazy man.

My granddaughter has a set of electric drums.

Trump gives himself an "A". Of course, he does.

Is high priced Cobia a fish flam?

The FBI likely undid Nixon.

Health care is hard, let the states do it.

Mike Milken said if you bundle the junk bonds together, they have less risk. The '08 mortgage bundlers did the same.

Some say Christians embracing Trump ruins the religion. Some think he's against abortion but I don't think he cares about it.

3-2-17 Thurs. No president can be accountable for every soldier killed in battle. Oprah for president. She's got lots of money and personality.

In 47 years, I have only had two office refrigerators. No freezers or ice makers.

Fox's Kennedy says the Trump administration stand that marijuana increases crime is nonsense.

3-3-17 Fri. Florida Trend says Trump's trade plan sucks and Hillary's not much better after she changed her stance.

The can of corruption that is the Trump administration is spreading like spilled paint.

A lying president is a slippery rock on which to stand.

The military Trump wants to rebuild was cut by republican sequester.

I ground coffee beans using a mortar and pestle.

Yesterday, it was the tooth of March.

Trump sleeps 3 hours a night? Might he push the wrong button?

Nothing like a Trump victory to make one want to redo the electoral college.

3-4-17 Sat. Putin, one of the world's richest men, could pay off Trump's debts with one check. Over 17 years, he has become king of Russia. No wonder Trump admires him.

Russian planes are often seen where Trump is.

Imagine the republicans get a dog, shave it, put a new collar on it, and call it a cat. That's Obamacare.

Cutting pollution regulations is the quickest way to boost industrial jobs.

Putin's empire resembles the Mafia. All his Oligarchs are wealthy thugs.   That is why it hurts them when individuals are sanctioned by our government.

3-5-17 Sun. Trump is projecting his own faults onto others. He's a creative master liar and he stirs the soup so that no one can analyze it.

For lunch I had chili, fried onion rings and for dinner, ice cream.

Sometimes I wish I had let them draft me but it was during Vietnam.

Remember when T. Boone Pickens using Mesa Petroleum took over Gulf or Philips Oil? Sort of what Putin is trying to do to the USA.

3-6-17 Mon. Gun vendors run more ads at tax refund time.

In Trump's world, friends lie for you, so he was mad at Sessions for recusing himself from the Russia entanglement.

Trump played the Obama race card when he claimed O had tapped his phone.

Trump lies hurt real people. The so called election fraud hurt those officials and this phone tap thing is off the chart.

Trump takes us back to 1950. No, wait, Disney already did that.

Who killed Jon Benet? Why run a show like that. Maybe it will result in a lead. Lots of crimes have been solved after 20 years.

Taxes aren't cut, only pushed around. Whatever cuts happen, are matched later by increases.

There is a new show, Nakid, Afraid and the Rose Bush.

3-7-17 Tues. The enigma of the Trump fan is emerging. First they hate Obama or Obummer. And then they hate Hillary or Killery. Folks believe O and H killed people. They believe O and H want to sell out the country. They like ostentatious displays of wealth. The Trump plane set the stage for the second coming. Hillary was right, many of them are deplorable, but saying it was her big mistake. Many Trump fans are marginally employed and angry about outside forces hurting them. Why smart people like Trump is more mysterious.

Transparency is Trump's enemy. Kickbacks in foreign countries is normal and Trump likes that.

Trump ego is larger than his concern for our safety.

Birther, wire taps, fake news, fraudulent elections, Trump lives in a sick world of rigging and self indulgence.

He has a short attention span, distrustful, bad temper, poor memory, lazy and trusts few. – John O'Donnell in the book, Trumped

He made his casinos buy, Art of the Deal and that is how it became a number one bestseller.

3-8-17 Wed. Strong evidence Trump colluded with Russians to throw election toward him. – Rachel Maddow

One voter said he was glad Trump not beholden to any special interests. Another compared him to Christ. At the core of Trump's appeal is hatred of Negroes, Jews, Muslims, Hispanics and Asians.

Trump admires Putin for his ability to laundry money and steal from the treasury.

Al Franken, former humorist, is now a hero. Ben Carson not so much.

Walking to school, texting, driving, texting, ooopps.

God's a novelist who gave us Trump to show He's the better author.

Does the reverse income tax encourage not working for a living?

Eight years of Birtherism and now wire tapping, I don't think so.

Rush Limbaugh compared Trump to Joe McCarthy.

Alternate facts are real to Trump fans.

By his own admission, Trump likes to fight, but with others doing it for him. He is a fan of boxing.

Russia tried to throw the election toward Trump because Putin hated and feared Hillary. Trump needed the money.

3-10-17 Fri. Trump has no loyalty to America. Would sell her out in a heartbeat.   He sets the moral character bar so low that he will be a wretched role model for years to come.

Julian Assange and Trump working together?

The republicans told Nixon to pack his bags.

Trump lives apart from his wives so he can ready the new wife for his charms. Teach her obedience and submission.

He doesn't tip. Stiffs everyone. Kings don't carry money.

How do you know when you are a HOE? Your boy friend brags about it on Facebook.

Rachel Maddow and Fareed Zakaria are my two must watches on TV.

Dan Rather on Facebook is a measured drip drip drip against Trumper.

Don't care what he says, watch what they do. – Rachael Maddow

3-11-17 Sat. Sean Hannity making policy for Trump?
Firing all the US attorneys helps to put Trump beyond the
law.

Don't need a state dept., we have guns. CNN is calling the
Yemen raid a massacre. The Muslim ban reeks down
through history. Dan Rather is writing a Trump book too.

Trump talked to a congressman today, beats Obama in
that regard.

Lies worked in the Trump business but can it work in geo-
politics?

Regulators sat on their asses as the 2008 crash happened
and now the CIA lets Julian Assange steal all our files.
Where is the competence, the energy?

The union shop workers check their watches while the self
employed work long hours with a smile on their face.

Cruise ships are too large. Most shipwrecks happen due to
greed, overloading and poor maintenance.

Trump was thrilled to buy all the Atlantic City casinos but
when the going got tough, he bailed via bankruptcy, took
the easy way out. Bankruptcy is unlucky or incompetent.

Old age OK with the medical community. We all die of old
age and the doctors say, it's ok. Why doesn't somebody
do something?

If there is no death in heaven, it might get kind of boring. We need change and drama to keep the zest in life?

For centuries, man sacrificed other men or women to God or gods. Enter Christ who God sacrificed for us. A strange turn around.

3-12-17 Sun. What would you say when you meet God?___________

Are there any fat homeless people?

Trump mind forgets authorizing an expenditure and gets mad about it again and again.

Pence can't lie very well and sticks out in the Trump bunch.

Marla was a sweet person who got snared by greedy Trump and today is known only as one of his exes.

A good war creates jobs so long as we don't get bombed.

Replace Obamacare with vouchers? Let states do it? Let states take the bad press. Let states kill the babies. Tax credit for health care?

Can I have your autograph. Crazed man jumps whitehouse fence. Maybe drones could aid in safety. Donald, don't insult your guards.

Would like to see 5,000 passenger cruise ship and crew evacuated. Just a drill. See how long it takes. See if they can even do it at all.   While we are at it, let's evacuate all people in a 100 story building. See how long that takes and if it can be done.

3-13-17 Mon. Trump said he would forgo the presidential salary of $400,000 a year but he fights over sums a lot smaller than that.

Donald and Tillerson taking the fifth over Russia ties?

Trump lies but what if he believes lies told to him? Is that Steve Bannon's job?

After 30 years in the same house, I mapped the sprinkler heads. Copy survey of house property and push each lever to see what water comes out. Did that 4 times which activates 6 heads. Welcome retirement.

3-14-17 Tues. The microwave is watching you. (Kelly Anne Conway's explanation of Obama wiretapping Trump.)

Republicans have had years to fix Obamacare. Talk about leading from behind.

Our tax refund equals our medical bills.

Trump keeps reporters busy for months over his own fake news stories.

I saw Obama skittering around the Trump Tower with wires, pliers and a nefarious look.

No matter how fake a story is, some people will believe it.

Deutsche Bank fined 7 billion dollars for laundering
money. Trump received Russian money. The only thing
not proven is, was the money Trump got laundered?
China paid record price for Manhattan tower owned by
Jared Kushner?   (Trump's son in law.)

3-15-17 Wed. Records are kept of money changing hands
between countries. Trump owes much money to Chinese
interests. No Trump in 2020 unless he shows all his taxes,
law coming.

Trump's business plan is to lie. From that comes much
evil.

Will illicit income be reported on a tax return? Ask Al
Capone.

"The people have to know their president is not a crook."
– Richard Nixon. That was when he became the first
president to show his income taxes. He was being
audited.

According to the '05 tax return summary found by Rachel
Maddow, Trump skitters up and below billionairehood.
2005 was the best year for real estate.

Trump going back on campaign promise and will keep his
salary. He may donate it later.   Did Trump backers force
Steve Bannon on him?

Trump water-boarded his mother.

A Japanese gambler won $6 million at Trump Plaza in one day.

Warren Buffett says for the average investor, buy the Standard and Poors 500 index funds.

Buffett once made a 6 billion dollar mistake. He traded stock for a company which value went to zero. The value of the stock he traded away would have been worth $6 billion, if kept.

I like the fact Trump is renewing pipeline construction.

46 Ethiopians were killed in a trash landslide. Count your blessings.

3-16-17 Thurs. Rachel Maddow looks like a man and laughs about it.

Remember when Democrats ran granny in the wheel chair ads being pushed off a cliff?   Or told viewers Republican death squads were coming. That's what we are in now with repeal and replace Obamacare.

My eye doctor billed $17,000 for one cataract surgery. Is that sustainable? How can any health plan stand that sort of charging.

Chocolate coffee cream best ever.

First it was the birther lie and now the Obama tapped Trump's phone lie. What a freak show.

No Muslim ban is allowed under Amendment one of our Constitution.

Paul Ryan and Mark Cuban seem like decent republicans.

3-17-17 Fri. Trump has put Rachel Maddow on the map and she is gleeful.

The FBI did surveillance on Mike Flynn and in Trump's mind, that's Obama wiretapping his phone.

Trump kills Pacific Trade deal leaving China to pick up the pieces and be the leader.

If Gorsuch is approved for the Supreme Court, the Muslim ban is OK.

Vietnam was prolonged because officials were afraid of being called unpatriotic. Tip O'Neill talks about it in his book, Man of the House.

John O'Donnell's book, Trumped, 1991, describes in exact detail how Donald manages. He bellows and bellows again, louder.

3-18-17 Sat. Other countries may be the best gauge of our president.

The constitution is silent on an insane president.

During WWII, the British planes dispensed tin foil strips to confuse the German radar. Trump does that now with his fake news.

If North Korea senses a US invasion, they might lob nukes on Japan and South Korea.

Trump has paranoid grandiosity and malignant narcissism. The British surveiled Trump, the Three Stooges were busy.

Trumpcare, you gotta pulse? You're OK.

If too many Americans adopt the Trump method of lying, we are done.

Would you rather be harpooned or caught.

I'm 74 and got my driver's license good for 8 years. With glaucoma and cataracts, I drive a large car and always stop when I hear the crunch.

Harry Truman didn't want a presidential library. He thought it should wait until after he died. He got no pension either. He made America great.

Dad was a Realtor in Palatka for 30 years. One of his first flips was he bought a house for $2,000 paying the seller $50 a month. He swept it out and picked up trash, reselling it for $2,500 and holding a mortgage at a 2% interest advantage. Read about it in Real Estate Dad's Way.

3-19-17 Sun. Trump's ticket to stay in office is a war with North Korea. The only excuse for his lies is ignorance and that is not good enough.

Chuck Berry, RIP at age 90.

E. F. Hutton used to own Mar-a- Lago in Florida before Trump.

Dad didn't like Meals on Wheels. It was a lot of food for him to pay for and he only weighed 140 lbs.

I can't sleep unless the dogs are barking.

Obama could but won't sue Trump for libel re wire tapping. It would be bad for the country.

Hillary and Obama are not an excuse for the Trump presidency.

Good lunch at V-Pizza and then on to the orchid show.

Man robs Wells Fargo, but they give him an IOU.

3-20-17 Mon. Trump has been a bullshi__er his entire life. – Fareed Zakaira.

Perry Mason by 1991 weighed 400 lbs and could barely say his lines. Lennie Briscoe of Law and Order had a part. Then Columbo of same time had no cell phones but there were hand held TVs.

Man walks to Mars. My train has sailed. Lab chicken eggscellent.

One day, a business will answer their phone.

Some of the Trump voters will miss their Obamacare.

So many of Trump supporters are ignorant of the downside as they stick it to the psychotic liberal black lovers.

3-21-17 Tues. What a Godsend Trump was for the Russians.

Not sure Trump can tell the difference between TV and real life.

Trump embarrasses me for the country.

Everyday I spent at the fish camp was a dad take me to work day.

Mother never worked after they married, but we didn't have much either. World War II taught us that women could work effectively.

Conrad made us "rich" as in Real Estate Dad's Way.

On our camp front porch, I'd listen to guests talk about their surgeries never dreaming I'd be having my own. Well, that day is here and no one wants to hear about it.

3-22-17 Wed. Rachel Maddow is Woodward and Bernstein times ten. Trump has noticed her. She'd better watch her back; she could be pushed out a window. Russians are dropping like flies.

Paul Manafort took Russian money. Could he turn on Trump?

Study needed to see if internet bots could sway an election sufficient to elect Trump. Trump was right all along, the election was rigged.

The market pulled back fearing a non tax cut, but a tax cut is wrong now. Inflation would happen.

Al Franken a better senator than comedian.   Gorsuch ok but Garland cheated.   Putin's new book, Art of the Steal.

Russians could out Trump.   Trump's new book is Killing O'Reilly.

Trump needs his rally fix to stroke his ravenous ego. Trump not as orange as before. Too bad, it was his lucky color.

The 2016 election will turn out to be the biggest upheaval since the civil war.

Trump's daughter is the acting first lady. Nancy Pelosi was Miss Lube Rack of 1955. Miss lube rack can be construed all sorts of ways. God fearing Trump fans fear the obscene. Chris Christie has been completely forgotten. My guess is Bannon would not allow Christie to play.

Whatever good you do is shared with God but whatever evil you do is all on you. The devil did not make you do it. Flip Wilson not withstanding.

3-23-17 Thurs. Manafort dripping in Russian cash while working on election of Trump. Hello President Pence.

Tillerson should quit. He doesn't have his heart in this.
He's not money motivated.

"Friends" would have me be quiet about Trump. Love of
country is supposed to keep me quiet. I'm not the same
guy they knew in high school. I should hope not.

Russian rules: 1. Dump pro Trump stuff on internet. 2.
Dump anti Hillary stuff on the internet. 3. Steal Hillary's
emails and laundry them through Wikileaks.

The market is sure to crash if Trump is impeached.

The narcissist Trump assumes all people are like him and
would steal and lie for money.

Credit Union now has a $5/year inactivity fee.

I saw Wizard of Oz as a child and it was terrific.

Got the car detailed and paint touched up. Great deal. 07
Mercury looks much better.

Bought mini-video camera at Best Buy for $80. Now I can
churn out a steady supply of commercials for my books.

The first video camera we bought was 1994, cost $1,000
and was as big as a car transmission and almost as heavy.

3-24-17 Fri. Trump is ready to let Obamacare die a
natural death. He will tell us for the next 6 months, the
failure to pass a replacement law was not his fault.

The Ocare pattern of failure may set in motion a moribund Trump term. The Tea Party, or renamed Freedom Caucus has made repubs the party of No.

CNN compliments Trump on his language style (lies) and gets the order (interview). Trump explains away lies by saying I'm president and you're not.

I say consolingly, Pence is better than Trump, but many people don't agree.   Pence would kill abortion.

There was a communist scare in the 1950's and a Russian scare today.   Obamacare may be worse for Trump than the Russians. Trumpcare upchucks.

Being Trump's press secretary would be like having hemorrhoid surgery every month.

ISIS gives lost souls a place to put their grief. At last, a reason to end it all in a blaze of glory as we gleefully join with Allah.

Russian murders of diplomats and former friends of Putin increasing at an alarming rate. Any of these tied to Trump campaign?

 Good role models needed. Books and movies too.

3-25-17 Sat. Don't expect a tax bill while Trump sizzles under Russia investigation. The wall might crumble too. The flailing Trump has energized Bernie Sanders.

Trumpcare fails. Dems jubilant. Blacks for Obama rolling in victory. Trump can't pour piss out of a boot.

The Trump stink ruins good republicans. Did Paul Ryan dumb himself down for Trump?   T owes $300 million to Deutsche Bank, a famous money launderer?

Will writing become interactive like Facebook is now? The paper book would still sell as a memento or souvenir.

Don't arm teachers. Some of them are already having sex with students.

Some dogs appear to smile.

Paul Ryan is the real president.

3-26-17 Sun. Sane people all over the world hope the USA can survive Trump's nonsense and foolery. He's a third rate pimp stick.

Has Trump learned you can't boss politicians? Trump says, This isn't hell and I'm not hot.

Seminole Electric may close unless Trump guts the EPA. Seminole, based in Tampa, uses coal to make electricity near Palatka. Fla.

Health care failure has exposed Trump as not caring for the people. Let it explode he says.

My dream: Trump forced out of office in a plea bargain reached over his collusion with Russia to throw the campaign his way. No jail. Pence quits, he's dirty too.

Paul Ryan becomes pres. T writes book, The Art of the Crooked Deal.

Science show: All those planets and moons with no life. Seems like a waste. Planet 9 is supposed to be out there. Ten times the size of earth. Pluto is the size of our moon and was discovered in the 1930's.

It's easier to remember talking points than to think about them.

3-27-17 Mon. Repubs will dump Trump en masse if they think he is toxic to their re-election.

Freedom Caucus likely to be worse for Trump than Dems. They say no to everything. Mighty Trump struck out. Next time he should try holding the small end of the bat. Bernie seems to still have a dog in the race, not Hillary.

The well meaning are often penalized. A lying president is worthless. Lying is easier than learning. Rhetoric is easier than understanding.

My new drug, Expimp, gets rid of your awful nose, trims it, shapes it. Side effects include nausea, bleeding, shrinkage, reduced brain cells and missing penis. I am working on a non-ageing pill. Supplies limited. Reserve yours now.

The take-away from Trump's health care debacle for me is he doesn't give a damn about voters or his promises to them.

3-28-17 Tues. Stock market down 6 days in a row.

Who will fall first, Trump or Putin?

Trump has plastered the white house with relatives. He knows you can't trust anyone. No one knows that better than a crook.

Trump insults the people he needs. As his approval rating goes toward 30%, the average voter knows better.

The message of Trump University is that education is optional.

Rachel Maddow has built a ring of fire around Trump, yet still no smoking gun. So many are involved, a squealer is inevitable.

Civilian casualties rising in Iraq.

Voters wanted a strong man but they got the Mad Hatter.

Trump stopped at Trump Gas and Trump Clothes on his way to Trump Golf and Trump Eats.

A pest control company has a new TV ad featuring Crunchy, the pet cockroach. Nice.

Listen to your TV. A week ago, it told me to change the batteries in the remote. Did I? No. Then after watching 1 hour 50 minutes of Columbo, the TV froze. Then I obeyed and scrambled the new batteries into the remote, in the nick of time.

Trump says health care had no democratic support. Gee, I don't think they got a chance to vote on it. Trump is making fake news normal.

The Freedom Caucus is still fighting the Indians.

Huma, wife of Weiner, is taking him back. It's hard to find a good man.

3-29-17 Wed. Rachel Maddow, 43, left Bill O'Reilly at the gate.

Is Preet Bharara our new Deep Throat? He is the fired New York US Attorney.

Trump and O'Reilly sort of became one sometime in 2016.

Why does Trump hold up a menu every time he signs an executive order?

Am I too old for Ivana?

Hannity and Limbaugh are Trump boot lickers extraordinaire.

Gorsuch being beat up by Garland.

Putin just bought Ohio. Trump aides say it was payback for Kasich.

Trump makes Sean Spicer into a comedian.

No wall unless it has solar panels.

Political parties include the liberals, conservatives, moderates and Duh.

Once individual voting is perfected, any official including the president could be voted out unless they maintain a 60% approval rating.

Rachel Maddow has discovered a ring of corruption around Trump that if it spills, it'll be like a bucket of open paint. Both Putin and Trump will want to kill her.

Trump under investigation for treason and still tax return is hidden.

3-30-17 Thurs. A three year old girl finds a hot water heater curbside, puts her arms around it and says, I love you, robot.

Trump threw the long ball to Russia. He accepted their help. He believed it was the only way he could win. All the polls were against him.

Trump made hay from reopened coal mine, took full credit for it. Dems pay attention. In a depressed area, each and every job is a big deal.

Melania has a new interpreter. Her daughter, Ivana will do just fine in the mother's role.

If Trump goes down, so will Pence; like Nixon and Agnew.

What are we to make of silver? The ad says buy it because it might go up in value. It's fun to collect silver dollars but in my family there were fights over who owned them.

The stair riding chair isn't so bad but the cost of the second floor, whew!

I have to pay rent for the hospital who did the surgery even tho it was part of a larger surgery and only took 5 seconds. This cost was never disclosed to me.

Bella, our wolf-Yorkie mix, is getting grey on her black back. We have another interesting dog, a hound-Chihuahua mix. He has big feet and big appetite.

3-31-17 Fri. Flynn to blab? Trump lame duck? Paul Ryan ok, no Pence.

Trump's new book is, I Want to Tell You. (O.J.Simpon's book)

Flynn at height of his fame. Was he corrupted by Trump filth or was he already dirty?

Tax cut in doubt. Health care was washed out in 5 days.

Trump thought about tanks rolling down Penna. Ave. on inauguration day, thought better of it, then lied about having the idea.

Nixon fooled us but Trump told us he lied as part of his business plan.

Spicer gives me acid reflux. Russia putting away their guns, they have Trump.

Trump ran for pres because he needs money. Kushner in over his head in $1.7 billion Manhattan skyscraper deal.

Trump new book is Art of the Flop. If Trump is ousted, we could get someone even worse, like Mama June.

Put the sharp edged planter right beside the entrance to the eye doctor's office.

Vinyl sometimes better than YouTube. When it comes to music, the "right" rendition can be hard to find.

$1,000 cash back when you buy a car. Don't be stupid. It's all your money or your debt.

4-1-17 Sat. Russia and Trump worked together to topple other republican candidates and Hillary. – Rachel Maddow

Trump putting on brave front but inside rotting. He's thinking about what to do after he quits. He's said he's not working with dems or freedom caucus. Who's left? He belongs in a TV show.

Does Hillary blame Bill for her loss?

I read a book about E. F. Hutton, Burning Down the House. The book didn't mention they were in the mortgage business and asked me to appraise a horse farm near Ocala, Florida, 120 miles from my office.

Jogging and biking is good for you, if you don't get hit by a bus.

If extraterrestrials come to earth, they will look like us. If hostile, they could just change the atmosphere until we are all dead. In order to get here from the stars, they would need control over gravity and be able to change one element into another at will.

4-2-17 Sun. If you are going to be bad, be really good at it. – Larry Flynt

Who lit Bernie Sanders' fuse?

Don't believe the time windows. Stanley Steemer was supposed to be here 2-4 but got here at 5-7 cleaning kitchen floor with suckita suckita machine drowned out the news.

Health care may be just too hard for anybody.

Trump is getting a long haired shaggy yellow dog.

The seller can make sure you can afford the house.

4-3-17 Mon. A lot of job killing rules and regulations have been pushed on the American people by politicians of both parties and all levels of government. They act like we have unlimited resources.

An arsonist in Atlanta managed to collapse part of I-85.

The last wall I know of is the Berlin Wall which was a political disaster for the Soviets. We don't need a wall, just a fence and road for our patrols. Perhaps there could be an occasional bunker or drone port.

A texting Texas 20 year old driver ran head on into a church bus killing 13 people on the bus. Texas has no laws against texting and driving. The driver is alive and will face many charges.

4-4-17 Tues. Trump's lazy and will delegate most of his presidency. 36 year old Jared Kushner now in charge of half of it. Jared's father was jailed for tax evasion and jury tampering. Kushner is married to Ivana, Trump's daughter.

Trumper is a good nickname. Dignified yet bellowy.

Syria war result of baby Bush destabilizing Iraq?

Hatred of a black president is keeping us from getting our required 9 Supreme Court justices?

A movie I don't want to see any part of is Snakes on a Plane.

Our 7 dogs all go nuts when wife Martha leaves and they anticipate her return 7 or 8 times before she actually returns. That's a lot of barking and running to the front window.

4-5-17 Wed. The stock market may eventually decide that competence is more important than money.

In 2013 Assad crossed the red line and Obama gave congress a chance to bless a war in Syria which they didn't do. Trump also said don't go during this time. Assad gassing his people worse than say napalm?

Trump signs anti-privacy bill. Better start putting money in the mattress.

Trump's 3 homes are needed to hold all the pictures of him. He has saved money on gold hair dye since winning the election.

Bill O'Reilly has just asked Bill Cosby for advice.

No Garland, no Gorsuch. Gorsuch seems like a good man.

Trump distracts by outrageous Twitter tweets. Is Pence sorry yet?

The Trump wall will cut countless ownerships into pieces and litigation will cost as much as the wall.

North Korea hacking into banks worldwide. They are world class hackers.

4-6-17 Thurs. Angel of St. Augustine Video put my video on Facebook and YouTube. It was a short read out of Real Estate Dad's Way.

O'Reilly tried to coach Trump. They are both sexual harassers yet don't understand what it is.

Trump's approach is hyperbole or lying. But is he also unhinged? Mental testing for presidential candidates should be required.

Rex Tillerson is "auto pilot" on the movie Airplane.

Our pool may not look good even from space.

The president serves 10 years. Eight in office and 2 being blamed.

The first vibrator was steam powered. (The science channel.)

Trump can't love Putin And Assad unless Assad promises to kill more kindly.

4-7-17 Fri. Trump bombs Syrian air bases. Most of the country already bombed. This puts the playdate with Putin in jeopardy. It was probably Hillary's emails that brought this on.

I'm not sure why we want to topple Assad. After all, the absence of Saddam hasn't helped.

Russia has a kleptocracy, that's a government where the leaders keep all the money.

Paxton Cooper was born to Jason and Kelly Cooper, my second cousin.

Poison gas is bad but napalm sticks to the body while it is burning.

Don Rickles died. To me he was not funny, nor was David Letterman.

When Kellyanne Conway got Sarah Palin's job, Sarah threw herself in front of a polar bear and was eaten.

The Navy has ordered a new $6 billion aircraft carrier, planes not included.

4-8-17 Sat. Did Trump bomb Syria to impress Xi, the president of China who was at Mar-A-Lago at the time of the attack?

A gas attack killed 1,700 in 2013 but Trump said stay out of Syria over and over again. Why go in now?

With the push of a button, one can take out a city.

Bombs often cost more than the value of the targets.

Bannon being pushed out? Don't let the door hit you as U leave.

Lunch at Zaxby's, the chicken place. Had enough for dinner too.

Did Hillary's pantsuits put Trump in the Whitehouse?

Does Melania wear shorter skirts when foreign dignitaries visit?

4-9-17 Sun. Did pictures of dead people inspire Trump to fire the missiles? Isn't the Trump Doctrine simply: Wheeeeeee.?

It seems to me that Trump seeks ratings more than anything else. You can't take the TV star out of the POTUS. And he is proud of being an idiot.   His brain automatically says, You are the one who is wrong.

He has been told not to call Kim Jung Un the little fat guy. Actually, a war with North Korea would help them.

Lincoln had to call coloreds property to free them, then he had to call them people to grant citizenship at war's end. Pretty tricky. Lucky he wasn't some ratings obsessed former TV star.

Tried frying eggs in Karo Syrup, not so good.

4-10-17 Mon. With Trump as an example, O'Reilly roams free. Cosby in background cheering Trump on.

Did Kushner push Bannon out?

You are not a president until you push the war button.

Is Trump irrational or unpredictable? Either way, he's proud of it.

Trump is divisive and has created more hate than any other president?

Kim gave us powdered muffin mix you heat in the microwave. Muffin in a pouch.

4-11-17 Tues. Alabama governor resigns after grabbing co-worker's breast. Trump grabs pu_sy and is still here.

No tax code changes unless Trump shows his taxes.

The office of the president naturally inflates ego but in Trump's case, is that even possible?

My next life could be lived on another planet.

N. Korea's Un worse than Syria's Assad as a threat to us.

United Airlines will pay a million times what they could have bought the guy's seat for. (overbooked flight, man dragged off plane)

Dogs run toward front of house dozens of times a day but only when the foyer rug is frazzled and flapped do we know the mail has come.

A very meager living is to be had speculating in baseball game tickets.

At this rate, the next president will be Mama June.

Patton had lousy people skills but he was right about the Russians.

Our new Supreme Court Justice is Neil Merrick Garland Gorsuch. There is now precedent that no court justice can be confirmed unless the president and congress are all of the same party.

4-12-17 Wed. United Air Lines and many other businesses take daily stupid pills.

Will Trump use the A. Bomb?

Dinner is supposed to work like this. When it's ready, I fix a plate and eat it. Then Martha says, I want cookies. So how do I uneat 1/3 of my meal? Martha is old school and must feed me and feed me and....

You take your girl to your bar and five hookers say hi.

Spicer says even Hitler didn't gas his own people, uh, wait

I don't mind a president using Twitter, but unrestrained use of social media has blown up our stupid factor hugely.

4-13-17 Thurs. When Trump fired the missiles at Syria, he put our Special Ops troops in a firefight with ISIS. If gassed children set him off, what will he do when ISIS beheads one of our troops?

Medical marijuana license signs popping up around Jacksonville.

Ben Carson was here kicking the walls of one of our troubled HUD apartment complexes. (Ben is Secretary of HUD under Trump.)

Tillerson has found his voice but still partly brain dead.

Clinton kicked down the door of loose morals setting the stage for Trump.

Help wanted ad for Fox News: Need 8 pm anchor, bellicose, loud, interrupts constantly, sexist, knows everything, has others write for him, crude, a bully. Who? Pres Trump? OK, give him an interview.

We don't text and drive but Martha coupons and drives.

Putting on my good shoes for Longhorns. Feel strange wiggling, a lizard was in my shoe.   Only in Florida.

Day after day of not running the heat or air makes me want to go out and buy a bucket of diamonds.

4-14-17 Fri. Trump taxes can't be released, it's too large. A summary will be, but who do we trust to compile the summary?

First we have to prove collusion between Russia and the Trump campaign. If so did it cost Hillary the election.

Trump is unpredictable and erratic because it's easy and it makes him get more attention. In his world, you can't be too famous and he makes no mistakes.

Obama tip toed past many a foreign war but after the disastrous baby Bush, that is what we wanted.

Glenn Beck survives on and on.

First strikes are always successful.

Discover Card easy to get, has high interest rates and not widely accepted.

4-15-17 Sat. Russia happy about Trump and North Korea. Does China care if N. Korea kills half a million S. Koreans. Maybe it's time to pull troops out of S. Korea.

Bombs good for ratings. Many don't trust Trump. His support team shapes him and keeps him on point, sort of. Trump acts on the last advice given him? – Dan Rather

Ted Kaczynski, Unibomber, was a genius but went mad. Crazy people don't froth at the mouth, shake or howl.

Don't blame Melania for no Easter egg hunt at the White House.

Lindsay gets a BS in psychology. Her first customer should be Barkley, our epileptic dog.

Who if anyone has studied North Korea to see what could/should be done? CNN goes into these countries and give us valuable info.

4-16-17 Sun. Happy Easter. Watched part of Ten Commandments. Moses is asked to choose a wife based on their dancing ability. Sexist as I'm sure it was/is?

It's hard to believe a death count in battle from a lying president. During Viet Nam, enemy casualties were routinely over reported making the war more difficult. Lies kill.

North Korean missile fizzled. Was it aimed at our navy forces?

Bannon and Kellyanne gone? Hope so.

Did Trump double cross the Russians by bombing Syria?

Olive Garden in Jacksonville surrounded by road construction.

Operating under pretense of replacing a ceiling tile, crooks installed a camera aimed at the safe and thus got the combination. Then stole cash and jewels worth ¼ million dollars; and some Viagra. Why would a strip club need Viagra?

A newspaper has rightly decided to publish all the names of lotto ticket buyer losers. The 400 lb paper will cost $125.

4-17-17 Mon. New electric planes are coming.

Trump must show his taxes to the FBI. Forensic accountants and intrepid reporters could uncover much.

Fareed says extreme Trump hatred is an illness. For instance, his decision to bomb Syria would be within Obama guidelines.

Garage sale: Bargain or junk?

He who cheats an honest man will live to see the honest man rewarded 10 times more.

4-18-17 Tues. Trump says, Drain the Swamp, maybe he means it literally, being a Florida property owner.

For sale cheap, one North Korean missile, $20.

Trump to North Korea: Our leader is crazier than your leader.

Washington, D. C. pays more in income tax than any state.

Kim Jung Un fires missiles at our navy. Communists don't believe in God but Un thinks he is a god and will gladly die in a bath of heavenly fire.   And, he wants you to join him in final glory.

4-19-17 Wed. In the future, a law will require all presidents to release their taxes and pass a mental exam.

Trump lies are corrupting our good people.

No wall, no health care, no tax reform, we can always bomb.

The diet is blown when we have his and her ice cream.

I believe the Fox Five talked all at the same time. O'Reilly gone for good.

Trump the showman is living his dream via executive orders. He is his own movie.

B-52s roamed the skies during the Cold War. Is that coming back? Shouldn't we remove targets from being near North Korea?

A lot of republicans think the Mexico wall is stupid and a waste of $.

39 mail carriers have been torn apart by our 7 dogs.

Is a porta-pottie an outhouse? Both can be a friend of the appraiser.

Trump does not understand Easter but he loves Christmas.

Barbara Bush had a husband and son as president. Hope Melania does not repeat that feat.

4-20-17 Thurs. Trump is emotionally incontinent.

O'Reilly is now in the No Work Zone.

Trump lies and the media notices. Gas prices up, time to steal some oil. Trump thinks he owns the United States.

Fox News: Help wanted.   We have tons of O'Reilly books, 50 cents each.   I heard Bill O and Bill Cosby arguing if drugs or bullying was better.   O'Reilly settled his first sex harassment suit in 2004.

Close the observation window and shoot death row inmates with rifles.

Don't hear much about Cuba anymore. Obama driven story.

Those failed policies of the past, can we get that back?

No one is irreplaceable. – Bill O'Reilly

People don't change but their bills get bigger.

There are few sick kids on the weekends.

Daddy Bush was mostly applauded for not going into Baghdad after winning the Gulf War. Too bad Baby Bush didn't follow suit.

I dreamed Trump hired me to appraise a proposed building. He was coarse and dismissive, not smart way to act toward your appraiser. When completed, the building was squat at 10 stories, wider than tall and it all fell in leaving a cloud of fine blue powder.

4-21-17 Fri. From top Fox reporter to just another muckraker. (Bill O'Reilly)

Trump is the most incompetent president but baby Bush was worse. (So far.)

The Trump sales method is repeat, repeat, repeat.

No more money worries for Donald Trump.

The menu had calories listed by each entre so I just got a bowl of soup. My daughter ordered me a salad and gave me a butter muffin. All is well until the gratuity cake arrived for it was my birthday. I wasn't sure I'd eaten too much until I staggered in the front door of my house and had to cancel dinner plans for the evening.

One of our dogs oinks. Has Martha been keeping a secret?

4-22-17 Sat. Good lunch at Cantina Laredo but I sense a new cook, manager or supplier.

Will Bill O'Reilly work again? Brain twaddle.

Hiding and lying poor way to run the government. Pay for play? Buy one of Trump's condos and join Mar Largo $200,000 and have dinner with Trumpy.

Nukes needed to wipe out 20,000 pieces of artillery aimed at South Korea. Or 4 MOABs equal one nuke. Every time there is a terror incident, the right wing fringe picks up power.

Dreams can take you where only God knows about.

This was taken from Facebook word for word: I wanna go on a date but y'all niggas don't be having cars.

4-23-17 Sun. My parents probably would have voted for Trump. Mother went along with dad who would vote republican even if it was a toaster running. Elect an outsider with no experience, OK.

Make American Great Again, Drain the Swamp, America First, these phrases are Trumps best and only work.

Don't fund the border wall.

Soon, Trump will require all men to wear the red tie.

Trump will buy waterfront Florida land to create Trumpland, an international haven for buyers who want to be close to the Big One. Millions of lots sold without regard for rising water levels. Oh damn, I hate it when that happens.

Recent movie advertised as more violent than the Godfather. Great.

Bill O'Reilly to keep working? Wouldn't radio be better than a podcast?

Venezuela takes General Motors plant. Somehow Trump will take credit for creating more American jobs this way.

4-24-17 Mon. Governing part of a party poor way to lead. Fights with congress rather than cajoling them.

Air pollution in China reaches us. Radioactivity in Japan reaches us.

Roger Ailes told the pretty Fox blonds they'd learn how to succeed in a hotel room.

Does Trump raise money at the rallies? He's more than a president, he's an infection.

Martians are paying for the wall.

Robin Williams said of George W. Bush; He's a comedic piñata.

Someone asked if you grab the nipples of nursing women who are doing it in public?

I told Trump to build a red tie factory in North Korea.

I opened the pouch containing the powdered muffin dust and mixed in half cup of water, baked in microwave. The result was a mini-blob that oozed onto the plate.

Amazing that there was a march for science and that we would need a march for science.

4-25-17 Tues. Need to see Rachel Maddow's legs.

Nixon, Clinton and Trump have each lowered the bar by welcoming sleaze. Was Hillary punished for Bill's sins?

Trump ordered his crown to be jeweled, spangled, bedazzled, and paid for by his foundation. Trump loves Wikileaks, the fix was in.

O'Reilly hiding under his desk. Michael Moore still standing.

Trump will have continuous pictures of Mr. Big, on the wall, sure to keep out rats and Mexicans. 100 days, no laws passed.

When young people get famous, growth slows. When talent fades, sex display grows. Brittany Spears set off a slew of low riding pants.

Elvis was right to shoot his TVs.

The trouble with vegetable soup is the vegetables.

Martha hits brakes hard, all the groceries I'd carefully placed near the tailgate shot forward leaving their bags.

Corrine Brown's fraud trial begins today in Jacksonville. She was seen with her mouth closed.

Trump to cut taxes on corporations to 15%? Does that include LLCs?

The 1990's TV show Columbo had 3 dead, 2 perps and one surviving perp. Busy night.

4-26-17 Wed. Trump cover up regarding Russia so like Nixon it's uncanny.   Lying is a Trump requisite for employment.

Russia did not invade Ukraine, Ukraine joined the Russian Federation. Words matter. Trump's war on the media is understood as a war on the truth.

Trump rode to victory on a horse of hate.

His daughter Ivana being "first lady" weird or cute?

Is Trump mentally stable? We learned with Reagan's last year that they have to be watched.

Texting and driving kills. Pit Bulls kill kids.

Trump ok with North Korea as their leader is crazy too.

What will a one foot increase in ocean levels do to our economy?

Flynn fraud hangs over Trump like the pendulum and pit.

Trump lied his way to power, promised everything to everybody and name called poor screeching Hillary into oblivion.

4-27-17 Thurs. Voters didn't realize billionaires don't tip. Billionaires may be corrupt but given Trump's lies, he's leader of the pack.

Jeff Sessions, the hollowed out attorney general is near bout worthless.

All dad wanted was to cruise the river with his fishing pole.

Let's grow our way out of any deficit with tax cuts; paaaleezzee.

Trump Tower has termites.

For sale: Hair salon in North Korea.

People put money in my bank account all the time and I don't know about it? (A hat tip to Corrine Brown)

It's hard for weather to be good when fires dominate the landscape.

The more tax brackets, the less time spent trying to wiggle into the lower one.

A farmer in a doublewide was heard to say: This inheritance tax is killing me.

King Trump summons the senate to the white house.

Lumber tiff with Canada could raise home prices. Builders don't need excuses to raise home prices.

Trump wall complete. Flying cars become popular.

Trump Beans mostly water. He didn't say how many beans in the can, fool.

Russia welcomes California into the Russian Federation when they secede from our union.

4-28-17 Fri. Just a few honest people could tumble this rotten white house.

Throw Mike Flynn under the bus? He is the bus. Will serve 6 months to 2 years in prison, or he'll sing.

Ordinary decent people choke on lies, which is why it's so hard to be a Trump employee or adversary.

Trump made a big deal of donating part of his salary to himself (his foundation) while taking millions from Russian oligarchs.

Trump buys large cattle ranch, then puts us on the leather money standard. His next book is: Achieving By Insulting

Pretty dumb for the South to fight for the 1% owning slaves. Bout as dumb as voting for Trump.

4-29-17 Sat. Flynn has dirtied Pence and Sessions as well as Trump. Trump blames Flynn on Obama.

I see Trump as the owner of 1,000 strip clubs. And, he'd be his own best customer.

Funniest Trump statement: "Believe me."

Trump loves bad guys like Mike Tyson who fought for him in the Atlantic City casinos.

There are no tax cuts, only redistribution. Tax load get pushed around like a mountain of mud. When feds cut, local raises them. When feds cut, deductions also fall.

Trump admits This job is hard and he misses his old life. His game of winning is won, it's over but he can't let it go. Still trying to figure out his job. Is it bullying the world for money?

4-30-17 Sun. Does Trump have a conscience? Is he a good speaker? Is he a Jell-O man?

Buy the book Two Paths by John Kasich.

When Trump skipped one of the debates to raise money for veterans; that was bold and creative. Never mind that he gave the money to himself. But when he skips the broadcaster's dinner, isn't that cowardly and divisive?

They kept the government open 5 more days, Halleluiah.

All we need is one written or recorded sentence: You help us win and sanctions on Russia will go away.

Loop Restaurant costs more than Chilis, but there is no tipping.

Republicans only care about the deficit when Democrats are in power.

Woodward and Bernstein are saying Watergate is back.

5-1-17 Mon. Dad pointed his cane at lamps, tables and chairs, telling me what each was worth, and then said, One day all this will be yours.

Trump seems to like other country's tyrants and despots. T has many needs but not you. Trump believes his own lies, that is how he flies.

It ain't right: Man beats his wife. Wife calls cops. Man attacks cops. Cop shoots man. Wife sues city.

Do in Un now or wait till he has 50 nukes and the missiles to put them on?

Republicans choke on health care; it's not in their DNA.

Reagan killed the middle class. – Elizabeth Warren

The four level house had the lowest level 2/3 under ground and the lot backed up to wetlands. Not good design in Florida.

We have a tomato and lime bush.

Trump skipped the media dinner in favor of a rally in Penna., where people applaud him recharging his ego. Meanwhile, back at the dinner, a comedian says the elephant in the room is missing. Vlad Putin couldn't make it.

5-2-17 Tues. Trump would have prevented the Civil War. Only John Kasich has the courage to stand up to Trump.

In the '90's, Barbara Bush's biggest fear was Larry Flynt. Now we have a revolutionary in office who would kill democracy and make himself king. Trump's appointees are low on qualifications like himself. This band of losers is more apt to follow Trump to hell.

Trump won't learn, already knows it all. History ain't important. His only loyal TV network, Fox, is riddled with sex and discrimination scandals.

School should teach students to vote and that the presidency is not wrestling. The fact that Trump could be elected is telling and scary.

Trump says all that stuff sober. No excuses. Trump and Un, what could go wrong?

A city attorney said immigration is a civil matter. I don't think so.

Don't put calorie count on menus. It's like my parents were there telling me to chew, eat slower, use my napkin.

5-3-17 Wed. Voters elected Trump knowing he had no experience but they presumed him to be a successful man who would learn stuff, but instead he hides, lies and covers up. Plus he's a nut job and a crook.

Comey dished on Clinton but not Trump. Why? Hope Hillary does not run again.

Trump has declared Saturday Kim Jung Un day.

Trump grabs pussy and it's locker room talk. Corrine Brown steals half a million dollars and it's bad bookkeeping.

Trump said he could shoot someone in the middle of Fifth Ave and keep his support. No wonder he likes Duterte, pres. of Philippines.

During the debates, Hillary tried to talk about facts while Trump stalked around, made faces and interrupted. So we elected him, wrestler in chief.

Cable news is like science shows, some speculation and partial facts.

Trump hates the media but the media loves him.

What is the difference between Kim Jung Un and Donald Trump? One is a crazed dictator and the other is a North Korean.

I'm not criticizing Trump, it's alternate humor.

Trump is like a snake in the living room. Some say pretty, I say get rid of it.   He's proved that government is hard.

5-4-17 Does Melania Trump have a college degree, probably not. Barron Trump has his own floor in the penthouse.

Trump shows pictures of the wall under construction but that is just maintenance of existing walls. – CNN

Rachel Maddow will be the next Bernstein but the path is long and torturous. Repub lawyers threatening her now.

By the time Barbara Bush was 75, she'd had 2 hip replacements and 2 toes removed.

Comey wrong to mention Hillary in public and not Trump.

Hillary should not share emails with Weiner and his wife.

Weight watchers: Avoid bowls of stuff which encourages automatic eating.

My dentist said: Oh My God.

FBI director Comey said tax returns are helpful in an investigation.

Cold fusion will control gravity? I have invented a convertible bus.

Barron Trump wearing tank top tuxedo to the prom.

Some men are called complex. Maybe crazy.

In Art of the Deal, Trump says his father, Fred was a tyrant. Maybe that explains his affection for Un, Putin and Duterte. Fred demanded fast work, done well. Maybe lies cover up inadequacies.

Ivana Trump, not quite grown, leans toward Eleanor Roosevelt or Hillary Clinton. A sort of anti-Bannon.

5-5-17 Fri. Nixon just a foretaste.

Twice during the Spanish Armada, commanders stopped to loot wrecked enemy ships. The Spanish commander was chosen based on social standing, he had no naval experience. The Spanish Armada had more priests on board than gunners. It was a war of religious conquest, a sort of crusade. When the battle was over, the English nobility wouldn't pay the victorious naval men.

Corrine Brown and Trump, two of a kind.

I hope last night's rain killed the 100,000 acre fire in the Georgia swamp.

Impeachment is about popularity.

Pre-existing conditions are hard to pin down as they get worse over time.

Bar-b-q restaurants have lousy salads.

5-6-17 Sat. The world seems determined to elect or be ruled by dumb bums.

Remember Beanie Babies? Kim had hundreds and Lindsay had dozens of them.

Maybe Corrine Brown can cry her way out of a conviction. Corrine is facing 24 federal counts of tax fraud and stealing from a charity.

Investigations create other investigations and the truth outs.

Walk in tubs have to completely drain dry before you can leave.

Kim Jung Un's hair mimics his grandfather's, but a few suck ups mimic the style, yet to catch on here.

Trump has made all of us question the truthfulness of everyone and everything.

5-7-17 Sun. Horses were used extensively in WWII. Tripods walking around spewing destruction still are with us too.

Please submit personality profiles on Donald Trump, Adolph Hitler and Joseph Stalin.

A growing movement wants Trump to be de-presidented via article 25 of the constitution.

Bill and Hillary have a strained marriage since she is now into the blame game. There is plenty to go around.

There would be no republican health care without Obamacare already being in place.

Dad worked until 87 and lived till 97. He'd sleep at his desk and in church.

Today it's a seller's real estate market but there are always good deals. Someone always wants out fast. Usually, you need cash to take advantage of this situation. If you don't have it, get a home equity line of credit, but don't use the money for a boat or vacation.

Print your pictures, at least the best ones. They stop time and if the object is gone, a picture is all you have left.

Trump makes Fox the state TV station.

5-8-17 Mon. Trump introduced the idea of fake news thus corrupting society for a long time. Like McCarthy and his communists in the 1950's.

Corrine Brown owes $800,000 in restitution.

110,000 acre fire in South Georgia.

Legs Diamond was killed by his own type of guy, other mobsters. In his early purse snatching days, he earned the name Legs because he could run so fast. He violated, there is honor among thieves.

Greg Gutfeld was good on the Five (Fox News) but with his own show, it's like the lid on the pepper can fell off.

Fox News outed Dubya's DUI 11 days before the election of 2,000, before they became Trump's bitch.

Christianity became Rome's official religion about 380 AD.

Dirty political tricks are normal, but not inviting Russia to help Trump.

5-9-17 Tues. After the 9-11 attack, Trump said his buildings are concrete not steel. Not so fast Trumpy. All high rises are concrete and steel. He said that because the steel melted in the World Trade towers due to being covered in burning airline fuel.

Rachael Maddow says Pence is a liar. Trump's only boss is the press, no wonder he wants them gone.

If Sally Yates were in Russia, she'd be dead.

Mike Huckabee says if no one smoked, overate, or sat around all day, health care would be affordable, oh, and don't get Alzheimer's or cancer.

Eric Trump brags about how well they are doing in Russia. Duh.

5-10-17 Wed.   Trump fires FBI Director Comey. Nation shakes.

Comey did seem to like spreading the news about Hillary. Where is Trump's loyalty?

Hyper partisanship ruining our country. It's all up to congress now.   Comey has lots of beans to spill.

Comey saw news of his firing on TV while he was in California. You're fired, more than just a TV show motto.

Kellyanne Conway shown on CNN but as usual, no sense.

It was all in Trump's book, Mein Kampf, I mean Art of the Deal, he lies his way to success and pushes back harder to all who offend him, which is everybody.

Trump and cronies lies are piling up like a wrecked train. Give Flynn immunity and let's start spilling those beans. When are the repubs going to start smelling this stink?

To hell with Obama back in office, I'd even take Dubya, who did real good by invading the wrong country but he only missed by one.

We need our old monuments. Are we to rewrite Tom Sawyer?

A guy in a big truck backed out into the passenger side of my car wrecking front door and damaging back one. He has no valid insurance due to tickets and fines. I now am sporting the plastic bag over windows like I've seen so many of over the years.

5-11-17 Thurs. 140,000 acre fire burning in South Georgia. Smoke is in the air.

Comey has a jar of secrets to be opened upon his "death".

Lenny the Nose Bobarino is the new FBI Director.

The media has a long memory and they forget nothing.

Kim Jung un played 18 holes of golf and scored an amazing 18. Trump said he was honored.

Some of Trump's people are so gross, Huckabee Sanders for instance.

Checks and balances work well except with the military where Orangeman has virtual free reign.

Spicer is off this week, out taking lying lessons. When Trump says, Believe me, You'd better.

Comey was investigating Kushner? This firing of the director will focus the FBI on Trump-Russia like never before.

Corrine Brown fraud trial continues in Jacksonville federal court. One juror replaced for "leaving it up to God."

5-12-17 Fri. Corrine Brown convicted on 18 of 22 counts of fraud, theft and tax evasion. But, she screamed, I built this courthouse. Hardly. Braggadocio didn't work this time. Maybe Trump can be next.

There is a new truth in town, Trump Truth, good only for 10 seconds.

Trump's nomination was Russia's lotto win.

Trump's legislative successes can be stated at this time to be zero.

He called Comey a Showboat. This president who worships himself. He cannot be interviewed as he is always bragging or campaigning.

My '07 large Mercury was hit, damage $1,700. I never wanted to trade it but this accident makes me wonder. My wife, Martha, thinks it's uncool to drive this large car but her cars are 17 and 19 years old. So I asked her would it be ok if I drove a '59 Cadillac? She said, Of course. So it's done. I'll just put fins on the Merc.

5-13-17 Sat. Do not brag about a good deal. I've heard people say, "I stole that." Why one time I bought an apartment building and the seller ended up paying me! Later a fire in that building killed a tenant.

Trump was elected because he is an unconventional businessman but what they didn't know was the extent of his psychosis.

Trump might not care if he's ousted, he's making millions off this gig.

The president has put us in the most danger since the cold war?

The trend is for doomed psychos to take a bunch of people with them when they commit suicide.

My wife Martha's loyalty to Trump is cracking but she chooses not to watch the picking at him.

Trump views the press like a felon looks on the police.

Make America Great Again, (for him).

Thank God Trump does not owe me money.

The man who hit my Mercury just paid $1,687 in damages for its repair. Neither one of us had any collision insurance. He is honorable and I am grateful and impressed.

The FBI will avenge Comey. Comey may have made some unfortunate political forays but he is honorable and didn't deserve to be fired.

5-14-17 Sun. The best thing Jimmy Carter did as president was to approve the loan to Chrysler Automotive.

You could buy a new car for $1,000 in 1928.

Thank you Robert for fixing our fallen window blind.

When dad entered a nursing home, it was a problem finding someone to cut his hair.

Trump Tweets makes the press secretary's job almost obsolete.

What do you do when your date takes food off your plate?

Where are the bills and laws. Trump is just defending himself. On the plus side, I did see Kim Jung Un in a western business suit.

The next president has to take some sort of test for basic knowledge and sanity. And to show his taxes. It otta be a law.

It's understandable that a lot of real estate people like Trump. The stock market liked him.   But not if it's perceived that he's unhinged.

Dad paid $10,000 for his restored 1,800 sq. ft. house in Palatka's historic district in 1963. He paid it off in 5 years. Read Real Estate Dad's Way.

5-15-17 Monday Nixon said the president is above the law. Not quite. The mid term election could turn the tide against Trump.

Trump might be able to pull a success in North Korea or Israel/Palestine.

Sears long slide. Their appliance warranty fell short. They built the 110 story building in Chicago. They kept the Regency Square store open for years for nothing and Walmart ended their life.

Dad was an efficiency expert in Ohio in 1948. He'd go into industrial plants and figure out how to speed things up and reduce jobs. This was to combat rising union power. Today the unions are gone but job reduction continues.

Trump is worse than Nixon because there are more lackeys around him. – Fareed's panel

Our Civil War freed the oppressed but a few years later, robber barons had reinstated the old system in a different way.

Remember George Wendt of Cheers? Well, he was a very bad man on last night's Columbo.

5-16-17 Tues. There are a dozen investigations open on Trump.

Saying Trump has dementia is just being kind.

During the campaign, T was loose and destructive. As president, he is insane and 6 years old. For a shining second, repubs thought they had another Reagan, but he's just another fraternity brat.

Repubs can either ditch this monster, or they can all go down at mid-terms.

Colossal ignorance of the head man and the corruption of close officials continues.

Putin and his friends hold the mortgage on Trump.

People had no trouble believing the lord is ok with slavery.

Patton said war is the greatest thing man can do, but what about the moon landing, interstates, cure for cancer.

In 2001 a publisher wanted $11,000 to do my book. Today it's just a few hundred dollars.

5-17-17 Wed. Keep a journal of important conversations and events.

Paul Ryan beginning to doubt Trump can lead.

It seems the bar was higher in Nixon's day. Nothing is getting done except Trump's defense. His fans are starting to not watch any news.

My wife Martha is turning against Trump but her pride defends him when I bash him. She voted for him.

Latest North Korean missile went 1,250 miles up. The space station is only 250 miles up. They have been hacking computers all over the world.

Hillary never came close to this level of destruction. Trump is like a boy with a new Corvette.

90 out of 100 people will believe Comey over Trump.

Trump trying to impress the Russians means they have something on him like a mortgage, tapes, something.

5-18-17 Thurs. Trump steps on himself time and again. He fires Comey only to be faced with Mueller, former head of the FBI.

Trump ran an effective campaign and sold himself to the baser among us but he is unable to lead.

There is a commercial on TV advertising holy water.

Trump is making the presidency irrelevant. Still whining about the media.

In 1792 the stock market was born on Wall Street, then just a lane.

Putin angry over the potential loss of Trump. Where could he ever find another like him?

Many Trump supporters have turned off the news and are out looking for Bigfoot.   Both sides are so dug in, it's like the civil war.

Every 50 years there has to be a Nixon. Everywhere Trump goes he destroys.

5-19-17 Fri. Pence dirty, Priebus dirty, McMaster better watch out, Get out or get sullied. Paul Ryan close to the flame.

Donald demands loyalty but won't give it and is throwing his campaign buddies under the bus.

T is worse than a lying president. He makes new truth up every day.

Investigations are unpredictable. Al Capone murdered dozens of people but was sent up for tax evasion.

In other news, my daughter found a cat on her way to work. She turned around, went home, made her daughter stay home with it.

Roger Ailes dead at 77. He was overweight and had health issues. A fall ended his life.   A brilliant man but overshadowed by lust. His bimbos are relieved. Some might be in the will. J. Paul Getty put his mistresses in his will. Right after Roger was forced out of Fox News, Bill O'Reilly was also fired for the same thing, sexual harassment.

If Trump is impeached, he will believe it is our loss.

Once a toilet is flushed, it cannot be unflushed. (Let's be sure about getting rid of Trump)

A Russian is willing to testify as to Trump's collusion with the election and removal of sanctions.

5-20-17 Sat. Kimberly Guilfoyle wants to be press secretary.

I can't believe T thinks firing Comey takes the pressure off him.

Trump thinks he won because of Russia. Trump is unmanageable and can't be interviewed. Paul Ryan, a good man, is awfully close to the flame.   T calls Comey a nut job.

O'Reilly says Ailes was forced out by "bad behavior". Sounds like he stole some candy.

If Hillary had won, Weiner would be secretary of communication.

Obama was president when I retired. He did dumb stuff, Ferguson, pre-judged racial criminal cases, IRS, guns to drug runners, regal attitude toward congress, but nothing is like Trump, who sets the bar so low as to be hazardous to the country's health.

Dan Rather gave us fake news and the internet exposed his error. Today, he is using the internet to showcase his views.

Nixon was Roger Ailes' first client and Trump his last. Crook bookends.

Russians are being exposed too and one will testify.

A toilet cannot be unflushed so be sure you want Trump gone before pushing the handle.

5-21-17 Sun. Trump in Saudi Arabia. He's got sand in his hair and oil in his pocket.

Car shopping a drag. I drew a disinterested salesman.
Killed the deal. I'm upset about having to trade simply
because someone hit my car.

Twenty Million Miles to Earth, 1957, black and white,
lizard from Venus, ok, in another movie there were cows
on the moon.

Trump is happy now, he's found the world's biggest
sandbox.

5-22-17 Monday Saw my old car on Columbo. It was
grand then.

Trump hates media yet he is on it 24/7. Media tracts his
lies.

Fox News has lost viewers. Maybe because O'Reilly is
gone. Maybe because they don't report any bad news on
Trump.

A child will turn down $5 if they want $10. A child will
refuse the reward for cleaning up their room so they can
not do it.

Ivanka got $100 million from the Saudis. Not bad. He
excoriated Hillary for doing something like this.

5-23-17 Tues. I traded in my damaged '07 Mercury for a
little 2014 Buick, 4 cylinder. It's red instead of white and
cute. I hate cute.

Gov. Kasich: I told you so.

Trump makes Nixon look good. – Susan Estrich

5-24-17 Wed. Trump's monetary worth is based on his feelings.

Hate needs a target.

Trump lied all his life in business and he let the lawyers clean it up, but now, he is president and is watched by an unforgiving press and people. His methods are flawed.

Ladies, date the man with the job.

Trump is making democrats out of many who were undecided.

5-25-17 Thurs. The Art of the Deal: Gather around all you crooked people and bow down to me.

Trump advocates are losing popularity and ratings.

Mar-a-Lago has a sinkhole but we all might get that.

Most rain since Hurricane Matthew. Ten frogs netted out of the pool.

The local news said that if you go to the doctor for a sore throat and he looks at your vagina, report it.

Kids go to concerts without telling anyone, unsettling for some Manchester, England parents.

In 1940, Washington, D. C. had 15,000 outside toilets used by 30,000 people. The good ole days.   Talk about a swamp.

Trump lies, makes up new reality and says wrong things. The media has 100% recall and he calls it fake.

5-26-17 Fri. Met Mike Malaghan, author of Picture Bride, in St. Augustine for dinner at Centro Piano Bar. When the food never came, he asked the server about it and we were told they have two restaurants and only one kitchen. Hooda thought?

Fox News blaming Obama for Kushner?

Montana congressman wins election even after fighting off a reporter. Trump ways are winning with some people.

I met a Trump voter in the check out line at Publix. I put the divider a little too close to his stuff and he slammed it down in extreme anger such that I left for another line. Road rage waiting to happen.

5-27-17 Sat. Still cool in the mornings. Soon summer will melt us.

Reagan said he'd resign if he became senile. Not very comforting.

Trump believes he can do no wrong. If he does wrong, he hides it.

Very hard to sell properties are now selling but sales have also slowed. They slowed in '06 at value's peak.

In the 7 years between the car I lost and the one I bought, lots happened to them. Lots of electronic gadgetry. I have a slow learning curve but will pick up bits and pieces now and then, when younger people are in the car to show me.

5-28-17 Sun. Shopping at Walmart is OK. Look for nipples under the thin T-shirts.

We are often defined by our quirks. Howard Hughes and his urine bottles. J. Paul Getty with his pay phone in the British castle.

Jack Welch made $100 million from GE during his tenure but gave half of that to ex wives as he traded them in for younger models.

We have no grills, only an oven.

Trump has to ride in a golf cart while the other European leaders walk.

European Street has Styrofoam dishes. Even soup bowls.

5-29-17 Mon. Memorial Day. A space plane will launch satellites. Anti missile technology will be perfected when we have to clean space of debris and junk we put there. We have polluted space.

Monica Lewinski had Bill's baby?

Jacksonville has a class action suit going over leaky pipes in your house.

Michelle O should not run for president as it would be a backlash from Trump who was himself a backlash from O, the husband.

Will Russians push Kushner out of a window?

Trump could lose his wife and daughter before the mess is done.

A TV door bell rings and 7 dogs become airborne off the couch and run to the front door.

The press won't worship Trump and that is the genesis of their war.

Kushner lie? Where would he get that from?

Ace Hardware has no fishnets.   Only Walmart has them.

"Take home pay" was invented in 1943. Federal taxes were withheld out of salary. Prior to that taxpayers were billed for the previous year.   The treasury was delighted with all the new money pouring in and gleefully spent it.

Saddam Hussein not so bad after all. Good/bad is relative in the Middle East.   Tribalism like our Indians before we killed them.

Many lonesome people cure it by going to doctors.

Mother died in 1987 but never saw a microwave.

5-30-17 Tues. Twenty minutes on hold for ATT re bad email when I was told to call another number.

Nixon collected crooks around him. That's what liars do. Not as bad as Trump though.

Air conditioning runs night and day now.

Some bad shrimp set off a rush of diarrhea at a local strip club. Three pole dancers and dozens of patrons were "affected".

Tiger Woods got a Florida DUI. He said it was the pills prescribed to him but too many of them. Subsequent testing proved him right.   DUI means driving under influence of drugs or alcohol.

Light speed can be exceeded by using spit.

Alan Dershowitz's support of Trump might be misplaced since all Trump wants from Jews is their accounting ability.

Pond cleaned. There are people who clean fish ponds. ATT technician fixed modem so now all green lights. (For a day or two.)

5-31-17 Wed. Tiger Woods does not deserve publicity. His career is over. He's just a rich Floridian with a successful sports past.

We stocked the pond with new fish. The birds are ecstatic.

It's hard to know who Trump is working for, us or Russia.

6-1-17 Thurs. Trump's party in the majority and still they are impotent.

Melania Trump, a former nude model, is out of her league.

Ivana Trump, the first daughter, is the real president. (Don't I wish.)

The Trump hate will live on long after he is gone.

Self worshipers are very lonesome people.

Saw two RPGs at the Avonlea Antique Mall. (inert)

Trump has paid clappers and Twitter bots to bolster his fan base and stroke his ego monster.

The Trump doctrine is; if Obama did it, it's bad. (Stupid but his base loves it.)

In 2000, we bought a new Chrysler Sebring convertible which just sits in the garage. Two or 3 cats lived in it, threw up and shed all over the seats.   Hence, the name Cat Condo.

6-2-17 Fri. Will Trump shatter the country? Pit one government against another within the US?

His speech pulling us out of the climate accord was flanked by praise speakers. And he waited for applause, sometimes too long.

Inexpensive natural gas is hurting coal and nuclear energy providers.

Bush carried a pocket knife in each pocket in case terrorists happened by.

Kathy Griffin gave me her head for safe keeping.

I dated Monica Lewinsky and Brittany Spears in one night in Palatka.

The U.S. joins Nicaragua and Syria in not joining the Climate Accord.

A lying president doesn't trust anyone. Art of deal gone flat.

6-3-17 Sat. Kathy Griffin can get her career back if she can learn to be funny. If not, get a real estate license. Holding Trump's bloody head is not a liberal or conservative cause, it's a matter of decency. Similarly, old monuments are not one cause or another's but a matter of history and should be respected.

Megyn Kelly withstood Trump's nastiest and rose above it. Her first interview with MSNBC is Vladimir Putin. Suck it up crying Kathy.

Trump said global warming is a Chinese trick to slow us down. Trump's environmental knowledge came from his own university. He's given ethics waivers to his close people.

If the kid does not ask for lunch money, he ain't goin to school.

Let God worry about climate change? We work as partners with God to do those things that need doing.

6-4-17 Sunday I walked over London Bridge in 1985.

Barkley hungry and eats after taking 2 days off. Seven dogs are so competitive over food they eat too fast and then throw up.

Kathy Griffin cannot out insult Trump. That is the one thing he is truly good at. 12 Republican candidates learned that the hard way during the campaign.

You get about 2 years between retirement and the day doctors take over your life.

6-5-17 Monday Al Franken's new book Giant of the Senate is about him, pretty cheeky.

15 of us celebrated at dinner Mark's birthday and Lindsay's graduation.

I've gone from 8 cylinders to 4. Ironically, it was 1981 when I bought a 4 cylinder Buick during the recession. They brought it to the house.

Kathy's head, Bill Maher's house N___r. It's all part of the Trump pussy grabbing era.

Trump is becoming known for stupidity.   He's making America small again. Dumb too.

The press stands between us and the Trump firestorm of hate.

Terrorists want us to hate Muslims in America.

Quit using Arab oil and the terror will slow down.

6-6-17 Tues. Rachel Maddow begins her second week of exile.

Kathy Griffin may as well keep bashing Trump, little to lose anymore.

Trump fans say don't worry about the tweets. Social media is not important. Believe me.

Trump doesn't like the Muslim mayor of London. Hooda thought?

Lyndon Johnson was as crude as Trump but a savvy politician.

An integrated electronic VA seems like a good idea to me.

Privatizing air traffic control. I don't know about that. Maybe if I trusted Trump.

New kitchen pipes were $750. This is one of the advantages of renting.

6-7-17 Wed. Trump having trouble getting a lawyer since he's not paid several in the past.

Rocket Mortgage push button, get mortgage. The procedure is the same for all mortgage companies.

Obama caused Trump without realizing it.

Trump has made lying a world sport.

Not enough crooks to staff top positions in the T administration?

Sessions out, didn't lie well enough? He's learned.

Make America Stupid Again. The National Enquirer president.

6-8-17 Thurs. Trump's attorney likely told top officials to clam up in front of Senate committee. Is attorney going to do their time? They should have taken the Fifth. The Trump machine needs oil.

If doorbell rings during dinner, well, let's just say Barkley ate half my What a Burger.

Jones College closes after 99 years. First wife and I lived in their tower in 1968. Tolls on the Matthews Bridge backed up traffic for miles.

My old $50 printer only lasted 9 months. This time I got one twice as tall and 3 times the money.

Trump will have an easier time losing weight in prison.

Government officials owe loyalty to the country, not Trump. The military must obey Trump unless the order is unlawful.

Not only Trump but dozens of others will be impeached.

6-9-17 Fri. Trump tweets send him packing? Due to his record of not paying lawyers, T is stuck with a real estate lawyer to defend him on a crime.

Firing FBI Director Comey to stop an investigation was naïve to the point of stupidity. There has never been a pres. like Trump. Even Hitler did some good before burning down the country.

A lying president reduces us all. T fans point to the crooked media and crooked Hillary as justification for Trump.

6-10-17 Sat. All during the campaign, T carped about a rigged election and it turns out, he's the one who rigged it.

The Russian election attack was equivalent to Pearl Harbor. – Dan Rather

Lying has always been done in government and politics but today it has risen to unbearable levels.

Toby, the Chihuahua's new name is: Football with Legs.

The level of honesty in government since Nixon has gone down so Trump may walk.

The white house tapes have been filed with the Trump tax returns.

With summer daylight hours, mail may arrive at 8 p.m.

I have 45,000 likes on Facebook. Thanks, everyone.

Trump says reduce regulations. Yes, but can we believe him?

Trump said the Empire State Building went up in one year. True, but it was built during the Depression so cheap workers were abundant.

Note to Paul Ryan: Trump will ruin all who defend him.

Man comes home unannounced, finds wife in bed with another man, Man gets up, dresses and leaves. Wife says What man? This is the Trump method of how he lives.

The worst day for me was when Jimmy Carter sent our forces into the Iranian desert to rescue hostages.

6-11-17 Sunday Many groups in our society seem to want their own language.

Pancakes for supper.

Adam West gone. RIP His Batman TV show in the '60's was funny, campy and enduring.

Being new to your field is not a defense for wrongdoing.

Karen saw a snake on our front porch. Our place is completely overgrown.

6-12-17 Monday We love our old shoes.

Trump glad about Comey's hearing? Dude, he just called you a liar.

Bill O'Reilly gone, Rachel Maddow up, bodes well for a more civilized TV and culture.

Trump knows it all and rejects people who could help him like past presidents.

We are drowning in our possessions, junk and stuff.

6-13-17 Tues. Trump fans say the media makes him lie.

Nixon acted normal but inside was a crook. Trump acts strange so inside him must be a lunatic.

Trump not worst president. He hasn't had enough time. Lyndon Johnson worst but T has so much potential. Baby Bush terrible too.

Puerto Rico wants to be a state. Hope it happens.

Obama campaigning for Hillary last few weeks hurt her as Trump fans combine Hillary and Obama into one big mess. It was hatred of O that elected Trump.

Trump has cabinet meeting where all but one worship him.   His first cabinet meeting was creepy.

The T personality has a lot of hate for others, insecurity and fear or paranoia. He had a tough father but T is also original and others can't be blamed for everything. Hitler had a bad father but we don't blame him for the Holocaust.

6-14-17 "You're fired" not working for Trump anymore. Governing is hard to do well and the clueless T is too proud to learn.

Sessions sweeping up Trump trash too big a job for this little boy.

Sessions: My daughter is not pregnant and the plumber did not do it.

If Trump is Caesar, who is Brutus?

People work for T out of patriotism but are soon squashed into a stinking heap of goo.

6-15-17 Thurs. The baseball shooting has put my posts in question as if I'm the cause of the violence. Trump won on hate and now it's coming back to him.

Trump stepped on his own tongue when he fired Comey. T is the president who never should have been.

What's taking the Cosby jury so long?

Trump rhetoric coming home to roost? He has demonized democrats and media. Words are bullets.

6-16-17 Friday Pence lawyered up, smart.

What's with five year olds graduating? We passed until 12, then graduated.

I am helping Corrine Brown collect money for her second trial. Leave bags of cash on my front porch.

6-17-17 Sat. Trump is sort of a Boss Hogg. I'd be happier with him if he managed a McDonalds. Making it harder to go to Cuba dumb.

Pence will be ruined.

Trump now has 4 lawyers. Can he pardon himself?

Lies are believed no matter how ridiculous.

Scalise's doctor very good at language but describing massive injury falls short, makes our medicine look primitive.

With 7 dogs barking and both Martha and I coughing, we can't hear a thing.

An insulted candidate is an insulted voter.

Trump's lovefest with Russia makes our foreign policy more strained and treacherous.

6-18-17 Sunday. Happy Father's Day. Arthur E. Cooper

Only 30% of people approve of Trump. 12 Trumpers now have lawyers.

Every computer expert used to be something else.

Robo vacuums are just toys.

The Regency Olive Garden is surrounded by backhoes. Road construction for 2 years now.

Bill Cosby walked. Larry King interviewed and Cosby talked about Spanish Fly. King didn't know whether to laugh or not.

Trump will make new law, not voluntarily.

Restaurants pack you in with other customers, babies and kids. And then blast you with music.

6-19-17 Monday Everybody's a genius for 15 seconds.

Oh, Yess, I'm the great pretender,,. Trump reminds me of the early evangelicals.

I am collecting for the Trump memorial. Please leave your pennies on my front porch. The monument will be the finest grade marble or plastic.

Bought a one cup coffee maker from CVS for $10 net after the coupons and discounts.

Businesses put themselves and you through a terrible mess with discounts, clubs, cards, promotions, etc. It took an hour to buy a cart full from Office Depot one Christmas.

6-20-17 Tues. Trump is hiding from the press and everyone else unless he can preen. T writing resignation letter as part of a plea bargain?

Billy Graham did not believe in evolution.

Welcome to the Trump attorney class on alternative reality: Here you will learn to say down is up.

6-21-17 Wed. Prior to Trump's campaign, we knew he was an asshole. During the campaign, more negatives emerged. As president, he is a nut-job.

Repubs have a dump Trump group forming?

Medical side effects may include nausea, vomiting and diarrhea but I'm so happy I took it, I'm dancing with my lawnmower.

Mattel introduces hung over Barbie and paunchy Ken.

People have died for the truth which is why Trump is so offensive.

I like billboards.

Dudley the cow died.   He caused Martha to not eat beef for a year. He was part of an internet fund raiser.

Jacksonville's Riverwalk downtown is growing and may become really great.

Stock owners are happy with Trump or his era. The taste of deregulation and tax cuts has investors salivating.

I hung a defective blind using 2 yardsticks. Martha said no. It was good enough for the Greeks and Romans.

6-22-17 Thurs. Two jurors voted not guilty in the Cosby trial.

With hacking all over the place, let's look back at good ole paper.

Ossoff, Ga. democrat lost even tho he spent millions.
After a while, people just tune it out. Even tho dems have lost 4 elections in deeply held republican states, they are ahead of where they were last time.

Billy Graham sold Christianity to millions around the world. Trump sold himself to millions here in the USA.

Trump has a worried dyspeptic look. Nancy Pelosi is the face of stupid for the dems.

I've been dieting since I was 25. Dad made fat jokes when I was in middle school. Make your kid tough again.

Honest people don't sound dead certain in politics which favors slickboys like Trump.

An autopsy of our citizen "killed" in North Korea should be forced to happen. This is an international incident.

6-23-17 Fri. The much maligned health care bill is just an outline at this point.   To go boldly where everyone has gone before is the wheelchair person's goal.

Russia practiced on Ukraine before entering our voter roles?

The USA has taken 4 years off to feed the rich.

Turn Trump loose on our zoning laws. Let's use the land we've got. What housing shortage?

Trump is the quintessential criminal, lies, overtalks, controlling and no guilt.

Repubs gutting O-Care but without O-Care, there would be nothing. Repubs can't do health care, it's not in their DNA.

Trump is taking the press conference back to radio, audio only and only after it's over and can be "approved". News management, cowards.

A woman was killed by an exploding can of whipped cream?

6-24-17 Sat. The head of the CIA is a Trump appointee. At times, Trump almost seems like a Russian agent. He sure sounds guilty.

Absentee voting will take a big increase to avoid cyber meddling.

Classic Trump: Confusion over tapes/recordings. Maybe, maybe not, same with firing former FBI chief. Birther BS. Fareed Zakaria was right, he's the bull shit president.

Verbal only press conferences. Sketches being made of the meeting, like a trial. Holy S, Batman.

Big divorce settlements mean lots of new larger boobs.

Trump is bringing back sailing ships where a crew of 300 to 400 was needed to sail and only 5 sailors died per voyage.

For good health, take a nap. Under Trumpcare, we all have to die at 50. The megatrend is employers don't provide health insurance anymore.

6-25-17 Sunday Every time the party shifts, we get new health care?

1,000 psychiatrists will be writing books on Trump. His election will be known as the Dred Scott of elections.

Doesn't T remember what happened to Nixon? Trump had to know about Russian hacks, he was briefed, but he did nothing then or now.

Speeches hours long are forgotten hours after they are done.

Who was driving the destroyer that was hit by the freighter? Are we letting machines do our looking? There should be 360 degree vision like a control tower.

6-26-17 Monday Styles change but beauty is constant.

One shooting per day in Jacksonville.

Trump believes bad publicity is good. The goal is get attention or media distraction, needed if you are a crook.

Health care very complicated and when half the authors of it are lying, the result is bad or zero.

There is fake news, but also fake history and fake science. Aliens have visited us before, and they built the pyramids.

Scientists who put down religion are blind. Where do hunches come from? Where does inspiration come from? Where do good ideas come from? Divine interaction is where.

6-27-17 Tues. I worry we going to have 9 Clarence
Thomases on the Supreme Court.

Do you have any quiet around your house? Time to not be
bombarded with noise? Quiet can be a beautiful thing.

Pence and Kushner have gotten name criminal attorneys
to defend them but Trump still has his divorce lawyer.

The Trump lie of the day is: CBO gives fake statistics.
(Congressional Budget Office)

Cary Grant's mother was committed to a mental
institution by his father and Cary never told where she
went. He was 11 and thought it was his fault. He had LSD
therapy later in life and realized the effect his early life had
on his whole life and also got his mother out of the place
and bought her a house.

For Trump not to fill many government offices is
malfeasance.

We will live inside all the time when the sun gets hotter.

A woman asked if I didn't believe in Jesus. I said Jesus
didn't destroy the dinosaurs.   And if he were here today,
he'd have a car.

6-28-17 Wed. Deutsche and VEB Trump's banks, lenders,
very questionable. One is fined for money laundering and
the other is just Putin's piggy bank.

Repubs eating their own, Art of the Dud.

A bug flew in my ear and I smashed it in there.

T threw so much BS during the campaign, it's now haunting him.   T so bad our allies around the world are ducking and covering.

Got hair cut, yet another barber has failed to make me look like Cary Grant.

Lightning burned a house in Nocatee, near where my daughter lives.

Don't worry Trumpers, he's going to fake jail.

6-29-17 Thurs. Trump's knowledge of science is: Earth, Wind and Fire. He's got his party in handcuffs. I am more afraid of snakes now.

First we had Rod Blagojevich and now Donald Trump. Drain the swamp: Ha Ha Ha.

For T to do nothing about Russian hacking is a dereliction of duty said Adam Schiff.   T sure became a lame duck quickly.

Trump has been compared to P. T. Barnum but I'm not sure that's fair to P. T. Piss on health care, T just wanna win! Don't miss my new book: Trump, the Thumb Sucking Years.

I can't believe Trump won the election by sticking out his tongue. Jeb Bush would have done health care by now.

Downtown Jacksonville: Enterprise Center sold in '08 for $162/sq. ft. and again in '17 for $48/sq. ft. The difference is occupancy. Kiss your tenants.   Experts don't know shit. It's all a guess, folks.

The stock market is simple like Trump. Health care fails to pass and it goes down.

I have invented a heart assist pump, like a hybrid car, live to 200. Leave $200,000 on my front porch.

6-30-17 Friday   If 3 senators defected to democrats, T would lose his majority.   Proof that T operative colluded with Russia to steal Hillary emails. T could be great except for the obscene part.

Trump is the only man who could "Go out" via atom bomb.

It is painful watching good people deal with Trump.

Trump has dissociative disorder, lives only for the present.

Sanders: The people elected a fighter. (Yeah, but they thought he was sane.)

Trump seems to have a fetish about women bleeding. What macabre is in his squirming brain?

Women are never happy with their appearance.

We had to put the vacuum cleaner together, AND we had 2 screws left over.

7-1-17 Sat. One by one, T supporters will fade. Even my wife is wondering.

Trump treats us like Russia treats us, keep pushing shit until someone eats it.   Have you no shame?

Jeep runs off road after flat tire. Fourteen people in it.

T hurts country and presidency with his abusive tweets. Proof he doesn't care about the country. T fights like a 12 year old girl.

Imma gittin new hair at Walmart.

Pull our troops out of South Korea? They are the excuse for N. Korea's war like posture.

T has hate build up syndrome. Pow, it's bled off and he feels better. Has no memory of raking anybody.

Our security system failed at the same window a handyman rehung a blind. Makes U wonder. One repair causes another.

Woman had her purse stolen so she runs him down in her SUV. He lived. Did she over react?

7-2-17 Sunday Russia investigation will end Trump reign. T wants a raise in pay.

The National Inquirer likes Trump. Hooda thought?

Don't buy a car during a UAW strike. Greta Van Susteren fired by MSNBC. George Zimmerman not dead.

The introducer often takes up most of the time allotted for the speaker's speech.

Trump won't approve Tillerson's requests for staff build up. T wants lackeys, not staff. Don't need no secretary of state, just more guns. Sadly, Tillerson believed Trump when he took the job.

7-3-17 Monday Leave troops in South Korea? They've been there 65 years already.

Trump appears mentally ill or on drugs. T defiant look reminds me of how Mussolini looked in old films.

The Indians were defeated because they were tribal, always fighting among themselves. Trump wants to make us tribal with him as the biggest chief.

7-4-17 Tuesday Happy Fourth of July!

Trump lies more than all living politicians combined. His Nixon was showing from the beginning.

Publicly successful people often have F uped personal lives.

Obamacare $500 billion. Trumpcare $27. Which do you want?

The world is afraid of Trump and what he will do to America and as America goes, so goes the world.

Bridgegate ruined Christie but he's better off than being a Trumper. He seems to be a rotting beach whale.

Brittney Spears rocks Israel. Hard not to love the girl. Trailer park girl overcomes. Shows world her pussy, no one grabbed it.

Make America Non Racist Again!

Dudley the Cow T-shirt arrived in the mail. Dudley was an injured cow on the Gentle Barn who recently died.

7-5-17 Wed. Twilight Zone on all day and night on Sci Fi channel. Two I hadn't seen. Rod Sterling forgot to write about a Trump presidency.

I invented meatloaf spaghetti.

Pence looks clean and scrubbed, but he lied about Flynn and the Russians. He's in it deep.

You do not want seven dogs with diarrhea.

More people trust CNN than Trump.

The world used to look to us for leadership and inspiration.

7-6-17 Thurs. Link to Trump Russia collusion died, he was 81.

Need mole inside North Korea. Conventional weapons at the border are the real threat.

Poland's alt right government promised Trump a cheering crowd.

Morning Joe ratings jump up due to Trump bashing them.

Today's TVs have glitches.

Un has surrounding countries by the balls.

Dogs scratch off on wood/laminate floor on one of their 100 trips a day to the front door.

Need coalition of South Korea, U.S., Japan and China to depose Un.

First Trump wants to stomp all of Obama's rules, then get funky with the alt right. Trump asks the Ayatollah for advice.

Trump said he was a founding father, who knew?

7-7-17 Friday Nasty name calling during our election made people stay home.

Trump so in bed with the Russians that he and Putin will have a baby named MoneyMe. T's constant media bashing is a defense against collusion when it is finally proven.

Trump's victory is the racist backlash from Obama's 8 years. T spews hate toward our media even overseas – Un-American.

To Trumpers, he is not a crook, just a great businessman. Everywhere he goes there are demonstrations both in America and abroad.

Emails are ok, but if it's really important, they will call.

A builder in trouble will always blame the appraiser.

Rush Limbaugh invented fake news and Trump put it in orbit.

Facebook is a political stew.

Trump should raise tariffs on China until they do Un in.

Deteriorating mental health is exacerbated by harsh words.

Un is the new Castro on steroids.

The Twitter Trump often clashes with the scripted Trump.

7-8-17 Saturday   Did Trump's long meeting with Vladimir Putin validate Putin?   We are probably strong enough to withstand Trump but why test it?

Mayor of New York and Gov. of Calif. going to Germany to apologize for Trump? Trump and Putin peas in a pod.

China is helping North Korea and themselves. There is vigorous trade between them.

Pence is batshit crazy but no one notices, he's out shown by his erratic boss.

You can tell when I'm clubbing by the cash bulge in my jacket. Is, You don't sweat much for a fat lady, still a good pick up line?

God bless air conditioning. Genius means losing sleep.

Books a Million: can't use e-card in store, their site is sticky, hard to manage, slow delivery too.

Fox: rioters. CNN: demonstrators. See the difference?

T asked Melania if he could keep Putin.   Damn, Russia is now a state.

Healthcare not nearly as interesting as the rotten media.

Fake news is given to news channels in the hope they will use it so the donor can them blow them up. Remember Dan Rather and the Bush bashing.

7-9-17 Sunday   Trump and Putin won't tell the truth, it's all up to Robert Mueller. Trump's defense is that he was clueless.

His supporters take him on faith while turning a blind eye to the oh so obvious flaws. It's almost like a secessionist movement, an abandonment of morals and reason.

Germany forgot to book him a hotel room? Ha! Ivana sat in for him during the meeting. Maybe he had to use the facilities.

Realtor open houses are few. In a seller's market, they aren't needed.

7-10-17 Monday   Trammell Crow said of Trump in the '80's: He can see all his buildings from his office but mine cover the earth.

Where would Florida be without fill dirt, ditching, air conditioning and bug spray?

Trump seems unhappy and worried that he will be robbed of some of his possessions.

Lamborghini vs Buick: You pay an extra $485,000 to get the second 100 MPH.

Trump can't arrange an eclipse of the sun. I like Ivana sitting in for daddy, she's better than him.

Russia is a huge source of $ for T. He is a businessman, right.   If only he could kill journalists like Putin.

Trump criticizes America when abroad, didn't Obama get hit for that too? A recent poll of Trump voters said 42% of them believe Judge Judy is on the supreme court.

The Obamacare tax will probably be on all of us someday. Trumpcare says let the states do it.

Trumpers love to say the media is no good. And Thank God for the National Inquirer, T's favorite paper.

T is more courageous and open hiding behind his Twitter a/c. Meanwhile, the world wonders who's really in charge?

North Korea's mission is to survive. Put them back together. Unite N and S. Korea, then our soldiers can leave.

Trump seems to lack faith in the future, out for the quick buck, the easy payoff. The Mafia is more believable.

7-11-17 Tuesday Lying only works in the short term, then you either have to fess up or be known as a fool. Reporters are forced to call Trump a liar because of the obvious nature of it and the frequency.

Trump is the best liar in the world. His course, Lying 101 covers such subjects as: Change the subject, Make up a new lie and Blame something else.

So many top Trump officials have met with Russians, I see a noose in the background.

Trump guts the EPA, makes sense, if you're a real estate man, you know new environmental rules can ruin land values.

7-12-17 Wed. Holy cow,crap Batman, Donald Jr. goes off with his own email, welcoming the Russians to the campaign. What colossal dumbass.

Trumpers, it's ok to change your mind. Mueller can't work if Jr. does his job for him. Repubs aghast, defecting, power slipping away.

Moby Dick rolls over with hundreds of harpoons. Big Trump quiet on Twitter, taking his attorney's advice.

Rachel Maddow thinks U gonna hear lies by the thousands in defense. Trumpers have turned off millions of TVs.

The beginning of Trump's campaign signaled a dirty kind of politician, not welcome in civilized society but we got him and getting rid is going to be hurtful to us all.

What Trump needs now is a war. Fox is backing down in their support.

Rush Limbaugh with his elite drive by media opened the door for hatred of the media. Then Trump with his hateful rhetoric.

Trades people listen to right wing radio during their working hours.

SNL did such a good job on Sean Spicer that the White House went off live video.

Lying is part of the job description for a Trumper.

Culture is a role model. There is a fine line between tough and mean. Trump has taken "winning" too far. Kellyanne Conway is an approved liaison for Russian spies.

Dust off Tiffany Trump. Why doesn't daddy like her?

7-13-17 Thurs. Since T owes big $ to Russian banks, they control him.

The really really tall buildings are in Dubai and Asia.

Constant lying is a part of extreme narcissism.

T says Russia is a fake crime. Fox is beating the Hillary basket.

Arnold Schwarzenegger could not get an acting job, too much body, name too long and that accent.

Trump blames media for all his problems. Those damn leaks. He hates the media but the media loves him. Viewership is up up up.

I'm not sure the billionaire personality is suited for government service. They generally are grabbers, takers and even thieves. Exceptions include Warren Buffett.

What happened to the wounded destroyer Fitzgerald? It has certainly dived off the news.

7-14-17 Friday   The first contact between Trump and Russia has committed suicide? Embarrassing Trump lawyers need anger management training.

Trump's an ass because he's tired. T's enduring legacy will be sleaze. T handshake with French first lady turned into an inspection.

Prayer not gonna fix Donald. He and Pat Robertson are two loons. Trump is a man who will live in infamy.

Martha wondered how much work Jimmy Carter really does on the houses. I'd be glad just to have him there. Good publicity.

Reading about Jim Morrison, the early years, dude, man died at 27.

The difference between an $800,000 house and a $ million house is the ceilings.

Melania Trump must be wondering if she could be doing something other than polishing her nails.

Give your house mates some time alone, away from you.

7-15-17 Saturday   Trump will leave legal messes long after his term is up.

Pence is looking more and more like Tiffany Trump, on the outs.

So many people duped. T told them he'd replace Obamacare with something better but that would require more government spending, the last thing a repub is willing to do.

We have a new secret police, the Kremlin.

It's Friday night, time to hit the clubs, smile, drink, dance, chat, charm, hit a pole, hit a VW, get pulled over.

I've invented a sleep pill that will knock you out for a week and make you lose ten pounds. Leave $ on my front porch.

7-16-17 Sunday   Should O. J. Simpson get out of jail on parole?

When I saw Jurassic Park, I thought you're gonna need a bigger gun.

All the President's Men on TV all the time.

Trump is good at digging his own grave.

I apologize for any of Trump's faults I may have missed in this book.

7-17-17 Monday.   What is the quickest way to be branded a liar? Hang out with Trump. Was the meeting with Russia legal? Probably not.

Rest in Peace, John H. Rogers. He was my boss when I moved to Jacksonville in 1968. He was a friend. Lived to be 92. He didn't have to work but laying around not in his DNA. He was a true southern gentleman.

How low can Trump's poll numbers get?

The movie Shadow has disappeared as well.

Had my first bacon sandwich in awhile.

7-18-17 Tues. Cruiser's Grill has the best fries.

Twitter is the president's soul. He was weaned too soon. The ppl don't like fakes. Social media tells who you are.

Dad never went to a doctor until he had symptoms, lived to 97.

McCain probably had brain surgery, not a mole above the eyebrow.

In Trumpland, the most often told story is the truth. He's still campaigning. He should be talking about policy.

Martha and I have 4 printers. We just learned that printers and copiers are the same thing.

Jimmy Carter should write a book on why his presidency was an utter failure.

7-19-17 Wed. Is Trump letting Putin have the world for cash? He seems to be a high national security risk. T knows there is big $ in laundering.

Kushner has thousands of meetings. How could he be expected to remember one meeting where a Russian had dirt on Hillary and another was a money launderer.

Laundered money is stolen money so it matters little if 30 or 40% is paid out to clean it. How do you launder $? Move it around from one bank account to another. Buy cars or real estate. Ask them in South Florida.

I have never had a car with a sun roof.

All republicans have to do to save health care is to add money to it.

Both a snake and gator near Betty's house. Disturbing or just Florida?

7-20-17 Thurs. From now on, you no show your taxes, no get president's job.

The OJ Show is looming.   The press knows where the red meat is.

T demands loyalty but gives none.

Pray for John McCain and the Country.

Help wanted: Honest men and women at the highest levels of government.

Trump lies worked in business. Customers either believed him or were too polite to confront. But in government, this is not true and the press is chewing him up.

T mad at half his staff because it can't be His fault.

Russia is a snowball.

Hillary stepping on coal miners made her sound cold blooded.

Florida voters went for Trump.

T and his supporters can't pass healthcare, so T takes his marbles and goes home. "Let it fail." I'm not going to own it. Him first, others last.

Blasting Sessions on Twitter very crude and rude. Sessions was Trump's first major follower.

7-21-17 Friday Sessions can't fire Mueller because he's recused from Russia. Trump would like the FBI to be his personal police force.

Trump lawyers trying to derail the Mueller investigation. Trump asks if he can pardon himself and kids. Even Nixon would not do that.

Mueller is following the money all the way into Trump's personal business 10 years back. Russia gets their hooks in you over time.

Trump is the money addict and Putin is his pusher. Money laundering can be very lucrative.

McCain should retire now. If he comes back, his enemies will say he's affected. (Brain surgery)

Trump says he will fire Mueller if he goes into his personal business. Mueller: Hold my beer.

OJ Simpson to be released on parole. OJ and Trump alike. Both narcissists. Neither assumes any blame for anything. Both can blather on and on about their virtues. Both professional liars. One killed, the other said they could...

OJ not in tune with the Trump times. George Zimmerman laying in wait for OJ.   OJ dated only white women but a black jury set him free. I hear he's gonna have a sleepover.

Trump twisting and OJ on the prowl. May both of them be run over by a slow bus.

For 20+ years my bank has been charging me for checks which they said were free when I opened the a/c. Got free checks at my new a/c down the street at the credit union.

7-22-17 Sat. Impeachment has no limits on what it can consider. Trump lawyers giving hints of what the problems are. T cares more about himself than the country and tests to the limit the strength of our government.

Money laundering is a mystery to many people. They think it's a tax thing rich folks do, but it's a crime. The mafia does it, drug runners do it. Trump.......

If Mueller fears termination, leaks will abound. T fired Comey, why wouldn't he fire Mueller?

SNL ended Sean Spicer's career as press secretary. (Saturday Night Live TV comedy show).

Funny facts bend to the will of the provider.

So many buildings are hit by cars, trucks, SUVs, etc. Buildings are big, damn.

Martha likes Stephen King but not Coneheads.

Which would you rather have, a sane liberal black guy, or a semi-senile, ego maniac, lying psycho as president?

7-23-17 Sunday A snake cut in two can still bite. Such would be a Trump presidency. Get ready for the biggest Hillary dump of fake news ever. He will be removed by armed police.

OJ is an affable oaf but he's still a psychopathic killer, beware. Women will line up to date him oblivious to the well documented dangers.

Never again will there be a president who doesn't show his taxes and get a psyche exam. That is the Trump legacy and a good one at that.

7-24-17 Monday May all bad TV actors get killed off.

Firing Mueller would end the Trump presidency.   The Russians are leaking too.

Ocean pollution is making fish sick and then us.

Trump likes quick fixes, no waiting, not good for deal making.

Say the tobacco industry gave T a billion $ loan on the Tower. Pay back when you feel like it. Then T goes out extolling the virtues of smoking and saying how good it is for you.

Bobby: I like you, Mr. Trump, you're a real screwball.

Ppl like T don't commit suicide. It's never their fault.

Doctors and hospitals need to go on a diet.

7-25-17 Tues. Trump excels at slander. Did Chris Wray, FBI nominee, pledge loyalty to Trump?

The Boy Scouts learned a lot at Trump's speech.

Stay in office, Sessions, make it harder to fire Mueller.

Yeah, we met with Russians, it was boring and we left early. Nothing discussed. We weren't really there.

Medicare for all, it is coming. Doctors don't even pretend to care now.

Trump proves you can't sell with zero product knowledge. Repubs sound like Pelosi in 2009.

Benjamin Harrison, 23rd President, had the White House wired for electricity in 1890 but was afraid to use it and stayed with the old gas lamps.   I understand.

7-26-17 Wed. By supporting Trump, Repubs sold their soul and our future.   So many ppl believe every word Trump says.

The senate has to vote to vote?

Sessions dug in and if he's fired, the Pence faction of the republican party will rise up.

Martha turns off Trump and watches Animal Planet. He's either stupid or crazy. As T sinks the nation, Russians are clapping.

Washington Post full of Syrians? Welcome to Trump's banana republic.

> 1.   No Russians. 2. Maybe a few. 3. OK, we did meet with them but it was short. 4. Maybe there

were several meetings. 5. Everybody does it. 6. It's not illegal.   7. If it is illegal, dems are worse.

We are all trapped in our own heads.

7-27-17 Thurs.   Trump thinks no one is smarter than him, a big handicap. His major tactic is to distract with another story.

Sessions was a senator with a solid base when he met his devil.

Both Martha's and my doctor is dismissive.

Even Rush Limbaugh can't understand the Trump-Sessions stress. Caring for people made America great. T doesn't understand that way of thinking.

Trump getting rid of 15,000 transgender people in the military? Small part of budget but big backlash.   Worse is his decision not to staff many important government posts.

7-28-17 Friday Trump needs a 007 hitman to take out enemies. One man can ruin this nation.

Trump lied during the campaign so now congress is bogged down in mud trying to make good.

There are 10,000 diseases on TV.

History is a great teacher but it's sound bites and semi accurate.

Trump hatches his Mini Me, Scaramucci, Trump's communications director for 5 days?

Russia is helping with the investigation via their TV. Is T the Larry Flynt of politics?   Larry says T is beneath him.

Banks anal, can't overpay a car loan.   The internet boosts power for all of us for good or bad.

Military leaders not bowing to T on the transgender ban.

People who fear being fired often leak material while they still can.

Some managers pit employees against each other. Some like dog fighting.

Fake news caused the recession. Mortgage companies lying about their product. Regulators asleep at the switch. Lying and Lazy, 2 legs of disaster.

President Trump is worse than candidate Trump.

 7-29-17 Sat. Jon Benet's death is her parents fault for making her look like a hooker.

I just learned how to spell Priebus and now he's gone. Not about to learn spelling of Scaramouchi.

Priebus never said anything. He talks but nothing comes out.

Anybody who is anybody has been fired by Trump.

Priebus out, Kelly in, my head spins, Hitler sacked his generals in the end but no help.

Trump knows all about leaking. He used to do it under the name of Baron Jones or something.

North Korea looking for love in all the wrong places.

Trump folds under push back. The military is apt to push back on the transgender issue.

Our first X rated president.

My wife dumped Trump for not doing anything.

7-30-17 Sunday   800 lies, and that's just this morning. Don't impeach now, you will know the time.

Work has begun on the Trump – Mt. Rushmore project. OMG, it's a giant dick.

Trump needs to get into the swamp to get anything done. He's not gonna wait for Obamacare to implode, he's gonna defund it.

Dammit, that's 10 times today I've been mistaken for James Bond.

Bernie Sanders has the only cogent health care message, and he's said it a million times. It's his only issue.

A person never knows when his courage or honor might leave him; that is why we pray.

7-31-17 Monday Welcome to our new world of lies. I didn't even know we had an ambassador of religious freedom.

Trump has created a big new cadre of comedians.

His supporters prop him up by saying how bad Hillary and Obama were. And to think, T does all that stuff sober.

Bill Clinton had a good tax plan. Bernie Sanders a good health plan. The Trump wall has been shifted to North Korea and China.

Asia and Europe together can be the new number one. Trump seems to want the destruction of America.

The U.S. is building a new mega base in South Korea away from the population centers.

Columbo ferrets out crime where no other can even see it.

The eclipse will be 90% in Jacksonville, even cloudy, the effect will be noticed.

Woolery Drive in Jacksonville floods routinely and the city ignores it.

8-1-17 Tues. Coming soon: The 15 minute career of Scaramouchie.

Nobody is allowed to cuss more than the D. Scaramouchie barely had time to wipe his feet.

The Trump library is ready. Two books, one is already colored.

In 1999, Jerry Falwell proclaimed the purple Teletubbie, Tinky Winky was gay. I see why Larry Flynt pilloried him.

Trump has invented the Tweet storm.

Obama shown light on racial problems and also inflamed them. He kept us out of war, spawned the Tea Party and created apartheid in congress. He was funny and likeable.

Let people know the truth and the country will be safe. – Abraham Lincoln

8-2-17 Wed. Just sell the stuff, quit with the games, discounts, credit cards, savers clubs. Walmart just sells it straight and cheap.

To Trump, the presidency is just another gig. He's obsessed with Putin and how he was able to steal all the money. Trump operates by bullying but that doesn't work well in government. Top people can make more on the outside so he has no carrot and stick to hold over them except their desire to serve and make a difference. He crushes all his good people.   He makes them into liars.

All of Trump's statements must be followed by; I wonder if that is true.

When Gov. Christie becomes an ex gov., he will apply for the job of being Trump's food taster.

Trump power is slip, slipping away.

The Trump personnel turnover is stunning.

Each time a storm is named, insurance companies save a billion dollars due to higher deductibles.

Seems like we should help Venezuela instead of sanctioning them.

8-3-17 Thurs. Tony Schwartz wrote Art of the Deal and said Trump uses a "truthful hyperbole". That was a spin of vastly understated amount.

Sure wish Nixon were alive to comment on this Trump mess. Is T killing the better angels of our nature? He's emboldened racism.

New immigration rules passed by Trump would keep out his own mother. Most of us know immigrants who could not speak English when they got here.

The first recorded lie by Trump was when he was 4.

50's cars were massive steel, 5,000 lbs, no mileage or safety, gaudy, rolling palaces, I love em.

In twisted Trump land, there is no climate change until water comes in the front door of Mar-A- Lago.

Congress wrote the Russia sanctions, not trusting Trump to do it.

A hated government does not long survive. – Seneca

8-4-17 Friday You never get full snacking.

May the Trump trial be presided over by 300 Mexican judges.

The news plays what Trump has said and he says it is fake. Mueller convenes grand jury.

Holly and Spanish Bayonet are very bad plants to have in your yard.

Scaramoochie dating Kimberly Guilfoyle of Fox News fame? Seems like a good fit.

Darwin withheld his book, Origin of the Species for 20 years because he feared he would not go to heaven.

General Kelly may become the real president.

My health insurance company sent me a pooper scooper. It's nice to be loved.

Tony Romas on Southside Blvd. in Jacksonville was gutted in order to become a Hooters.

Trump lies in order to build up his ego. I call that a sickness. He lies to create a self, magical thinking, one of the legs of evil. – Scott Peck

All us amateur authors hope to hit word lotto.

A life of ease is a difficult pursuit. – Cowper

8-5-17 Sat. A 1998 Law and Order is about the press, still topical.

Trump builds a perfect self, so he never has to admit he's wrong. He doth deny too much. Some voters support an official even after conviction.

Yall remember the Great Recession, caused by crooked banks, lenders, brokers, insurers, clients and regulators? Don't we need an honest president?

Prosperity cannot be divorced from humanity. – Calvin Coolidge

UGH: That feeling you get when you click on "read more" after a post and it's 10 pages.

8-6-17 Sunday The war on leaks is a new arm on the war on the media. A stable president has fewer leaks. Some of his helpers lose their jobs in a week.

OJ and Corrine Brown are both single. Just sayin.

Jay Leno's Garage: '57 Buick has speed buzzer goes off if exceed preset speed. That'll fix em. In '07 I was on My Space.

Soup bowl too large for spoon. Two spoons disappeared before I retrieved them thus figuring out the problem.

A man's true wealth is the good he does in this world. – Mohammed Several FB friends said it should be Jesus.

Trump supporters are screaming how bad Hillary is/was. Sorry folks, no go. She did think her campaign was "unsinkable."

Sarah Palin lost and Trump won. Where is the honor in that story?

8-7-17 Monday Construction costs soaring due to lack of workers.

Trump hates truth and his own people, where is the success?

Pence for president?

The swamp is growing.   Dad never lost faith in Nixon. Dad was an ideologue, not a thinker. Rhetoric is easier. Mother was a thinker but as a women, voiceless in those times.

Al Gore said Trump was elected by the 30 second sound bite. TV and social media are key.

If the ocean rises one inch, that can mean 2 feet during storms, the right tidal action and water build up. Trump won't care.

8-8-17 Tues. Trump knows the public forgets quickly. Last minute undecided voters won it for him. The Comey releases sunk Hillary yet Stupid Trump fired him. His trust rating is now 30%.

If a Ross Perot type candidate ran in 2020, T could win a second term.

Should Josh Phillips get out of jail? Remember when he was 14 he killed Maddie Clifton who was 8 and hid her body under his waterbed for a week. The Florida Supreme Court ruled you can't sentence a minor to life in prison.

Trump is taking over Taco Bell until the wall is paid for.

A 50' crane helped take down a huge oak near our house. We got our 500th load of pine straw which is why our yard is 2' higher than anyone else's. Martha loves pine straw. A stack of it is leaned up against the garage.

Trump's base is headed up by David Koresh and Jim Jones.

Trump's abortion knowledge is near zero.

I'd make a mashed potato mound, dig a hole in the top, fill with gravy, then cut the side so gravy ran out, Look out!, run, dam broke!

8-9-17 Wed. We are now crazy like N. Korea. China could invade N. K.

The Trump presidency seems like a vast sickness, an invisible blanket of disease.

No presidential news conference except Twitter. T creates his own media channel, all things Trump, a world of constant praise. The National Enquirer endorses him. Is Trump buying Twitter followers?

America speaks with forked tongue, Trump and his aids.

Should I go to a doctor who advertises on TV?

Trump said he'd keep his intensions quiet, another lie.

The exuberant stock market is based on expectations.

Trump and Un, 2 little boys with a nuke in each hand. What could go wrong?

8-10-17 Thurs. The Trump mind is: push employees around, you will never need them to help you. He's living a movie, top people pulling away. Makes enemies all over the place.

N.K. takes a few practice shots at Guam?

We got a Wounded Warrior calendar. Martha quit giving to them when it was revealed they kept most of the money.

Build cameras into guns. If camera can't see, gun won't fire.

FBI takes Manafort's files for criminal investigation.

Limbaugh says T doing crazy act for Un's benefit. That's no act! Trump would start a war to gratify his ego? Bush did.

They that govern the most make the least noise. – Selden

8-11-17 Friday   You've noticed Trump's shitfaced facial expression. What would you call it? Who me? I didn't do it. You caught me. I don't care…….

Free the North Korean slaves. Not everyone's gonna survive T. Un better be afraid of him, I know I am.

J. Edgar Hoover and Tolson dressed up in women's clothes. Secretly, at night, Trump dons his Superman Cape.

Where did the N.K. hatred by Trump come from? Out of the blue we gonna nuke them? Could he be distracting the media from Manafort and the other players?

Better to shun the bait than to struggle in the snare. – John Dryden

N.K. is doing well now. But the U.S. is still the bogeyman keeping Un in power. Now Trump has more than validated that view.

Trump delegates And does it himself. Chaotic management leads to deadly mistakes.

8-12-17 Saturday   There are still grown-ups in government but the Child in Chief is dangerous to us.   The Art of the Deal is the Way of the Steal. He has already stolen from you.

Trump ragging on Mitch McConnell.

I still like Fridays even tho my career is done.

Trump's staff has to figure out what he really means.

T has decided to borrow from all his employees.

The right wants to get rid of red light cameras and recycling.

This book, What have We done !!! is prophetic. The logo WW!!! is right on target.

Paul Bunyan Cooper just axed a fallen limb and hauled it out front.

Once every 1,000 years comes a leader this bad.

Send military into Venezuela? OK, then Chicago.

8-13-17 Sunday   TV commercial: baby sitter charges $30 then adds $20 in hidden fees. She is wearing high heels digging into the foot stool. Pretty slick.

Repubs cringe over Trump weakness on KKK. T: David Duke? I don't know him.

The media is the voice of the people and the people are saying, We don't like you Trump. Supporting media is getting weaker.   If Rush Limbaugh bails, you know he's done.

Trump when he was 27 put together the failing Commodore Hotel deal with the City of New York. He received tax abatement and the city received profit sharing. He renovated the hotel and it did well but the city began to miss their money. Before it was done, T bilked the city out of millions of dollars. Crooked then, crooked now. He kept 2 sets of books.

8-14-17 Monday   There are fewer secrets these days.

Obama did not speak of Islamic terrorists because he did not want to impugn the innocent ones.   Trump won't speak of White supremacists because he likes them.

Trump's fuzz speak keeps us off balance, confused and enrages the media thus increasing attention. He wins, we lose. Trump is full of hate and expresses it all the time.   A liar is often corrupt to the core.

The fake news portrayed the run over Charlottesville girl as fat, slutty and a victim of road rage.

We have gotten to know Trump. What's to like? Leaks might save us.

Trump won, North Korea can win. One nuke into California cities and they've won regardless of what we do to them.

I vote to leave historic statues alone. Are we going to rewrite Huck Fin?

Tell the truth and shame the Devil. – Rabelais

It's hard to hate close up. It was tempting to kill surrendering Germans but our troops held back. After capture, the Germans could not believe we were not going to attack Russia. Only Patton new the wisdom of this.

8-15-17 Tues. Remember Rosie O'Donnell vs Trump? He creamed her because he is the insulter in chief. I felt sorry for her and embarrassed by him.

Trump campaigns all the time and even has TV ads praising him.

Tree cutter to bid job by looking at our Google picture?

Bannon should go. – Scaramoochie   But Bannon is Trump's connection to the Alt-Right and that's a big part of the Trump base. Trump's second speech better but still insincere. (Charlottesville killing)

Eisenhower is the first president I remember. They say he did little but the interstates were built during his terms. Quite a lot, I'd say.

8-16-17 Wed. There is going to be a hanging. Trump is the destructor. I went to a Klan meeting in college, boring, cross burning, but now T has given them new life. I hope repubs get rid of T before Mueller does.

We can still lose the Civil War. Bannon half under the bus. I can't believe Trump still has 34% support. Send him a white conical hat.

Zillow seems to be rocking real estate like nothing else.

Who said, Kiss my grits?

8-17-17 Thurs. The Alt-Right shows some people have a higher hate content.

We are ready for the eclipse, cataract glasses.

Trump is such a big disappointment I can only image the joy at his departure, up there with first born, marriage, college graduation.

No new trial for Corrine Brown !

Vystar Credit Union won't return my calls or answer emails.

Trump won by winging it, no need for him to change now.

Pence is being groomed for president.

8-18-17 Friday   The military has separated from Trump on race. T wants a private military to better serve him.

Most of the media calls out Trump's lies.

Get the Confederate museum here in Jacksonville.

Trump's fantasies are actually war crimes.   He's not resigning until he pardons everyone.   He's addicted to TV and also hates the coverage.

Rush Limbaugh said the number of white supremacists is about equal to the number of trans-gender people here. Nice of him to link them in this way.

8-19-17 Saturday   Goodbye Steve Bannon, the propagandist. Kept Trump level. OMG, what now? Bannon was hired so T could get campaign money from a billionaire.

Pence is a professional politician.

Bannon gonna have fun at Brietbart shooting at everyone. Bannon was the worst of Trump yet T has plenty of worst left.

The "jobs president" has been abandoned by dozens of CEOs.

Trump is dying of 1,000 cuts most self inflicted.

One man can F___U_ the whole country.

Bannon gave Trump a soul, dark though it was.

8-20-17 Sunday   Dad got a new hip in the nursing home and he didn't even know it.

I bet they don't tear down the old slave market in St. Augustine.

Only democrats are now left at the white house.

I found a 2016 penny and it is thinner than older pennies.

8-21-17 Monday   Jerry Lewis died at 91. Martin and Lewis kept me entertained as a kid and when they broke up, I felt like it was a divorce.

I never thought about statues until a week ago.

The economy is like a great rolling ocean and no president can do much about it.

At best, Trump is a shallow thinker with no thought given to backlash or downside. At worst, he is delusional, as with the numbers voting or attending his inauguration.

Here in Jacksonville, Florida, we have 90% coverage so I plan on watching the eclipse from the street in front of my house.

If you go up in space say 50,000 miles, the moon will appear larger and the eclipse effect will likely diminish.

Is Trump crazy, too sick to lead? Is he between Nixon and Hitler? These questions are being asked with seriousness after Charlottesville.

8-22-17 Tues. Candidate Trump: Get out of Afghanistan now. President Trump: Maybe we'll stay awhile.

The eclipse still provides good scientific information today. Eclipse is being re-run at 10 pm. Eclipse glasses now only $10. Trump called off the eclipse as fake science. Doesn't like the competition.

Trump and family break Secret Service budget.

Destroyer McCain hits tanker in Indonesia. Doesn't anyone look out the windows anymore?

Steve Bannon is now ready to fire, aim. Sarah Palin gets her GED.

A lying president complains about fake news? Paalleeeeze.

8-23-17 Wed. Trump is making Russia happy, not us. Strong arm ok in Mafia, not politics. Repubs: Impeachment likely.

Pardon Joe Arpaio who is only up for 6 months? Who is showboating now?

Trump likes fighting period, winning secondary. Drain swamp means piss everyone off and appoint unqualified people to high posts.

Rich guys are not gods. Trump vs McConnell. My $ is on Mitch.

Science is right on the eclipse but not global warming?

Bravado got Trump elected, and it will get him deposed.

8-24-17 Thurs. Trump is good at dividing people, pits groups against others, like with his staff, sits back and enjoys the match.

Attendance at his rallies thinning. We have 2 Ts, scripted and off the rails. Two for the price of four. Salesman, liar, president, we weep.

Trump is building a cult following. For what reason we can only guess. He has no idea of what good health care is, he's just mad he lost.

His crooked media shtick is wearing thin.   Slow and steady, justice is on his ass. New in Washington? He could learn it in a day.

8-25-17 Friday   Trump's total gaffs burn the brain.

It has been reported that Carl Icahn got millions from a Trump insider affiliation/position.

The Steele Dossier on Trump Russia corruption is almost totally verified.

Which one is more corrupt, Trump or Kushner?

Who believes Mexico will pay for the wall?

Without immigrants, Trump would have no wives.

Clapper says Trump unfit to lead.

In Jacksonville, the house and apartment are now of equal desirability according to statistics and sales.

Remember Trump saying, Take the Iraqi oil. Now he has a similar goal in Afghanistan, mine the minerals. That would validate the Taliban position that we are in this just for profit.

8-26-17 Saturday   I was a centrist but Trump has made me a democrat.

Trump's Alt-Right qualifications have been validated completely.

Good luck Houston. Flooding from Hurricane Harvey. 3,500 FEMA trailers left in the field after Katrina in 2005.

The power of the corrupt to corrupt those who look up to him is almost absolute.

Hillary could not process how many people hated her or how the simian Trump could win.

Leaks and his own hand will impeach Trump.

8-27-17 Sunday One crook pardons another one, they take care of their own.

Dad boxed in college so we followed it but when Cassius Clay changed into Muhammad Ali, I moved on.

This is a lousy job if you don't steal. – Gov. Claude Kirk

Earthquakes are caused by promiscuous women. – Iranian cleric

Fox News trotted out the sad Joe Arpaio so many times, ugh.

Cracker Barrel is fun, has good food, cheap but the noise level is so high you feel you have to hurry up and get out of there.

8-28-17 Monday Not evacuating Houston, Texas for Harvey big mistake in hindsight. What happens if same storm hits Jacksonville, Florida?

Al Gore dumped his mistress right after his divorce was final. What does that tell you ladies who are dating married men? Often, mistresses are less accomplished and attractive than the wife.

The pardoning of Joe Arpaio sends a message to all the Trump/Russia buddies: I've got your back too. Trust me and you will get off if you keep quiet. Do you feel lucky punk? Do you trust Trump?

8-29-17 Tues. Developers with big egos will get needed money from any source no matter the risk. Trump and family have many ties to Russian banks/lenders.

Houston's 2.5 million people are really 5 million if you count the illegals. Perfect storm or global warming.

Trump's lawyers have lawyers. At some point the lawyer becomes an accomplice. Russia and Trumps are inter-twined. Trump ran for president for the money.

The warm/hot Gulf had something to do with the storm's severity and difficultness to predict. Preppers have been rewarded.

Trumpers think God sent him, that he is some kind of deity.

Wait 2 months to see a doctor and you get an assistant. Do you worry if you have two illnesses lawyers advertise on TV?

Big dogs knock down fences.

Trump's presidency is the anti-Obama's. Melania likes Michelle's speeches though.

Is Trump the worst president ever? Not yet. In terms of actual damage there are worse ones but he is potentially the worst as he could, would not mind destroying our system entirely.   And he's only been in power 8 months.

8-30-17 Wed. Houston police speak Spanish. The area is flat and they have placed growth over drainage.

Preachers who get rich, risk the wrath of the flock.

Melania Trump in 5" heels arrives for her flood.

NK shoots missile over Japan. Isn't that like shooting into a house? Everybody is just so relieved it didn't go to Guam.

8-31-17 Thurs. Trump was borrowing from Putin during the campaign. Trump cannot pardon state crimes.

No zoning in Texas means dangerous chemical factories mixed in with houses and schools.

Mountains of incompetency evidence pilling up against Trump, but I fear, the only way to get rid of him is if the economy collapses.

A Jacksonville policeman shot a drunk 13 times.

Al Gore calls the Houston flood a rain bomb from global warming.

Obama golfed during Katrina. He wasn't president then.

Harvey too nice a name for this storm. I'm calling it Pussgrab.

All my exes are from Texas!

9-1-17 Friday   Technology does not replace caring for people.

Joel Osteen has gotten rich filling a need. He motivates people with Christ lurking nearby. A pastor can be rich but not showy.

The 1963 movie, VIPs has moguls stranded in an airport. Today, they'd just take their own jets.   Elizabeth Taylor and Richard Burton had a love-hate relationship on and off screen.

Trump reminds me of Goldfinger without the charm.

Banking can be ethically challenged.

Un has a new missile, the Long Dong.

The capital of Texas is Austin.

All new laws should reference where the constitution justifies it.

9-2-17 Sat. I have done 15,000 appraisals in my life and am now looking for one of them. Court ordered summons where my report is part of the case.

Martha's brother has congestive heart failure. Sad but the body gets so wracked with pain, dying is good.

9-3-17 Sun.   5,000 things a day must go right for us to keep living.

The Indians have not progressed in part due to hanging on to their old culture. They won't allow autopsies for example.

Texas is the last bastion of right wing freedom. No zoning, no rules, no regulations. Did this contribute to flooding from Hurricane Harvey?

Trump can't stand his staff, only his family who has learned how to bow and scrape.

9-4-17 Monday   North Korea vs America about the same as the colonists vs England in size. Un knows we invaded Iraq and thinks nuclear power will save him.   Give him a seat at the table but stay loaded and aimed.

Hillary accepted Bill's affairs, seems a bit opportunistic.

Trump is the bull who carries around his own china shop.

9-5-17 Tues. During the campaign, T said we have a movement. I think he was referring to white supremacy. Trump's love for the alt-right has un-nerved many republicans.

Trump has enlisted Godzilla to take a look at NK.

Raise the debt ceiling and cut taxes? WTF

Gen. Schwarzkopf had it right, engage with maximum force.

A teacher must prick egos and make them work hard so they can learn.

Bernie Sanders is the Ralph Nader of today.

Tim Tebow fans will want to read, How the Lions Ate Tim Tebow.

9-6-17 Wed.   A corrupt politician is being investigated. Several crimes will come to light previously unknown.

Trump's rubber mind has made Putin the world leader.

DACA for all immigrants? (Deferred Action for Child Arrivals)

Trump's main road is immigrants are bad. Non white people are bad. Sessions is a hick.

Trump's plan to scare Un has failed bigly.

Remember hurricane Andrew blew away the Miami weather center.

Bought non cook easy to open food for Irma. Poptarts. Ate them all the first day.

10,000 septic tanks in Houston flooded. We have a problem.

9-7-17 Thurs. Facebook admits they sold ads to Russian operatives to badmouth Clinton.

Irma, Cat-5, has sucked up sharks validating that awful movie.

Trump gets Ivanka to bow at meeting. A visual treat to move the crowd. Trump deals with dems – good.

Bernie Sanders is the democratic tea party.

Draw down your pool if hurricane coming.

Three hurricanes are now boiling in the Caribbean.

All North Korea wants is South Korea.

Bobby Kennedy was against college deferments from the draft. He thought it elitist. Me too, but I took full advantage of it. Vietnam was no WWII.

9-8-17 Fri. Trump Jr. not as good a liar as daddy. Trump and friends all crooked so how will Mueller know when to quit investigating?

Irma and Jose, if the right one don't get you, the left one will. Two hurricanes for the price of one. Global warming, anyone? Trump is building a great wall to keep out Jose. I didn't want gas until I found out there wasn't any.

9-9-17 Sat. Flooding two floors up could loosen foundation so that a tall condo falls over in hurricane winds.

How do you hunker? Liquor store closed. Leave the duct tape off your windows. Today, I look out over a sea of junk food. Hallelujah! Limited water but plenty of Sprite Zero.

Trump made a deal with democrats to raise debt ceiling. Lots of debt OK.

Trump is very into the media, it has made him what he is and can tear him down. His ego is god to him fed by money and praise.

Rachel Maddow is still in danger, not from Trump directly but one of his many crazed fans. Lucky most don't know who she is.

I began smoking by taking a few out of mother's pack. By college I was fully into it and hooked for 12 years.

9-10-17 Sun. Hurricane fringe being felt. TV makes it sound like power outage is mandatory.

Anderson Cooper forgot Irma's name and called it Irene.

Some people are praying the storm goes somewhere else. Not very God like.

Kaepernick is getting a real estate license.

The Times Union delivered the paper. Worth every penny.

9-12-17 Tues. Missed Monday due to Irma. Both our baths have windows so it's the hall for the safe room.

This storm may set a rain record. Fox's Sheppard Smith called Janice Dean the weather machine.

Out of 25 cranes in downtown Miami, 2 fell. Thankfully, trees bend most of the time. Is Rush still here, how bout Trump?

Irma bigger than Harvey. A moment of silence for 9-11. During Matthew our power was off 24 hours but only 19 hours for Irma. The JEA, Jacksonville Electric Authority, may have learned from Matthew, one year ago.

Two generators going near our house. Are mufflers illegal?

Our back fence blew down so our neighbor now knows our dogs. The pool is brown and has wall to wall branches. Getting lawn furniture out of a pool is a lot harder than putting it in. Remembered candles, forgot matches.

9-13-17 Wed. Cool sunny day. What a difference.

Russia wanted Trump to be president too badly.

Trump was doing a tower deal in Moscow during the campaign and asking Putin for help.

A high level book is coming on Trump/Russia. T: Only liars need apply for high level positions. What other kind of person would a lying president want? It's the president's job to learn the truth. How can he do that when he just makes it up?

Trump's new book is: Praise for the Ayatollah.

Un knows crazy Bush toppled Hussein for being offensive. He also knows who's in the Whitehouse now is even more thin skinned. Bush toppled a dictator with no nukes while Trump lets Un who has nukes run free.

Did yard work all day long. Tired as only physical work can do.

In 20 years, cleaning the ocean will be a big employer. In 10 years, the electric car will be normal.

The Florida Keys, God bless em, have never held much appeal for me.

9-14-17 Thurs. Hillary seemed unhinged on the CNN interview.

In Russia, they shoot dissident journalists and Trump smiles inside. Trump gives Russia a state to pay his debts. The media pumped up T during campaign and now he hates them for exposing his lies.

Trump brought hate and nudity to the debate. Hillary brought decency and competence. T lined up Bill's mistresses, paid 0 taxes and stalked H and the audience ate it up. Trump lives for good ratings.

Remember when the Joker fell at the end of the movie and kept on laughing even dead? That's today's Hillary and Bernie.

Nixon was a crook but he got a lot done. It took 2 years to nail him. Trump runs a 24 hour campaign all day, every day.

A retired cop friend of mine said of Trump, "He talks like us." Does that mean prejudice?

9-15-17 Friday   Hillary is talky, even boring, the ultimate sin for a politician.

Un seems to be saying, Come-on, let's all die, it'll be fun. Sen. Moynihan was ready to bomb him in the '90's when his nuclear program began.

Trump working with dems has enraged his base and conservatives. Some repubs are blocking Mueller.

Office Max and Office Depot merged. They have a complicated system of rewards or discounts. My discount card has been inept since the merger. Even after discount, the ink was $33, so the answer is, Walmart, where the same ink was $21.

9-16-17 Sat.   Like Apple, Facebook, it seems placed their own interests above the country's.

A Home Advisor member said after I cancelled the appointment that the calls cost them $50. She just wanted to let me know. True or not I threw that name away.

Russia massing troops near Belarus.

Hillary is toxic to democrats.

There is no limit on how long a dog can bark and we have seven of them.

9-17-17 Sunday   Should the polygraph (lie detector) be admissible in court?

If I watch a one hour show on one channel and a 30 minute show on another channel, I should be able to avoid most commercials, right? Not so much.

After Hurricane Irma, there are many acres of tree trash waiting to be picked up, yet, I can't see where anything is missing. The town is still very green.

Social media is to enhance your life, not replace it. Trump is still making the media his bitch.

The Chicken Ranch in Nevada is for sale, $2.6 million. No word on whether that includes the girls.

Every year North Korea ties up a trillion dollars of our military assets and they have been doing it for most of a century. Who's the crazy one now?

Firing missiles over Japan or any country is an act of war.

Sanctuary cities are so numerous, they seem to have been approved by the people.

The decline in books is real, but writing has changed from paper to social media where every day, my friends write the equivalent of several books.

Hell is calling ATT, the vestige of the original telephone company, Bell Telephone. The day after he left, system goes down.

9-18-17 Monday   Hillary stalks Trump. I like it.

Putin wants to destroy democracies worldwide and he may be behind the sound attacks on our diplomats in Cuba.

Son in law, Dave to run in Iron Man in Chattanooga this Sunday.

Trump has a chance to fix NK. He is crazy enough. No past sane presidents have been able to do it.

Martha looses toothpaste top and squeezes it in the middle. Robert Downey 6' plays Charlie Chaplin 5'1". Is this right?

Our frothy leader is continually baited by the media. Rose asked Bannon if Trump was smart. Sort of, he rises to the occasion. He is a good attack dog and drops criticism of himself unless it portrays his inability to draw a large crowd.   Is Trump the most hated man in America?

9-19-17 Tues. The FBI picked Manafort's front door lock to serve search warrant. Mueller is handling this like a mob case.   Russian radio now in Washington, DC.

Generators don't work if they flood.

Is Hillary a sore loser? Many dems say she should just go away.

If we had not gone into Korea in 1950, what would it be like today?

Do not mistake toothpaste for rectal cream.

Listening to good books or reading them does not make us authors.

9-20-17 Wed. Frankenstein comes true, not by stolen corpses but by parts made in a laboratory.

In Trumpland, the truth is whatever was said last. This is a seething sea of mental illness. Hitler had little trouble getting demented people to follow him.

As the Russia probe tightens, some of T's top staff and family will flee the country.   Thug Trump has been using campaign funds to pay his legal bills. There is a white power hand sign. Not only does T lie constantly but he makes up facts.

Melania may wake up some day to the golden trap she has fallen into.

9-20-17 Wed. T's UN speech was raw, disrespectful and dangerous. Unhinged. Thuggish.

Obamacare is as good as we can get?

Nikki Haley of the UN scares Trump. Nothing is worse than a competent woman who might run against him.

Trump believes all Obama stuff is wrong. Or his supporters think it is.

You can get high top jeans for only $800.

9-21-17 Thurs. Lara Trump, Eric's wife, just had a baby and has dropped out of the news. Kushner and Ivanka will be back.

Realtors are wondering if they should warn ocean front buyers of the impending dangers.

Trump and Russia both untrustworthy so they either get along or fight.

Jack died 3-16 and Ben died 9-17 so my wife, Martha, has no siblings left.

Make and sell a sound system so your Ford Pinto sounds like a Lamborghini.

Melania Trump gives goody goody speeches but why bother when her Thug husband runs rampant over everyone.

Nixon had his tapes and Trump has emails.

9-22-17 Friday Trump stealing government money hand over fist.

Un calls Trump out. Let's fling a few atom bombs, just for fun.

Loreal heiress leaves $40 billion estate. Trump's new tax plan leaves it untaxed. I know this is so important to his supporters.

Trump did well with China if you trust China. We trusted Iran yet T harangues that deal all day long.

The media focuses on individuals and thus adds value to human life while T denigrates groups of people and calls others names.

The Germans said of Patton, the lack of war will kill him. Patton died Dec. 1945 in a car accident.

The UN, United Nations, was founded to prevent war. Trump spits on that tradition.

9-23-17 Sat. Would Trump insult McCain again? Yes, he's that stupid. God bless McCain.

There is no Dotard in Korean language. What they called him was fire ringed stupid old man.

The jelly fish has no brain yet it sleeps.

We order Chinese food delivered once a month but they have no record of us and no speaka da English.

The pool service got the pool blue again after 2 visits but it's now full of leaves from an early fall dump.

9-24-17 Sunday Some yard trash has been picked up from Irma. Gas mileage on my 4 cylinder Buick is about the same as my former 8 cylinder Mercury.

Trump gets a package from NK labeled, My Sweet Baboo, naturally he opens it. (It's an H bomb) Are NK quakes part of their atomic testing?

Some women's only job is boyfriends. Power of words, habit is often an addiction as in smoking.

Clinton and Bush: Everyone should own a home. Not so today.

9-25-17 Monday   NK let CNN in for a tour. We ain't so bad. In fact we're kind of cute. Some beautiful scenery. Lots of nice buildings and cell phones, all government controlled. Few cars. Bikes are big. Pictures of leader all over. No God, just leader. China has greatly aided in their prosperity. A lot of NK stuff looks familiar. Taken from us by China and reformatted into Korean. China loves NK. China transforming them from dependent to ally. Makes sense.

Mrs. Columbo has no first name. Dave finishes Iron Man.

Repubs: Let states do health care.   Uhuh.

Trump only knows how to campaign. We have George Wallace back again.

Trump blasts NFL. You'd think he'd be helping Puerto Rico get over their storm damage.

Many people cheer Kaperdunk.   Jacksonville Jaguars win in London.

Trump to repeal and replace Iran deal.   Uhuh.

9-26-17 Tues. I remember a 1952 comic book about nuclear war here in America. The hero pilot took an A bomb rather than let Washington be blown up. Now with Un and Trump, it could happen.

We exploded 100 H bombs in the Pacific before Kennedy halted testing.

Is Manafort in Iraq? Is he coming back?   Is Trump ever going to do something good?

Kapperdunk's original point has been lost. Has Trump turned it into racism? Maybe should not mix sports and protest. Maybe protest on your own time, not on the job.

Does Un think "rocket man" is funny? Weiner warms it for 21 months in federal care.

My granddaughter Lindsay and her step daughter Madison got on CH 4 local news regarding Be Kind to people. I'm proud.

9-27-17 Wed. A lying president cannot command respect, cannot lead. All T's close ppl have lawyered up or should. Spicer has a diary. DEA head quits, said T has no respect for the law.

T: Even tho the Puerto Ricans are poor, we gonna help em.

Chubby Hubby is an unfortunate name for ice cream. So is Moose Tracks.

Rommel and Doenitz were great commanders squashed by a weak leader.

Wind breaks the weak branches.

NK has sunk SK ships and shot our planes out of the sky. It's about time for some ass whoopin.   NK has declared war on us because of T's language.

If I could be other ppl, I'd be McCain over Trump.

9-28-17 Thurs. Russia is very hostile toward us, Donald. I believe it was Russia, not Cuba who tried to hurt our diplomats. Facebook has entered the world state confused.

Trump pummeling North Korea just makes them more important.   The T atmosphere has allowed Roy Moore and his type to rise back up.

Women rejoice. You can drive in Saudi Arabia if your husband lets you. Political arguments are all about who gets the last word.

Puerto Rico needs leadership. T could not lead out of a paper bag. PR will be his Katrina. T paying his Russia lawyers out of inauguration $. His buds not so much. Tax cuts do not pay for themselves.

Apparently, dogs do not get hoarse from barking. Milkbone has made a treat with a hole in it for easy dispensing of pills dogs need. Hallelujah.

9-29-17 Friday North Korean executions are carried out by banks of machine guns such that nothing is left of the body except a red spot.

Trump tax plan: $50 for you, $1 billion for me.

The latest career crook to be exposed in the Trump WH is Price of HHS. Trump likes crooks, he feels at home with them.

In T land, the best liar gets all the marbles. He creates reality with instant lies covered up by more lies. We saw this in OJ Simpson too.

Spitting on our country is a poor way to protest a valid issue. (NFL kneeling during Anthem)

Crowley Shipping of Jacksonville, Florida gave a boat load of supplies to Puerto Rico but forgot about getting the stuff distributed.

Is Trump going to Hefner's funeral? I'm taking Melania. Hugh Hefner brought class to men's magazines. Lucky he got Marilyn Monroe for his first issue. Playboy goes limp 10 minutes in tribute.

9-30-17 Sat. Tom Price out at HHS. Too many tax paid trips. I giggle when Trump complains about other's ethics. Press is sniffing for others like Price. There are about five. Does T ever wish he hadn't demeaned the press? I doubt he's that smart. High turnover shows T vast incompetence. Trump news comes Friday at five.

China will not give up NK or give up on them but they would take em over.

Trump flies over Puerto Rico on the way to golf and pitches a few hamburgers out the window.   A million Puerto Ricans could move to Florida.

RIP Hugh Hefner. The Playboy founder rebelled from the puritanical way he was raised.

Lady Di asked me to the Ball but because I was a commoner, I had to stand by the door and introduce people who came in. Behold Marshall Zukoff and his brother Marshall Jackoff.   Then I had to leave because of throwing water balloons.   (dream)

Warren Buffett is known as the burger chomping billionaire.

10-1-17 Sunday. Kushner is a ticking time bomb. US citizens are up against the world's best liar. T puts lies into other's mouth.

Did Hugh Hefner go to hell?

Roy Moore and Trump. Where is the cave man?

Sonic attack in Cuba on our diplomats could have been done by the Russians or all a lie meant to undo what Obama has done.

Trump is so afraid of criticism, he criticizes everyone else.

10-2-17 Monday Trump's house of lies will come down. Trump care works because you die. Top business ppl saying T is a dumpster fire.

There is a great need for labor in Houston, Florida and Puerto Rico. Can anyone see inflation coming?

OJ is out. White ladies grab your valuables. I bet he was a prison hero. Got to knock off two white ppl and got away with it. Headed for Vegas and the showgirls.

As I was in bed before sleep thinking of Trump the word Self-God came into my mind.

10-3-17 Tues. Shooter had a love-hate with Las Vegas. Big gambler, probably not a Muslim.

Life in America, the game show: Come-on folks, 59 dead, who's gonna top that? Most soldiers in Vietnam didn't kill that many.

AR-15s in stores, what could go wrong? Our first shooter with a social security card.

Gun control sounds bad. Instead use gun management or gun regulation.

He had a brother, ex wife, girlfriend, neighbors, etc. But no trail or hints of desperation. (Vegas shooter)

It's a movement folks, TrumpPutin. Seems T still running against Hillary. Is she the face of the democratic party?

10-4-17 Wed. Trump tastes foot in Puerto Rico, says, That's good. Trump threw bread to the beggars so he didn't have to touch them.

Laws easily bent by money. Feds might seize shooters estate for victim relief.   News hijacked by shooting.

If you couldn't be bothered to vote, you get Trump.

Repubs say dems took God out of schools and that is why we have shootings. God makes insane ppl too.

Dogs hunt for mailman from 4 to 6 pm. Dozens of runs at the door.

Vietnam has been called a misadventure.

10-5-17 Thurs. Rachel Maddow takes a lot of time off and they never tell us when she's gonna be gone or for how long. She's worth the wait.

Ben Carson sure is quiet.

If Trump fires everyone, won't it be hard to get replacements of quality? I doubt he cares. Is Tillerson the latest grist?

The Nevada shooter had a love hate with gambling, probably much like his feelings toward his father.

Melania Trump sounds like a talking doll.

Two hours at the vet. All sizes of dogs. Unique sense of community. All the people bound by a common interest.

Our piles of yard trash by the street have been there as long as the pyramids have stood.

10-6-17 Friday John Kelly, Chief of Staff, had his phone bugged.

Puerto Ricans call Trump a pendejo. (asshole) Inside the paper towels thrown by T is a flashlight.

After Jim Brady and Reagan were shot, automatic guns were outlawed but that law expired.   The NRA wants every American to carry a gun. They write most of the gun laws passed by republicans.

Repubs say we have shootings because dems have made us Godless. I don't think even God believes that.

Nevada shooter Paddock carried 23 weapons in 10 suitcases up to the rooms.

10-7-17 Sat. Corker: Tillerson, Mattis and Kelly are our firewall from chaos. Kelly and Tillerson are now hanging by a thread. The firewall is melting.

Trump manipulates the media all the time.

The 9-11 attackers kept their plans quiet for a year while they trained and planned it.

Firing from 32 floors up must have been like a WWII bombing raid. He tried to hit airport fuel tanks and maybe explosives in his car.

Trump's huge tax cut will just cause inflation and more debt.

Bannon feeding T lines on the failed Iran deal?

How much more can T attack the press? The British have a recall system. We need that.

10-8-17 Sunday Trump's sloppy language could start a war with North Korea. Un knows how to insult Trumpy.

Trump speaks on another man's molestation of women. Sad.

Shooter was an SOB but nothing foretold the Las Vegas shooting.

We ate at Copelands which has every Sat and Sun a huge buffet. Crowds cram around the tables but we forsake the extra plate for $2 more.   Leaving however, I have to admit I thought I could grab a sausage and no one would know.

10-9-17 Monday I miss letters from people. I still send a few.

We have a ceramic turkey on our dining room table.

OJ wants $5 million for his first interview out of jail.

20,000 phones and purses were left in Vegas and are now being returned to owners or heirs.

Lying is a disease and Trump is spreading it like never before. Also the notion that you can lie your way out of problems.

401k funds with Puerto Rican bonds may be a sell.

Trump turnover is so high, it's hell for us. Many have left because of Russia ties.

10-10-17 Tues. Trump's first wife, Ivana, called herself the first lady which in a way she was. (hyperbole) Melania took offense.

Trump was brought to us by Russian ads on Facebook and other platforms.

Puerto Rico, the forgotten state, will hang around Trump's neck like a dirty toilet lid. History will fester this hurricane problem into a mega failure.

Trump says he invented the words, Fake news.

The Northern California fire grew to 25,000 acres in 24 hours.

One of my FB friends moved the yard trash left over from Hurricane Irma off his grass. A kind soul and more energetic than me.

10-11-17 Wed. Weinstein counselor is Bill Cosby. Ailes, O'Reilly, Bill Clinton, on down the line. Weinstein's beautiful wife left him.

Agonizing long time before cops show up at Las Vegas hotel shooter's room.

If Trump is not mentally ill, he's close enough to get rid of. He's evil.

Voters threw a brick through a plate glass window when they elected T. Dems better notice.

Tillerson, an Eagle Scout, wanted to quit when Trump made his speech to the Boy Scouts.

Pence, Sarah Sanders and Conway all speak perfect Trumpeeze.

My Mercury is gone. My old shoes are gone. Old stuff is good stuff.

Corker may garner support from repubs who are not retiring.

Trump wall approved but only for 6".

10-12-17 Thurs. I don't think I would have held up a severed Trump head image for laughs. Cathy Griffin not around for this year's New Years Eve.

There is only a 30% chance Trump will finish his first term. – Steve Bannon.

I asked Facebook what is a choke, after watching Jay Leno's Garage and found out.

Girls in the Boy Scouts?

Does NK have submarines with nuclear missiles near our coasts? Trump doesn't care about deaths, nothing is his fault.

Trump would shut down our free press in an instant if allowed to do so. – Jake Tapper

10-13-17 Friday Why do girls want to join the boy scouts?

Trump's main agenda is killing off Obama's agenda.   A former Trump lawyer represented the Russians in the Trump Tower meeting.   Nixon is the top legal precedent for Trump.

Trump's god complex diminishes the advice of others.

Trump says the rising stock market will pay off the debt. Huh. That's a slick one.

I went to a new dentist. Initial consultation is only $75 but soon the big bucks become apparent. $900 for 3 fillings all close together. Digital x-rays enlarge the mouth, teeth, cavities, scary. Expert marketing.

10-14-17 Sat. The wall is Trump's only agenda except for bug spraying Obama's agenda. Are his voters that racist? Yes.

Mueller will find T unfit for office, at the very least. Many ppl who voted for him may now realize they made a mistake but would not admit it.

Priebus singing like a bird. Manafort got $60 million from Russians while he was Trump's campaign manager.

Cousin Jonathan's foreign policy was on his T-shirt, Nuke Iran.

The phone has sunk to a new low. Collections, scams and sales.

Name calling not good for diplomacy.

Obamacare one tough nut.

We replaced our 42" TV with a 55" one.

10-15-17 Sunday Puerto Rico is prime for a Russian takeover or some other power to influence.

North Korea could be responsible for our short romance with Cuba. They could have introduced the sound guns that ran off our diplomats.

10-16-17 Monday Melania looks so miserable it's making her look ugly.

Larry Flynt is offering $10 million to get Trump impeached.

Did Tillerson call Trump a moron or not, yes.

Any kid could be the next Leonardo da Vinci. Take them to the library or bookstore.

All good things are wild and free. – Blank book cover

10-17-17 Tues. Trump said Pence wants to kill gays.
Pence not very bright. – New Yorker, Rachel Maddow

Many close to Trump now facing bankruptcy over Russia legal fees. The T presidency can be summed up as: Chaos.

How many of us insult people you will need? Trump does. McConnell standing beside Trump, if looks could kill.

Heaven and hell same place, only difference is mindset.

Hillary fell coming down stairs in heels, with coffee, and broke a toe, or the Russians threw a banana peel.

10-18-17 Wed. Puerto Rico's festering mess is coming for Trump like a steam roller. Media savvy T should get this off the news.

Wells Fargo held up, gave IOU.

NK hacked our battle plans from SK.

Pence makes visitors pray?

10-19-17 Thurs. Sessions lies almost as good as Trump. T will be done-in from within, like Caesar. T is a brilliant politician but vicious and untruthful.

There is a Benghazi in every administration.

Making racism legal again.

Maybe T shouldn't call survivors of fallen troops.

10-20-17 Friday Gen. Kelly goes political, better at it than Trump. No experience T and no experience Tillerson, what could go wrong?

Chad, one of our best allies, is now on Trump's travel ban. Could be reason 4 soldiers killed in Niger. Trump won't say, he's a coward.

CIA chief now lies for Trump. Trump has no tact, no caring. Dylann Roof tried to start a race war but T is doing it.

There is no discrimination in the army, even in the '60's when I was in it.

Trump will stop at nothing to shut down the free press. Truth kills his ego, his everything.

Your surgery on the internet? Then cheap knock offs will be done in basements.

When we do get to Mars, it's 30 million years too late.

Roomba meets dog turd. Turd wins.

Wet spot ceiling? Could be leaking ducts. That can crash a ceiling.

10-21-17 Sat. Decency laws will be passed because of Trump. I will post about him until he's out of office. Rather than showboat us into a war, his main danger is to spread corruption all over our land, make it normal. Geo. W. Bush had to speak up about it.

Corruption is easy to get, hard to get rid of.

Trump sleeps 4 hours a night, eats hamburgers and steak and buys gold rimmed mirrors.

Cut corporate taxes and the bosses will pass the savings along to the workers? Uhuh!

Trump speaks like a man who learned to talk before writing was perfected.

10-22-17 Sunday Name the Las Vegas shooter___________

Trump has a fake Renoir and a fake Time cover.   Forbes lists his net worth at $3 billion, not the $10 billion he says. CNN keeps track of his lies which T says is fake news. If the fake is fake, what's real?

Trump to pay his buddies legal bills for T-Russia? Ha Ha Ha

Many voters thought T would straighten out after being elected. Ha Ha Ha.

Bill O'Reilly has a clear conscience after he paid off 6 women, last one $32 million?   Bill is a Trump double.

The T stain is spreading to hurt formerly good and innocent people.

10-23-17 Monday I chose my career at age 19 after 3 hours thought.

Our children are being raised by televisions.

Government is the ultimate blame game.

Have to watch some Fox due to Martha. They say the media is so mean to T. Never has a president been so mean and hostile to the media.

T paying associate's attorney fees so they don't roll on him?

It will take 10,000 workers to undo the Trump harm. Trump = O'Reilly.

The press conference is just a T parrot session. T is a press driven leader.

Canada is our largest trading partner. China's president Xi is personable like Reagan.

Fireworks boom half the nights now. One of our 7 dogs is afraid of it.

10-24-17 Tues. All advice is based on partial information.

Bannon is Trump's Cheney. Trump's new book is: Al Capone not so Bad. Trump has spilled a huge bucket of hate over America.

ISIS and locals combined to kill our 4 soldiers in Niger.

So, all news outlets are fake except Fox. What would a jury say?

O'Reilly brought down by journalists. He said, I am not Harvey Weinstein.

A young war widow vs a lying president. Oh my. Sooner or later, a black will be lynched.   Trump is protecting Putin or vice versa.

Hello fall, free air conditioning.

Trump fueled hate against the NFL has filtered down to the Florida Gators.

Former Gen. Kelly, now T's chief of staff, has been corrupted by T.

Cutting taxes will grow us out of the deficit. Ha. Ha. Ha.

If you want to simplify the tax system, get rid of corporate tax altogether. Individual payments would increase but it would be simpler.

Howard the Duck or Killer Klowns from Outer Space. Which is the best movie?

A 3 year old Jacksonville boy died when he fell into a ball park septic tank. Who left the lid off?

10-25-17 Wed. Trump gets money from Russia. That alone should send up red flags. T lawyer Cohen loud and profane, hooda thought? A lying president has no respect for laws either.

Bannon may run for president after Trump destroys himself.

When T insults NK's Un, he is also insulting the people's god.

Either be like Trump or get out, the repubs seem to be saying. Corker, Flake and McCain are getting out.

Fox News seems so surprised when ppl don't like T. Maybe it's because he's a huge A__Hole. Dems starting impeachment?

Either elect an honest man or pass hundreds of laws meant to rein him in. T wants 100% justice for himself.

Hundreds of TV medicines all bad when taken with alcohol.

Three year old boy fell in a septic with fiberglass lid at a ball park. The conservative city of Jacksonville saved $20 on the lid and cost a boy's life. They better get out their checkbook.

10-26-17 Thurs. Senate and house committees drop Russia investigation. Tom Steyer starts a brilliant TV ad campaign to get rid to Trump.

Trump will self impeach. – Geo W Bush   Trump to impeach Hillary. Trump is either a compulsive liar or mentally ill.

George Will said of Pence: A sycophantic poodle. On Trump, has a 6th grade mentality and doesn't need reality.

Trump is old, fat, eats a lot of meat, no exercise, little sleep, how does he even keep living?

Paddock's father a bank robber, brother arrested for child porn, the answer to the Nevada shooting is simply bad genes.

RIP Fats Domino. By all accounts, he was a gentleman.

Cutting taxes when we have 20 trillion in national debt is stupid and reckless.

Hominy for lunch aka butter soup.

10-27-17 Friday   Trump is entertaining but that's all you are going to get.   Many big money people on his side.

30,000 auto deaths a year, 30,000 gun deaths a year, 64,000 overdose deaths a year. T's fight against opioids is not funded.

T thinks wall will keep out the Puerto Ricans.

If you can't hold it, do you really own it? – TV ad for buying gold as an investment. Remember brand X?

10-28-17 Sat. Drones to Mars.

A lying president is inherently corrupt and if he doesn't fall on one charge, there will be another. Look for bribes.

Which comes first, trial or impeachment?

Pence knows a lot, he could leak, but he'd go down too.

Use a Certified Financial Planner for all you investment/estate needs.

Puerto Rico needs a Berlin Airlift size effort but with so few votes, well you know...

10-29-17 Sunday A brain surgeon (Ben Carson) knows nothing about housing. (Director of HUD)

Florida Trend Magazine devoted an entire issue to Water World or as the seas rise. Pretty bleak.

Fox News has given us the opinion: All politicians lie. Gee.

Stop the mortgage interest deduction at one million dollars.

Give baloney for Trick or Treat.

Will we miss Trump? He is very entertaining. Comics love him.

Bella (Yorkie from hell) aka known as the frizz queen, needs a case of Brylcreem.

Do we even deserve democracy when 100 million ppl don't vote?

10-30-17 Monday Trump holding country hostage? T: My tax plan gonna give U $4,000, believe me. After Trump, Christie ain't so bad.

Mueller handling The Trump/Russia investigation like a drug gang or mafia. The felon will be rousted at 6 AM.

Fox reports on the Hillary-Trump-Russia scandal, it's all one thing.

Corker and Flake resist calling T a liar out of respect for the office, but do say he is untruthful. Fox News in Trump's brains.

Trump has brought the country to a cold civil war. – Bob Woodward

80 year old John McCain who has brain cancer is the only one standing between Trump and us (disaster).

I predict Flynn or Manafort will be arrested.

Puerto Rico has 15 generating stations so I think the high transmission towers were blown over. Should be relatively quick fix and not tremendously expensive. The real problem is the system has a negative net worth and operates in the red too.

10-31-17 Tues. The courts will rule you can't pardon a person if you are a party to the crime. If T pardons anyone connected with Trump/Russia, impeachment is certain.

Trump was an illegitimate pres. from day one. The $ involved in this scandal is up there with Bernie Madoff.

Manafort – tax evasion. Can you say Al Capone? Papadopoulis wore wire for 3 months? T has not drained the swamp but rather added mosquitoes.

Luxury is the most overused word in English.

Facebook will have to disclose who pays for its ads. Greed snowballs.

Before the Civil War, slave owners families married into other slave owning families. This aristocracy was the 2%, southern royalty. That is how they got the other 98% to fight their war. Slaves were given as wedding presents.

Fox News says repubs are going to fake jail. This historic day gladdens the hearts of all who desire integrity in government. Democratic victories in certain states.

11-1-17 Wed. Manafort seen polishing Trump's plane. Could Trump run away too?

Lone wolf takes 8 lives with a truck in NYC. He survived police gunfire. Waterboard him? Fake Florida driver's license?   He wanted to go to ISIS heaven.

Papodouplios unknown one minute, internationally famous the next. College grad did not know our basic laws.

If 15 people around Trump are indicted, he will say they are just washroom attendants.

11-2-17 Thurs. Steve Jobs was an ass, but a smart ass.

Steve Bannon is the real president.

Trump guilty of collusion with Russians. – Adam Schiff

Guantanamo (Gitmo) is a legal zoo. Trump should know better than to send him (NY driver) there. We need a real leader, not a fake president. Who is the real terrorist?

We are lucky if anyone remembers even one sentence we said when our life is done.

NY perp lived with 2 bullets in him. Now he gets to love on ISIS. Jacksonville police take notice. You don't have to kill everyone.

Manafort up mainly for tax evasion and money laundering.

Bike paths should have car barriers.

If you don't know how to milk a cow, you will never have to milk a cow.

Trump has to criticize, it's part of his DNA. Only problem is he's so ignorant, he doesn't know what to criticize.

11-3-17 Friday Republicans are run by the far right. — Chuck Schumer

It is likely Trump will fire Mueller. His business breeding, he just won't be able to help himself.   T does not understand separation of powers.

I was never in a car seat and never saw a kid who was.

Dad made fun of me but he also complimented me. Elixir for a child. He continued when I was grown and I began to see through some of his BS but still.....

Sessions better quit lying. (He's no Trump.)

It Takes a Village, is all I remember from Hillary's old book. It's a good title and has stuck with me.

Trump's new Fed Chairman is a moderate, Thank God.

Fox News actually is pushing the Hillary Russia scandal. Oh brother!

With 3 arrests, Trump is sweating bullets. How will he hold up when there are 15 arrests? Or when they come for his family?

When Harry Truman was a boy in Independence, Mo., Negros were not allowed in stores or the library.

11-4-17 Saturday Carter Page looks high. The Trump administration lies or covers up. Sessions can bring T down yet T berates him every time a Russia revelation is made.

Twitter turns Trump into a "drunk driver". Will future presidents use Twitter? It could be useful and time saving done right. Have someone read it before it is dumped and dump once daily.

When T says give NY terrorist the death penalty, that results in no death penalty. (Guy who drove truck down bike path.)

The senate is getting mad at Jeff Sessions, the attorney general. They will keep at him until he spills the truth.

Our justice system is the envy of the world, yet T trashes it. Moron!

Trump's tyrannical father made him mean and suspicious. Terrified of criticism.

All T has to do to North Korea is teach them how to borrow money. He's now in Asia. Will he come back?

Can T pardon himself? He can't pardon others if he was complicit in the crime. The courts may stew over this for years.

11-5-17 Sunday All the mass shooters have failed lives whether they adopt ISIS or not. And, they blame us for their troubles.

White House staff at transition: I have never before seen such massive incompetence.

60 women claim Weinstein molested them. He's going to jail.

Trump is bashing our justice system because he's a suspect.

Sarah Huckabee Sanders cleans the pigsty.   A tax cut for corporations is great for stocks and 401ks.

Hillary is history. Get the Felon in Chief.

11-6-17 Monday Saudi Arabia pays for a lot of terrorism around the world.

Trump is temporary but his lies, hatred, bigotry and racism going to be hard to get back in the bottle.

26 dead in Texas small town. Shooter went after a church. This is now a national game or sickness, almost a fad. Nobody kills Americans like Americans.

A president Trump is Russia's dream come true. T built his empire on lies so naturally his cronies are liars as well.

Hillary put more money into the campaign and that is why Bernie fell by the wayside.

Science is the search for truth.

Manafort dumps Trump.

Men and horses wore gasmasks in WWI.

Both parties are lost, say hello to Independents.

Management of people is hard, everyone can't do it.

President Ford was shot at twice, both times by a woman, both missed. One missed because a former Marine grabbed her. Then the press outed him as gay and his family disowned him.   It was 1975.

11-7-17 Tuesday Wilbur Ross, Trump's commerce secretary, linked to money laundering and Putin.

Saudi Arabia internal power struggle threatens our oil supply.

Are Kushner and Flynn next on Mueller's hit list?

An American idea has taken on solid root. A suicidal man decides to go out in a flash taking many innocent people with him.   Use an AR-15 when going to war, you are really mad at the deer or you want to kill a lot of people.

Now the Japanese know Trump's a moron.

License guns like cars. Publicize the deaths by town and date. Keep a running total. Maybe public awareness can bring these bought and paid for officials into line with public thinking.

11-8-17 Wed. Christie was the pre-Trump. Some candidates use the Trump ideas because it worked once. Trump is Babe Ruth except he can't hit.

The extra hour God gave us is still with me. Oh, wait, God didn't give it to us, we did.

Bought the Hugh Hefner commemorative book full of bunny pictures. Did he F all of them?

11-9-17 Thurs. Trump meddling in the CIA trying to turn the Trump/Russia investigation into a dead end.

Dems swept elections but don't brag. Bragging invokes Karma. Women won big in the VA legislature, a backlash from Trumpism. Trumpism is a new word meaning all things crooked.

T has met his match with lil Un. That guy can match T insult per insult. Repubs will abandon T en masse when the critical point is reached.

Doctors should share more with patients as to what's in our files. I should have been given copies of eye scans for years but I had to ask to get even one.

11-10-17 Friday Trump eats campaign words in China. He dissolves state dept. He can bend the world to his will, or shoot.

Mueller will be fired when Trump's family is arrested.

Welcome to Trump Nuts: Chock full O Crimes.

There will always be Trump supporters, those who like the Mafia, those who like violent movies and we will always have money launderers.

It seems most mental cases live in the USA. (shooters)

Trump offers knowledge that anyone can be president.

11-11-17 Saturday Trump has called the media the enemy of the USA and the opposition party. So now the media is collecting victims of sexual abuse and parading it all over the election cycle.

It has been 72 years since an atom bomb was dropped in war. Will Trump's unending ego make him do it again?

I get my gold from Rosland Capital and my art from Family Dollar.

Trump's finest hour was his win over Hillary, an event he relives at every opportunity. First Trump, then Roy Moore. The party of pedophiles.

Are evangelicals ok with rape. Is it just too much enthusiasm from the male? After all, woman is a rib from man. Oh, it happened so long ago I don't remember. Then, there is the truthful: I don't know her.

11-12-17 Sunday Trump is loyal to Putin because of the money.

Lying is criminal if others are harmed.

Define and differentiate between Donald Trump and Roy Moore.

Trump and Moore have set off the media on a 24/7 pussy grabbing hunt.

Santa Claus will pass the republican tax bill.

11-13-17 Monday Liz Smith dead at 92. She said, Trump is a horse's ass. She covered the first divorce and sided with Ivana.

Trump could at least try to lie well.

Hannity makes a good Trumper. His sponsors are leaving his show on Fox News.

80 year old John McCain, complete with brain tumor, is the only thing between us and Trump insanity.

As America's national debt increases, our power declines. Stupid politicians and greedy voters have cut taxes too much.

Our success as a nation has been insured by inclusivity, all are welcome, all contribute. Lately, congress has been using only half its people.

11-14-17 Tues. Alabama's biggest newspaper said Roy Moore should get out of the race. Girls ages 14, 16, 17 and 18 have come out saying he molested them. Sean Hannity of Fox News supports Moore. Keurig pulled out of being a sponsor. Hannity told his viewers to wreck their Keurigs.

Trump lies and so can you.—T shirt slogan

Everybody wants illicit stuff but most of us keep it under wraps. Drunks say it's a hobby. Molesters think the kids want it.

You believe this tax plan will help you, from the lyingest administration ever known?

Korea was divided into north and south after WWII to help place the occupying Japanese. It meant nothing until 1950 when the north invaded the south. North Korea is still mad at us for stopping them.

11-15-17 Wed. Trump is in so deep with the Russians, the USA is second fiddle. Trump stole the election by telling lies so skilled we had never before seen the like.

Major repubs have rejected Roy Moore as a senator. AG
Sessions only remembers when the press remembers.

If you don't hate evil, you are already in hell. Trump is
much worse than the one Liz Smith knew.   T crabs about
Moore's morals, ha ha ha.

John Brown, Kappernick, Snowden and Trump, all traitors,
or not.

Trump stirred up Rocket Man to get his military spending
approved? Naw, he's not that smart.

11-16-17 Thurs. Hate for Trump may result in the election
of some unqualified democrats.

Remember Tom Price, ejected as Health Secretary over
excessive plane use?   Now comes Roy Moore, ejected
over excessive teenie bopper use. Trump asked Moore for
pointers.   Is Alabama crazy?

Charles Manson near death? Damn.

Without bi-partisan government, each administration will
just undo what the previous one has done.

Bill Clinton was a serial abuser of women but he was
punished adequately and ppl forgave him.

Sex abuse simmers for decades, then ignites. A good
reporter is often the match.

11-17-17 Friday A red hot real estate market has
rejuvenated the time share market.

All comics push boundaries and Al Franken fell off the edge. Women in movies get subjected to too much kissing etc. Remember Stuart Smalley, sort of an effeminate character. Maybe it's fitting that underneath, he's a rogue.

George H. W. Bush patted some fannies. Joe Biden also known as creepy Joe. Interestingly, Trump is silent on Roy Moore.   Bill Clinton apologized, took his punishment and moved on.

Tax bill slight of hand and takes away health care, deep six it now.

Trump is a god to his followers. The preaching politician, Roy Moore gets forgiven time and again, without end.

Ted Kennedy remains the poster boy for woman abuse when in 1969, he and Mary Jo Kopechne drove off a bridge. She drowned while he swam away and waited a day to tell police. Senate ok with it.

11-18-17 Saturday If 2 porn stars meet after a long separation and he forces her to have sex against her will, that is rape.

Anita Hill was screwed twice.

No Trump official is honest yet he is a strong role model. The media really hates T but for good reason. Trump looks older, where is that Botox?

Jessie Jackson has Parkinson's disease.

Russia has contributed significantly to Trump's wealth.

It didn't take long for the Keystone Pipeline to burst.

Hard to eradicate the smell of burnt toast. You don't need all the refrigerator parts.

General Douglas MacArthur was no friend of limited war. When canned by Truman for insubordination in Korea, he was a god, but time soon judged Truman to be right.

11-19-17 Sunday Bill Clinton quit the presidency today to be with Monica for the rest of their lives.

Many people did not admit to pollsters they were voting for Trump.

We need good health care and decreased national debt.

Made the long and tedious drive to the Mandarin Civil War Museum as it was in Jacksonville. Martha bought a frog with teeth and I, three books.

No funny Joe, No screechy Elizabeth, No Hillary, so who ______________?

Read/buy Anne Cooper's book, Second Life, her autobiography including my cousin Jonathan who is in my book Almost Alcoholic. (Not yet published)

11-20-17 Monday Martha drove while eating a Whopper. Thanksgiving looms and I sense an approaching whipped cream bender.

Charlie rocked em at Callahan High School.

The Kushner marriage to Ivanka was arranged since he is part of a large real estate empire too. Those kids are borrowed since Martha says he is gay.

How to Murder your Wife is playing by Roy Moore.

Trump is consumed by greed.

11-21-17 Tuesday Trump tactic is delay, delay, delay. Works well in business and in politics.

Was Al Franken set up? Why don't these guys use hookers or escorts? First Trump, now Moore, ugh.

First our TV went black and now it's ¼ in Spanish. Comcast fix it.

Trump said: We are now the United States of Putin. Come-on, it'll be fun, believe me.

We are paying for a full congress but only getting half + one.

Lying by Trump is his mother's milk.

11-22-17 Wed. Trump firing prosecutors. This is corruption so massive it threatens to makes us a second rate power.

Trump straddles the fence, uses confusing language, wants to have it both ways, but sort of maybe endorses the pedophile Roy Moore for the Alabama Senate on the grounds that the opposing democrat is bad.

Win at all costs, child molesters ok.

The present wave of women who have been harassed reminds me of the Communist scare of the 1950's.

Charlie Rose naked? Al Franken targeted?

On this day before Thanksgiving, I will have whipped cream on ice cream and pancakes.

11-23-17 Thursday, Happy Thanksgiving everyone.

Trump SoHo in Manhattan is buying Trump out, paying him to get his name off their building. A generation after Nixon, it's playing out again.

How to be a millionaire, start out as a multi-millionaire and work for Trump. Tax cut coming, believe me.

Leave Mike Flynn's defense money on my front porch. I'll make sure he gets it. Trump never met a spy he didn't like, Wikileaks.

Enough to eat is given in America but even here, there is not always enough, and world wide, there are still famines.

11-24-17   Friday, Black or otherwise. Gone with the Wind is 5 hours long with commercials. I played with Charlie and her blocks on the floor. Trump glued his brother's blocks together, effectively taking them away, the destructor.

11-25-17 Saturday Trump is gaining weight. I'm glad to be hungry again. Leftovers now more than manageable.

North Korean guards faced with overwhelming temptation to run into SK. One did so, was shot, but lived.

Dems need to find good candidates and show up to vote. Then, it's goodbye Trump.

11-26-17 Sunday Only the first Men in Black is really good.

Malia Obama smoking? Her dad did.

Trump is apt to appoint the most federal judges. Skip voting and then bitch about the president. I don't think so.

Mott accidentally buried his grandmother in their back yard. – His mother

Trump lied about being Time person of the year, but he knows his fans believe everything he says. He's trying to go around Dodd Frank, a financial protection put in place by Obama after Bush crashed the economy in '08.

I knocked Christmas shopping outta the park by buying 11 gift cards.

11-27-17 Monday Febreze stinks.

The Obama election kicked off a new civil war.

Trump tax plan: A roll of paper towels for you, a paper mill for me.

CNN, How Trump Won: He lied his way to victory. He surprised himself on how easy it was. He shoulda done it years sooner. Easier than real estate. Real estate is too ethical. What a shell game.

11-18-17 Tues. Trump destroying the NFL? A hotel in Panama is taking his name off the building.

Gutting the state department reminds me of Hitler firing his generals because the war was going badly.

The T tax policy is because the rich need more money. T prefers lies to truth, so is unfit for office, but maybe we'll get lucky.

Meghan Markel of Prince Harry fame is part black.

Why don't women grab men by the crotch?

Management textbooks don't say don't give one man two jobs. That is a basic given. T bought himself a Christmas gift but told Melania it was for her.

Trump: Obamacare stinks or it will when we get finished with it.

11-29-17 Wed. Trump has Russians coming out his ears. There is a criminal mentality. T feels Nixon was right and the damn newspaper was wrong.

Trump lies about CNN are evil. He is spreading poison around the world. His tax plan is a lie just like his campaign.

Christmas touches all of us in one way or another.

11-30-17 Thurs. 19 Russians are linked to the Trump campaign. He is awful close to $ laundering. He looks like Darth Vader in the long coat.

There is never just one allegation of sexual misconduct. Billy Bush did all of us a favor, yet he was fired. Matt Lauer was a randy fellow.

Trump winks that violence against Muslims is OK.

Trump doesn't need a state department. He knows it all.

I guess this is the wrong time to issue my new invention, glasses that see through clothes.

As women's issues rise in importance, these are bad times for the likes of Moore and Trump.

12-1-17 Friday Kate Steinly's killer not guilty? Not even of manslaughter? Damn, this is bad for dems. Reminds me of the OJ verdict.

There is enough now to put Trump away even if Mueller disappears.

New tax law numbers fuzzy as they always are. So we must trust the government. Do you feel lucky, Punk?

Conyers is 88 and still groping. Wow, just wow.

Trump is a praise addict, it's like a drug to him. The tax bill being rammed though so you don't smell it.

Fox News is doing an hour of topless news in honor of Trump. Trump could be tried for murder.

Lesbians are after Moore.   I wouldn't grab you if you weren't so sexy. Matt Lauer could tweek his technique.

12-2-17 Sat. Time to clean the crooks outa the white house. Trump denies the Flynn guilty plea is any problem. Flynn guilty of lying to the FBI, a minimum charge, lots of singing to come.

Tillerson called T a moron and T does not forget an insult.

Wells Fargo now has a Christmas saver's club using bitcoin.

Michael Moore dated teen girls?

Trump created a cabal of Russia leaning conspirators. Flynn to get 2-5? Trump lawyer said Flynn was an Obama man. Yeah, and Obama fired him and told T not to hire him.

How effective is Secretary of State Tillerson going to be with his replacement hanging over him.

Will disgraced general Flynn be another John Dean? Will he end up picking up trash from alongside the highways?

12-3-17 Sunday   Trump lies ok in business but not acceptable with the special prosecutor or the media.

The male has always grabbed a woman to procreate the species and it's hard to stop now.

Hillary lost to a skinny black guy and a fat old white guy so give it up.

If you buy the Trump tax plan, I've gotta bridge. It is by and for robber barons.

Kushner will make a nice addition for any jail.

The white house has roaches, yes we know.

Trump accuses others of what he does; crooked media and rigged systems.

12-4-17 Monday Was it wrong to let attorney's advertise?

Trump eats twice what a normal person does, yet no health report and no taxes shown.

Eggnog can be overdone, easily.   But should be sold year round.

Welfare and farm subsidies are 1% of the budget yet repubs think it's murder.

Publix ice cream is 2 for $10. So what's one? Doesn't say. $9, $8, no, turns out, one is $5.

Our take home pay is out of our hands yet people think politics is not important.

12-5-17 Tues. It's time for families of military to get out of South Korea?

Martha's cousin Ward is a good painter but his pictures tend to be drab especially after hanging on our walls for 30+ years.

Trickle down presumes a philanthropic nature of individual ppl but not corporations.

If dogs want to wear clothes, they will buy them.

Billy Bush says, Not so fast Donnie, I saw you say it. And you sound like a high school guy.

Howard Hughes business plan was to leave and come back months later and sure enough, things were better.   If a drugged paranoid man can become a billionaire, then Trump can be president.

Trump's confusion props up his lies. (for a short time) Lying on this scale is something new. He's got to come down as a lesson for our kids.

Trump insults the FBI trying to diffuse and minimize Mueller. Would he then dump the whole country to save himself? Of course.

FBI Director Comey gives Trump the election and T fires him. T is dragging his attorneys down into his crimes.

No need to watch Nazi shows, we have our own.

Trump and Nixon are now appearing together very regularly. If all the officials were like T, we'd be in medieval times.

There will be a Trump Scale of Dishonesty for future use. Like Pinocchio's nose.

Jeff Sessions is not long for this world. Next felon to fall? Pence shaky too.

Religion and GOP on life support because of Trump.

12-6-17 Wed. Trump enables Moore. Bannon, the wife beater, likes both.

Trump could be sex sued and indicted for fraud at the same time. Deutsche Bank laundered $ through Trump ???

Nixon knew justice could be obstructed and resigned.

Trump, God, guns and rape. Has a nice ring to it.

Unemployment at 4%, who is left to hire? What's next is inflation and high interest rates.

The Jacksonville Morgue is overwhelmed thanks to the Opioid crisis. Bodies on the floor, inadequate cooling.

Dad voted republican because Conrad voted republican. Conrad was in the highest tax bracket, we were not.

Didn't matter, dad followed his god anyway. Like Trump followers.

The government owes us 1. Fiscal responsibility and 2. Military readiness. And whatever else they can afford.

Conyers is the proof we need mandatory retirement in congress.

Howard Hughes had detectives follow prospective girl friends to see who they were dating.

The new tax law punishes democratic states due to elimination of state deductions.

12-7-17 Thurs. 1941, A date that will live in infamy.

Donnie Jr. has taken lying to the next level. Make up the facts and then make up the reason for the facts.

Gravity causes aging.   The rich don't marry, they merge.

Al Franken is effective and should quit when Trump quits.

Howard Hughes bribed Richard Nixon, ran over a man killing him after leaving a bar, but bribed a juror and got off, bought movie actresses, a man Trump could like.

The Peter Principle of 1969 states that a manager will be promoted to his level of incompetence. Trump proves the principle.

12-8-17 Friday All pinched women are now getting revenge or justice. There is a virtual tidal wave of sex allegations.

As Trump shrinks our individual values, the value of the nation declines as well. Trump Jr. makes dad look smart.

His fake teeth failed him at the Israel speech. The snakes are wiggling in the pen. Trump dragging Fox News and the GOP into the pit of hell.

Steve Bannon makes more noise outside of government.

12-9-17 Saturday Trump, Bannon, Moore, Duke, see the problem?

Despite these despots, dems still need to come up with a positive plan.

Has Ben Carson battled any brains since he's been secretary of HUD.

Past the age of 70, there is no longer any need to wrap Christmas gifts.

I've got flying carpets. Leave $ on my front porch.

Even crooks need the truth. Roy Moore laments the passing of slavery.

Trump going for the Alabama scuz vote.

12-10-17 Sunday Freezing this am.

How can 32% of the people support Trump? He's the best liar in the world. Fox says the Mueller investigation is biased. Trump will divide the nation into his loyalists and everyone else.

The Mucinex Booger's agent has warned either raise his pay, or he will blow. 41% of ppl prefer the Booger over Trump.

12-11-17 Monday Trump shuts down internet, too much criticism. Did T choke on his Moore endorsement. Is Moore too off the chart even for Trump? If Trump isn't Hitler, he's close enough for government work.

During an afternoon of TV watching, there are enough commercials to also read a book.

Ben Carson went in to fix Trump's brain but it was MIA.

I am offering plastic surgery for only $10 as I've never done it before. That is what we got with Trump.

I'm charging the dogs for barking. How will they pay? I'm taking it out of their allowance.

12-12-17 Tues. Many religious people are crooked. Pence is the token religious guy for Trump, now ignored.

Mueller is getting very close to exposing Trump and ppl like Jeanie Pirro with Fox News are getting virulent.

Eva Braun was the most loyal woman ever.

Hitler says he did not start the war, the Jews did. And he didn't lose it, the German people did. He killed 5,000 Germans after the failed assassination attempt on his life.

Tax preparers are really loan companies.

Roy Moore is a sex predator and that is the good news.

A lying president is like your optometrist saying you have hemorrhoids.

Trump is all about the now and his support of Moore will backfire.

12-13-17 Wed.   Roy Moore went the way of George Wallace. Trump: No baby, No bruise, No problem. Are bigots sexist too?   One bigot is an anomaly, two a pattern. Moore gotta gun and a horse. Trump opened the door for Moore.

Anne Cooper's book, Second Life, is valuable if you have lost a loved one or know of someone who has.

Twitter OK for a president, but not if he's nuts.   A documentary has been made of the T accusers, all 12 of them.

12-14-17 Thurs. Two Trump judges turned down by repubs for no experience.

Moore won't concede, like Trump, F___ reality. Bannon looks like a drunk and Alabama voters agreed.

Russia took Eastern Europe and then Berlin, WWII. Show the story of Hitler to middle school kids and maybe we can avoid another Trump.

Trump's pussy grabbing is becoming a millstone. Trump's grip on power is slipping away.

12-15-17 Friday   Is Bannon Rosemary's Baby all grown up?

Trump asked Putin for a job. Trump likes other crooks but has trouble getting along even with them.

Moore won't concede because of mice, the mice in his head.

That time of year when the meal takes forever and then it's the wrong meal. Do you eat it or be late getting back to work?

12-16-17 Saturday Trump, like Nixon, has no class. You can't pardon a crook if you as president are part of the crookedness. If Mueller disappears, another one takes over.

Trump is a bully and bullies are cowards, so T might leave the country. Crooked media, crooked FBI, it's all so crooked.

J. Edgar Hoover ran the FBI for 37 years. He got so powerful they were afraid to kick him out. He died in the Nixon administration, who appointed a man with no experience.

Buy on the internet because it's easy but the delivery man kicks your package over the fence.

We didn't eat the dozen donuts, we gave 4 to Lindsay.

God wants Moore to keep fighting?

Put all the tax on the individual and eliminate business tax altogether. Now that's simple. And business will cut prices because they care.

Trump will come back as a tree in his next life. That way he can be more useful.

The near win by Moore shows the evil around Trump spills and grows.

12-17-17 Sunday When the pres. runs down the FBI, it makes it harder for them to do a good job. Trump always looks anxious like he might lose something.

Some people want fireworks 24/7.

The supreme court is the arbiter of any Trump created constitutional crisis.

Workers get a tax cut for 1.5 years, then it goes up. Gotcha.

For Trump to do nothing about Russian intrusion into our election, seems to me like treason and if he fires Mueller, obstruction of justice.

Nancy Pelosi was Miss Lube Rack of 1955.

For months a convenience store with gas has been under construction on the way to our house.   I was hoping it was a WaWa, but alas, it's a Circle-K.   It's fun to say WaWa.

Trump could be the first pres. to fire 2 FBI directors, one present, one past.   Comey and Mueller.

12-18-17 Monday Who do you trust, Mueller or Trump?

Hitler has also been used on the democrats, but before the war.

Regency Court shopping center sold in 2007 for $25 million and sold again in 2017 for $5 million. The difference was occupancy.

Between Nixon and the novel 1984, we have Trump all figured out.

Facts can be found to back up any opinion.

11-19-17 Tuesday Hillary Clinton sank the Pequod. Track Palin married a moose. Mueller says to Trump, Good job.

Wife no cook, no problem, hamburger mixed with eggs, lucky we have dogs.

Trump hugs himself during speech. Needs fighting like an addict needs drugs. He's smarter when fighting according to Bannon.

Trump campaign rife with Russians, spilling over the sides.

Omarosa firing oversold. Senators and judges falling over pussy grabbing, why not the president?

People had a hard time mocking Obama for fear of being called racist, but Trump has opened the door for that, wide open.

Trump cares deeply about the California fires. Ya think?

Without debt reduction, we cannot do the great things anymore.

12-20-17 Wed. If you have colluded with Russians, Trump will pay your legal bills, believe him.

The tax bill is for a one term president. It's also a health care bill, slick. Rush it through speaks of panic or sneakiness.   Trump keeps his own taxes secret. Returning $ to the people insane when we owe 17 trillion

Pence will be best known for his lies.

The Peyton Place book/movie explores the notion, are women inferior.

Don't trains have engineers? Don't ships have captains? Doesn't anyone look out the window anymore?

Our military thinks UFOs are real.

Depose Kim and give NK to China. Then we can go home savings big $.

12-21-17 Thurs.   Some repubs are tying to discredit Mueller and the FBI. The Trump bile has spilled and spread.

Trump likes other crooks. Wells Fargo gets biggest tax break.

The 2001 audio book is much better than the movie.

If people won't say what they want for Christmas, get them chickens.

My politics is simple. Take the best from both sides. The Reagan tax cut caused a recession and a tax on social security. It's time we called this man a clown pres.

12-22-17 Friday Trump told Chris Matthews that women who get abortions must be punished. Is this the pillar of Trump's evangelical support?

To Trump, lying is normal, but not so for our legal system. Trump asked Comey for loyalty before firing him.

12-23-17 Saturday   Repubs leaking info to discredit FBI and Trump/Russia. Trump needs loyalty like the Mafia. T afraid to give a press conference. Damn fake news might be on to him.

Labeling one side crooked demeans all of us especially the side doing the labeling.

12-24-17 Sunday Have you seen, This is an apple ad on CNN? Even Trump knows his wall is crap. He signed a lot of secret bills while on the golf course, believe him.

12-25-17 Monday Merry Christmas. Trump shrinks USA while China expands. MAGA means isolation and America is in poverty. In his first year as president, T has gone from king to almost king. These are the good things Trump did in his first year._____________________

12-26-17 Tuesday Trying to surprise people is a losing battle. I'm glad Christmas is over. It's well intentioned but seems invented by stores. I did get Trump hair, cotton candy. Adds more to my awful diet this time of year.

12-27-17 Wednesday A lying president leads us down the Hitler road. Discrediting the FBI can be treason.

Is Trump our dead skunk in the middle of the road?

The biggest story of the year is our on-going acceptance of gun violence in America.

Trump owes $ to Russia. We owe $ to China. One world.

Normally, a leader has an intellect and a will to fix problems, but this one just bellows, changes his mind and fires people.

Jack Webb in his show Dragnet, got millions of people to smoke. Today the tobacco companies have been marginalized. We can do that to the NRA as well.

If Trump doesn't want Puerto Rico, Castro does or some other foreign power does.

12-28-17 Thursday Trump is a godsend for hundreds of comics.

My wife Martha loves Trump. She's smart but love is dumb.

Seven months later, Trump realizes firing Comey wasn't enough. So now he tears up the whole organization. Repubs are stained for all of history.

Arthur Miller was on Dick Cavett but great as he was, I want to know about the Marilyn Monroe marriage.

Do you remember Vermithrax Pejorative? It's from a movie.

There is a 75% chance Mueller will recommend impeachment for Trump and if the dems take over in 2018, it's a done deal.

The cheese cake knocked on the door and I let it in.

Obama insults Trump and I doubt T even knew it.

ISIS hates everyone.

Melania Trump is the most inactive first lady of all time? Did she dig for gold and end up with Styrofoam?

Prince Harry to Trump: I'm so sorry, your wedding invite got lost in the mail.

12-29-17 Friday   Keeping people off balance is a poor substitute for morals and clarity.   Trump sort of rats himself out by his own tweets.

Why the truth matters, ever had a lying dentist?

Moore lost due to voter fraud? Right out of the Trump playbook. Fraud is my friend.

Provable Trump lies run 5 a day. – Washington Post

China violates UN sanctions against NK and Trump cuts UN funding. Duh.

Red light cameras gone in Florida. My Buick Verano will not be built in 2018. According to TV ads, auto insurance over charges us $700 a year.

Former first ladies don't do well as presidential candidates.

12-30-17 Saturday   Even Trump supporters wish he'd quit tweeting.

The heart of negotiation is lying but both sides know that and settle in a middle ground. Trump has taken it further and made it a part of his soul.

I'm glad he gave weapons to Ukraine but with his record of lies, did he really do it?   Or will he really do it?

Trump supporters call me sick and deranged, another Trump playbook thing. Bashing T does not make me sick but I would get sick if I did not bash him.

Trump hides his taxes and his health report. Voters can't believe his over whelming mediocrity. A billionaire should be smarter.

12-31-17 Sunday   Trump denies Russian interference in our election so he won't fight it. Incompetence.

Comey should not have spoken in public about Hillary.

Iran's people mad about kings keeping all the money.   And spending it on foreign intrigue and fancy living.

We invaded Iraq because they might have large weapons. We know for sure NK has them, so where's the invasion now? Is a NK blockade next?

Trump is ceding his presidency to Gen. Kelly and others, hopefully competent.   T is lazy and confused.

Trump supporters don't try to justify him, they just say he's the boss.

Weiner has flopped out again.

1-1-18 Monday   If Trump had the power, would he unleash a dose of super inflation to bail out his over mortgaged real estate empire?

Trump admires Putin who admires Stalin who killed 3 million Russians. Just arrived, 2 tons of Trump toilet paper.   Long live T on another planet. MAGA (Make America Great Again) really means enlarge other countries making us smaller.

I finally achieved Red Skelton hair.

Thanks for reading.   Don't miss my next book, Blow Hard.